DOCUMENT MANIPULATION AND TYPOGRAPHY

The Cambridge Series on Electronic Publishing

Editor: P. Hammersley

The purpose of this new series is to publish books in the exciting and topical field of electronic printing and publishing. The series will attempt to cover all aspects of electronic publishing, including:

- Matters relating to hardware, software and standards concerned with transferring authors' words and images to the printed page;
- Document delivery – electronic methods of reader access to publications, full-text database publishing, CD-ROM delivery systems and the impact for libraries;
- On-line publishing systems and distributed publication systems – the impact of networks on the publication process;
- Human factors, relating, for example, to document structures for readability, editing aids, expert system-based interfaces and type and page design.

While there will be some overlap with other areas of computer science (such as information retrieval and computer graphics), the series will concentrate primarily on works concerned with publishing, and so should provide a scholarly and specific survey of developments in this subject-area.

Titles will range from graduate-level texts to multi-author edited works.

DOCUMENT MANIPULATION AND TYPOGRAPHY

Proceedings of the International Conference on Electronic Publishing, Document Manipulation and Typography, Nice (France) April 20–22 1988

Edited by
J. C. van VLIET
Vrije Universiteit, Amsterdam

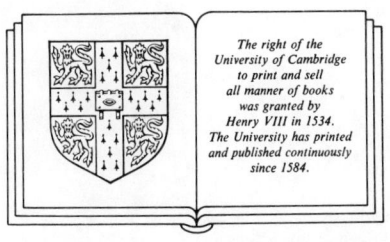

CAMBRIDGE UNIVERSITY PRESS

Cambridge

New York   New Rochelle

Melbourne   Sydney

Published by the Press Syndicate of the University of Cambridge
The Pitt Building, Trumpington Street, Cambridge CB2 1RP
32 East 57th Street, New York NY 10022, USA
10 Stamford Road, Oakleigh, Melbourne 3166, Australia

© Cambridge University Press 1988

First published 1988

Printed in Great Britain by Billing & Sons Ltd, Worcester

British Library cataloguing in publication data available

Library of Congress cataloguing in publication data available

ISBN 0 521 36294 6 hard covers

CONTENTS

Organization — vii

Preface — ix

CaminoReal: an interactive mathematical notebook — 1
D. Arnon, R. Beach, K. McIsaac & C. Waldspurger

Active paths through multimedia documents — 19
P.T. Zellweger

Visual structure and the transmission of meaning — 35
R. Southall

Automatic recognition and representation of documents — 47
L.D. Wilcox & A.L. Spitz

Structure recognition of printed documents — 59
R. Ingold, R.-P. Bonvin & G. Coray

Hard copy rendition of ODA-documents — 71
J. Behrmann-Poitiers, H. Keil & H. Loebl

Well-established document interchange formats — 83
J.-M. de La Beaujardière

The formal specification of the document structures of the ODA standard — 95
W. Appelt, R. Carr & G. Richter

Specifying structured document transformations — 109
R. Furuta & P.D. Stotts

Defining document styles for WYSIWYG processing *D.D. Chamberlin, H.F. Hasselmeier & D.P. Paris*	121
Image processing aspects of type *R.A. Morris*	139
Optimal line breaking in music *W. A. Hegazy & J.S. Gourlay*	157
Drag: a graph drawing system *H. Trickey*	171
Hypertext: the way forward *P.J. Brown*	183
Abstraction and integration in IDE, an editing and formatting environment *M. Kaplan*	193
Intent-based page modelling using blocks in the Quill document editor *A.W. Luniewski*	205
An introduction to Gargoyle: an interactive illustration tool *K. Pier, E. Bier & M. Stone*	223
FAXICOLOR: workstation for mixed-mode document composition in hospital environment *R. De Sousa, L. Shaofeng & G. Vaucher*	239
Vidura – an interactive multilingual publishing system – specification & design *S. Nath, S.N. Pattanaik & S.P. Mudur*	249
Synthesis of print-quality cursive script based on a model of the human handwriting mechanism *E.H. Dooijes*	261
Chinese character processing system based on character-root combination and graphic processing *Fan Cun-Chang & P. Zini*	275
Systems used	287

ORGANIZATION

Steering Committee
Jacques André   INRIA-IRISA, Rennes, France (*Chairman*)
Brian Kernighan   Bell Laboratories, Murray Hill, USA (*Vice-chairman*)

Program Committee
Jacques André   INRIA-IRISA, Rennes, France
Patrick Baudelaire   DIGITAL PRL, Paris, France
Richard Beach   Xerox PARC, Palo Alto, California, USA
Charles Bigelow   Stanford University, USA
David Brailsford   University of Nottingham, England
Heather Brown   University of Kent, England
Giovanni Coray   EPFL, Lausanne, Switzerland
R.W. Davy   Chelgraph Ltd, England
Richard Furuta   University of Maryland, USA
James Gosling   Sun Microsystems, California, USA
Vania Joloboff   Bull Research Center/INRIA, Sophia Antipolis, France
Brian Kernighan   Bell Laboratories, Murray Hill, USA
Peter King   University of Manitoba, Winnipeg, Canada
Dario Lucarella   Universita di Milano, Italy
Pierre MacKay   University of Washington, Seattle, USA
Robert Morris   Interleaf and University of Massachusetts, USA
J. Nievergelt   University of North Carolina, USA
Vincent Quint   INRIA/IMAG Grenoble, France
Brian Reid   DEC Western Research Center, California, USA
Alan Shaw   University of Washington, Seattle, USA
Hans van Vliet   Free University, Amsterdam, The Netherlands

Organization − Secretariat
Thérèse Bricheteau, Elisabeth Many,
INRIA-Service des Relations Extérieures, Bureau des Colloques,
Rocquencourt - BP 105, F-78153 LE CHESNAY Cedex (France)

PREFACE

EP88, the international conference on *Electronic Publishing, Document Manipulation and Typography*, is the successor to EP86, the international conference on *Text Processing and Document Manipulation* organized at the University of Nottingham, England, in April 1986 by the British Computer Society. EP88 is organized by INRIA (the French Institute for Research in Computer Science and Automation) that organized, in 1983 at Rennes, France, an earlier conference on this topic.

The EP88 program continues the themes from EP86, which was mainly concerned with document structures for interactive editing and with document standards. However, other themes are emerging with applications for exotic languages and multilingual systems. Very new themes appear in EP88 as well, such as active documents and document recognition. The phrase *Document Manipulation* will surely not have the same meaning in the next decade. Unfortunately, the one hundred papers submitted to the EP88 program committee did not contain enough acceptable material related to *Typography* or to *hypertext*. Invited papers fill these gaps in the program.

I would like to thank all the authors and organizers for their help in making the conference possible. Special mention is due to the Program Committee who had the difficult task of selecting the papers, and to the editor of this book who, as for the EP86 Proceedings, will make the proceedings available at the conference. All of us, working on Document Manipulation, appreciate how difficult it is to get a homogeneous book from heterogeneous papers.

Jacques André, Rennes, December 1987.

CAMINOREAL:
AN INTERACTIVE MATHEMATICAL NOTEBOOK

DENNIS ARNON, RICHARD BEACH, KEVIN MCISAAC, and CARL WALDSPURGER

Xerox Palo Alto Research Center

ABSTRACT

Four broad categories of mathematical software are numerical computation, mathematical typesetting, computer algebra (symbolic mathematics), and "technical electronic mail" (mail that contains formatted mathematical expressions). Powerful and sophisticated systems are currently available in each of these categories. Simultaneous, integrated access to all four types of functionality is not yet realized, however. CaminoReal is a working system that addresses this need. It is part of Cedar, the programming environment of Xerox PARC's Computer Science Laboratory, and is used in conjunction with Tioga, Cedar's multimedia document editor. Printing and management of other document components, such as text, graphics, and voice, are provided by Tioga. For computation, CaminoReal offers a built-in algebra package based on the notions of objects and domains, plus access to "algebra servers" on a network. Mathematical expressions are exchanged among CaminoReal, Tioga, and these algebra servers in abstract syntax. Our current servers are the Reduce, SMP, and SAC-2 computer algebra systems. This document has been produced using Tioga and CaminoReal.

> *There is no 'royal road' to geometry.*
> Euclid, said to Ptolemy I

1. Introduction

1.1. *Overview of CaminoReal*

CaminoReal is a system for direct manipulation of mathematical expressions, whether as part of a technical document or as inputs and outputs of computational engines. Its user interface offers interactive, syntax-directed, two-dimensional, WYSIWYG editing of mathematical expressions, placing or fetching such expressions in or from formatted documents, and two sorts of computational facilities: a built-in algebra package and well-known algebra systems such as Reduce [Hearn82], SMP [Wolfram85], and SAC-2 [Collins80]. The internal algebra package is based on an object-oriented paradigm that supports polymorphic procedures. For example, one can easily create and perform simple arithmetic on matrices of polynomials with complex number coefficients, or matrices of such matrices, etc.

CaminoReal has much in common with other recent work, but we believe it has two unique features as of this writing: the tight coupling of its computation facilities with a sophisticated document system, thereby opening interesting opportunities for computed and interactive documents (details in Sections 3, 4, and 5), and its access to computational "algebra servers" on our local network (details in Section 4). These capabilities have been facilitated by building it upon the rich base provided by Cedar, the programming environment of the Computer Science Laboratory at Xerox PARC [Swinehart86, Donahue86]. CaminoReal is closely linked to Tioga, Cedar's multimedia document editor, which provides facilities for printing and management of other document content types such as text, graphics [Pier88], and voice [Zellweger88a]. The screen, mouse actions, and keyboard input for CaminoReal and Tioga are managed by the Cedar viewers package (as for most Cedar tools). A viewer is a window that can be scrolled and resized, and which can have buttons and pop-up menus that invoke commands. The mouse is used to point and select text or expressions.

CaminoReal implements a recently proposed [Arnon87] standard architecture for "mathematical systems" that provides for interactive editing of mathematical notation, display of math in its traditional two-dimensional appearance, symbolic and numerical computation, and technical document production. We have found this architecture useful, and we summarize it in Section 2. Section 3 discusses Meddle, CaminoReal's interactive mathematics expression editor, and Tioga. Section 4 covers Algebra-Structures (CaminoReal's built-in algebra package) and algebra servers. In Section 4.2, we explain why associating domains with mathematical expressions can be a significant help in document creation, proofreading, and computation.

CaminoReal supports the creation of "interactive" technical documents. For example, the user can browse a typeset draft of a technical document on the workstation screen, select, edit, and compute with mathematical expressions in the document, and insert the resulting expressions back into the document. One can extend this paradigm to the notion of a "computed document," that is, a document with embedded computations. Two examples of computed documents are mathematical form letters and spreadsheets, which we discuss in Section 5. CaminoReal is one of several current experiments with active documents in Cedar [Zellweger88b].

1.2. Previous work

In the 27 years since J.C.R. Licklider presented the notion of man-computer symbiosis [Licklider60], there have been continuous efforts to define and build such "symbiotic systems" for mathematical work. Clapp and Kain's Magic Paper system [Clapp63], Minsky's MATHSCOPE proposal [Minsky63], and Martin's Symbolic Mathematical Laboratory [Martin67] appear to be the earliest. Numerous papers chronicle subsequent progress and offer pointers to the future [Griesmer71, Sundblad74, Ng79,

Berman79, Hearn80, Hearn82, Allen81, Foster84, Engeler85]. There is much current work relevant to CaminoReal [Bloomberg87, MathSoft87, Smith86, Spirkovska86].

Following Licklider and most of the authors just cited, we do not in this paper consider the questions of "intelligent behavior," learning, or automated reasoning in mathematical systems. These are issues of compelling interest, but we believe that certain more mundane topics deserve priority at present. Some examples of topics we exclude are: "mentor" and problem-solving capabilities projected for MACSYMA [Martin71], English-speaking MACSYMA Advisor [Genesereth77], artificial intelligence aspects of mathematical systems design [Calmet87], tutoring abilities of a calculus environment [Suppes87], and theorem proving and heuristic reasoning functionality [Bundy86].

CaminoReal, like most similar current work, builds on certain hardware and software developments of recent years. In hardware, these are: (1) high-resolution screens and printers, (2) pointing devices, e.g., mice, (3) high-speed networks, and (4) personal workstations. Important software developments are: (1) the emergence of large collections of sophisticated and powerful symbolic and numerical algorithms, (2) the rapid diffusion of high-quality electronic publishing systems that utilize the hardware base just enumerated, and (3) the broad acceptance of certain user interface paradigms for interactive software, such as WYSIWYG editing, direct manipulation [Shneidermann83], menus, windows, holophrasting [Koved86], icons, and browsers. Certain of these developments originated at Xerox PARC [Crecine86], and most are well integrated into the Cedar environment. We view electronic mail as a form of electronic publishing and, in fact, multimedia, WYSIWYG Tioga documents are routinely exchanged by electronic mail in Cedar.

Previous work on mathematical systems has not dealt conclusively with the integration of documents and computation. There have been a number of translators for converting the internal expression representations of algebra systems into typeset quality output [Wactlar64, Foderaro79, Fateman87]. However, this has been a one-way path. Once the conversion is done, one cannot subsequently access the expressions for computation. Although a number of interactive WYSIWYG mathematical systems, such as MathCAD [MathSoft87], MILO [Avitzur87], and INFOR [Schelter87], allow the production of some sort of document, only INFOR could be said to support professional-quality typesetting for text and mathematics. However, it has no provision for other media, such as voice or complex graphics, and is not currently connected to computational systems. Recent multimedia document systems such as Diamond [Crowley87] and Andrew [Morris86] support a range of media, but are only beginning to support math in documents and do not yet address the issue of computations with the math in a document. The experimental PEN system [Allen81] had some of the same goals as CaminoReal; its design decisions are a continuing resource as we attempt to build systems of broader scope. Spreadsheet systems can be said to integrate documents and computation, but they are typically limited in the types of documents that can be created and the media that those documents can contain. For us, documents such as multimedia technical papers, automatically generated logs, and audit trails (see Section 5.2 for a discussion of the latter), are crucial parts of a mathematical system. Furthermore, we want all of the documents in our system to be "interactive." That Tioga and CaminoReal provide a professional-quality publishing system may be gauged by the fact that this document has been produced with them. Tioga/CaminoReal documents are interactive. Hence we call CaminoReal a system for interactive mathematical notebooks.

2. Standard mathematical systems

2.1. *Introduction*

The material in this section is adapted from a recent workshop summary [Arnon87]. We postulate that there is an abstract syntax for any mathematical expression, which consists of an operator and a list of arguments, where each argument is (recursively) a piece of abstract syntax (cf. [McCarthy62]). Functional notation, Lisp S−expressions, directed acyclic graphs, and n-ary trees are isomorphic representations of abstract syntax. For example, the expression $ab+c$ could be represented in abstract syntax by the functional notation Plus[Times[a,b],c], or by the binary tree:

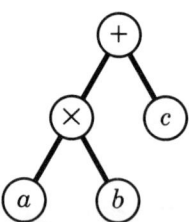

A "Standard Mathematical Component" (abbreviated SMC) is a collection of software and hardware modules, each with a single function, which, if it reads mathematical expressions, reads them in abstract syntax and which, if it writes mathematical expressions, writes them in abstract syntax. A "Standard Mathematical System" (abbreviated SMS) is a collection of SMCs, which are used together and which communicate with each other in abstract syntax over "wires" that connect them. In Section 2.2 we identify five possible types of SMCs. Any particular SMS may have zero or more instances of each.

2.2. Standard mathematical components

2.2.1 *ED - math editors*

An ED component edits abstract syntax to abstract syntax. A particular system may have editors that operate on other representations of mathematical expressions, such as bitmaps or TeX math notation [Knuth84]; however, such editors do not qualify as EDs.

2.2.2 *DISP - math displayers*

DISP components are suites of software packages, device drivers, and hardware devices that take in an expression in abstract syntax and render it. Two examples might be (1) the combination of an abstract syntax to TeX translator, plus TeX itself, plus a printer, or (2) a plotting package plus a plotting device. A DISP component may or may not support "pointing" (selection) within an expression it has displayed. For example, a DISP that renders onto a printer probably doesn't, but a DISP driving a display screen may. If pointing is supported, then the DISP must be able to pass back the selected subexpression(s) in abstract syntax.

2.2.3 *COMP - computation systems*

A COMP takes in an expression in abstract syntax, performs some computation on it, and returns the result in abstract syntax. Examples of COMPs are numerical libraries and computer algebra systems.

2.2.4 *DOC - document systems*

The simplest example of a DOC is a text editor allowing abstract syntax representations of mathematical expressions to be stored in documents. However, a DOC need have no relation to printing, so, for example, database, hypertext, and electronic mail systems are all possible DOCs. Essentially, a DOC is just a system that manipulates certain data structures (which we may think of as "documents" or "databases") in which we can "park" multiple math expressions represented in abstract syntax.

Note that if math is editable in place in a document, this is not part of the DOC *per se*, but the result of cooperation between a DOC, an ED, and perhaps also a DISP. The interactions that occur among the various components when editing an expression in such a situation are: (1) the DISP and the ED process the user's input and modify the abstract syntax representation of the expression, (2) the DISP queries the DOC to be given an area (typically a box) within which to display the new expression, and (3) the DISP paints the expression in the given box.

2.2.5 *MAN - system managers*

It is the function of a MAN to coordinate and connect the ED, DISP, COMP, and DOC components that comprise an SMS. Typically, an SMS has one MAN component, although it might be able to switch between several. SMSs may vary greatly in the face they present to the user, and such differences may well arise from the differing amounts of "knowledge" or sophistication possessed by their MAN components. MAN components do whatever is necessary to make the other components play together and perhaps more besides to make life easier for the user. For example, abstract syntax provides a syntax for communication among SMCs, but leaves unspecified the semantics of sentences in this language. Thus, if the function (i.e., operator) names of the abstract syntax used by an ED component differ from those used by a COMP, the MAN provides the translation. The user of an SMS need not, and is encouraged not to, understand the naming conventions of the particular components it contains. As another example, a MAN may have some "knowledge" of the relative merits of several COMP components for different tasks and provide automatic routing of computational requests to the most appropriate one.

2.3. *Further notes on the overall architecture*

A typical SMS (e.g., CaminoReal) will have a WYSIWYG expression editor that consists of an ED and a DISP that are much more closely coupled than is suggested here. For example, the internal representations of abstract syntax in an ED and a DISP (such as a tree of boxes), might have pointers back and forth, or the two may even share a common data structure. This is acceptable, but it should always be possible to access the two components in the canonical decoupled way. This would mean that the ED should be able to receive a standard abstract syntax representation for an expression plus an editing command in abstract syntax (for example, Edit[expr, cmd]) and return an abstract syntax representation for the result. Similarly, the DISP should be able to receive abstract syntax over the wire and display it and, if it supports pointing, be able to return selected subexpressions in abstract syntax.

Since abstract syntax is human-readable, any text editor can be used as an ED. However, many users of an SMS will only want to interact with mathematics that has a typeset appearance; they should not need to know that their system talks abstract syntax within itself or to the outside world.

Katz' recent proposal [Katz87] and others in the typesetting and document communities, distinguish the form (appearance) of a mathematical expression from its content (meaning or value). It is a thesis of the SMS architecture that such a distinction cannot usefully be made. Rather, we claim that abstract syntax can convey form, content, or both, and that its interpretation is strictly in the eye of the beholder(s). In other words, "meaning is just a handshake between sender and recipient" [Arnon87].

3. CaminoReal as a prototype SMS: basic editing, documents
3.1. *The expression editor (ED and DISP)*
A stand-alone interactive expression editor called Meddle is "in control" when a CaminoReal tool (i.e., viewer) is instantiated. Meddle's user interface paradigm follows Tioga quite closely. Multiple selections are made via a mouse pointing device. Operations upon the selections are initiated both from the keyboard and from mouse activation of menu commands. These input actions are parsed by a user interface management system that uses state transitions rather than a formal grammar specification. Incremental modifications to the expression are updated on the display after each keystroke or mouse action. There may be more than one CaminoReal tool active at any one time. Meddle provides several "creature comforts" suited to interactive editing of complex notation, especially the undo command and various scaling operations to improve the readability on low resolution display screens.

Meddle's internal data structure for mathematical expressions is n-ary trees, with operators as interior nodes and atoms as leaves (i.e., abstract syntax). For each operator, there is a template that defines its displayed notation. The components of such a notation are zero or more glyphs representing the "operator name," a notation for each subexpression (these are either atomic notations or, recursively, notations of the same sort), and any desired additional glyphs. For example, the summation template specifies that a Greek sigma, Σ, be used to denote the operator and that there be three subexpressions: a lower bound, an upper bound, and a summand. Such templates are written as procedures in the Cedar language and dynamically loaded with CaminoReal. When templates are first presented, any unfilled subexpressions are represented by placeholders (☒). CaminoReal tools are initialized to contain an expression consisting of the single placeholder ☒.

If, for example, we replace a selected placeholder with a summation template (chosen from a menu), we see

$$\sum_{☒}^{☒} ☒ .$$

If we then replace the summand placeholder with an indefinite integral template, we get

$$\sum_{☒}^{☒} \int ☒ \, d☒ .$$

We may continue to fill in placeholders, eventually arriving, for example, at

$$\sum_{i=0}^{\infty} \int \frac{1}{x^i} \, dx .$$

One may select a subexpression corresponding to a subtree by pointing at it and clicking the mouse; the actual selection is the "smallest" subexpression whose bounding box contains the hit. This strategy insures that Meddle constructs only structurally correct expressions, at the expense of freedom to manipulate all the glyphs in a notation. The intention is that additional operator templates be added to accommodate new notation rather than permitting the user to rearrange subexpressions arbitrarily. To facilitate keyboard entry, a complete set of navigational commands is provided, such as select parent, sibling, or child of the current selection.

Meddle depends on four types of selections: primary, copy, move, and keyboard. The *primary selection*, made by pointing and clicking with the mouse, establishes the focus of most operations. The *copy selection*, made by chording (holding down) the keyboard SHIFT key and clicking the mouse, supplies the argument for copying a subexpression to replace the primary selection. A *move selection*, made by chording the keyboard CTRL key and clicking the mouse, supplies the argument for moving a subexpression to replace the primary selection. The *keyboard selection* is a "primary selection in progress" for keyboard input of multi-character identifiers and numbers. If, for example, a primary selection exists and we strike 'M' on the keyboard, then a new keyboard selection of M is set and replaces the previous primary selection. If we next strike 'a', we get a new keyboard selection of (the identifier) Ma, whereas if we next strike '↑', the keyboard selection M is converted into the primary selection, wrapped (see next paragraph) with a superscript template, and we get $M^{\boxtimes}$ with the primary selection set to the superscript placeholder. When two or more selections are active at one time, e.g., primary and copy, the selected expressions can be in different CaminoReal viewers.

Modifications to the primary selection may occur by either a *replace* or a *wrap* operation. In replace, the subexpression in the primary selection is deleted and a new subexpression, determined by either keyboard input or a menu choice, is inserted in the expression tree. In a wrap, the primary selection is retained and replaces one of the placeholders in the new subexpression. For example, consider the first placeholder in the addition template $\boxtimes + \boxtimes$ as the primary selection. Typing the letter 'r' replaces the first placeholder with r, resulting in $r + \boxtimes$, and subsequently typing the key '↑' wraps a superscript template around the r to produce $r^{\boxtimes} + \boxtimes$ (whereas replacing the r with a superscript template, chosen from a menu, would produce $\boxtimes^{\boxtimes} + \boxtimes$).

All editing operations are available via menu buttons; certain common ones can be invoked from the keyboard. We have not so far succeeded in harmonizing the goal of simple and uniform semantics for selections and wraps with the goal of supporting standard operator precedence in keyboard input. For example, one might expect to type the keyboard sequence 'x↑2+1=0' to enter $x^2+1=0$, but we actually require 'x↑2⟨CTRL-P⟩+1⟨CTRL-P⟩=0', in which the ⟨CTRL-P⟩ keystroke invokes the 'select parent' operation.

Previous mathematical expression editors include the Xerox Star [Xerox86b, Becker87], EDIMATH [Quint83, 84], DREAMS [Foster84], MathScribe [Smith86], MILO [Avitzur87], and INFOR [Schelter87]. The Star editor has existed since the mid-1970's, and although we, like many others, have been influenced by it, Meddle has been designed and built from scratch in Cedar.

3.2. *Character sets*

CaminoReal deals with the challenge of presenting the rich collection of multilingual and technical symbols in mathematics by utilizing the Xerox character code standard [Xerox86a]. This standard assigns a unique code (possibly 1, 2 or 3 bytes long) to each symbol and subsumes several international standards, such as ISO and JIS, as well as *de facto* standards, such as the AMS T$_E$X math symbols [Knuth84]. Fonts that conform to the Xerox character code standard have mathematical symbols in standard code positions. Should a font lack particular symbols, a backstop "kitchen sink" font with a glyph for every code is automatically substituted. The scalable font algorithms in the Cedar Imager [Swinehart86] insure that symbols appear on the display or in the document with appropriate size and shape information.

Nonetheless, there remains the challenge of entering symbols that do not occur on typical keyboards. CaminoReal employs a tentative solution by using menus for special symbols and Greek letters. Other Xerox systems employ the attractive techniques of virtual keyboards to map keys into arbitrary character codes, and abbreviation name lookup translations, to map token identifiers into symbols [Becker87].

3.3. *The integrated document formatter (DOC and DISP)*

The integration of mathematical content into a Tioga multimedia document is accomplished by defining a mathematical object class in Tioga. One part of this class definition is the specification that the "data" for particular mathematical objects (i.e., expressions) in documents are strings. The actual string used for a given expression is just a linearization of Meddle's internal data structure for it. Thus, moving expressions between Tioga documents and CaminoReal tools is straightforward. Also included in the Tioga math object class definition are (Cedar) procedures that return a bounding box for an expression and that paint it into a given imaging context. These are merely slightly revised versions of Meddle procedures for similar tasks. Mathematical objects in Tioga documents may occur either in-line (i.e., within a line of text) or displayed (i.e., set out); both uses can be seen in this paper.

Tioga actually views a math object as a single, decorated character, so expressions can be Tioga selections just as any other character. Putting this another way, mathematical expressions in Tioga documents are indivisible units: they can be moved around within the document just like text, but there is no way to get at subexpressions while they reside in the document. Thus math in a Tioga document cannot currently be edited "in place," but must be extracted into a CaminoReal tool, edited there, and reinserted into the document. However, the expression evaluation operations provided by the CaminoReal tool interface (cf. Section 4) can operate equally well on Tioga and CaminoReal selections. Thus computation on expressions in documents can be performed by simply pointing at them (in the document) and invoking the desired actions in a CaminoReal tool.

4. CaminoReal as a prototype SMS: computation

CaminoReal provides two methods for algebraic computation, both accessible through the same tool interface: (1) an experimental domain-oriented package, AlgebraStructures, executed locally in Cedar, and (2) several traditional algebra packages accessed as algebra servers over the network. One may evaluate expressions at several levels of detail, from selected subexpressions to complete expressions to entire documents (see Section 5.1 for an example of the latter). The result of an evaluation operation may either be presented in place or in a new CaminoReal tool. The combination of these computation facilities and the interactive editing environment, especially the latter's undo command, provides a handy tool for exploring complicated expressions.

4.1. *The AlgebraStructures package*

The Cedar AlgebraStructures package supports a limited set of algebraic operations defined within mathematical domains. Primitive (built-in) domains include general expressions, booleans, Cedar integers, arbitrary precision rationals, Cedar reals, and Cedar complexes. Constructors for building new domains of sets, sequences, vectors, matrices, and polynomials over suitable existing domains are provided. The application of the AlgebraStructures evaluator to a Meddle expression proceeds bottom-up: given an operator and domains for its (evaluated) arguments, a suitable domain (general expressions, if nothing narrower can be determined) and value for that operator's subtree is determined. Every AlgebraStructures domain has procedures for generating Meddle representations of its elements, which are invoked to display the result of an evaluation.

For example, if we create the following Meddle expression in a CaminoReal tool:

$$\begin{bmatrix} 1 & 0 & -3x & -x^3 & 0 \\ 0 & 1 & 0 & -3x & -x^3 \\ x & -15x^3 & -1 & 0 & 0 \\ 0 & x & -15x^3 & -1 & 0 \\ 0 & 0 & x & -15x^3 & -1 \end{bmatrix}$$

and apply the AlgebraStructures evaluator to it, its domain will be determined to be 5×5 matrices of polynomials in x with integer coefficients. Evaluation of the (1,1) element of the matrix finds its domain to be the integers. We can select the matrix and ask for the operations available on it, which causes AlgebraStructures to evaluate it to determine its domain, and then display a menu of the operations available on elements of that domain. For the matrix, one of the entries of this menu is Determinant, which if selected yields a result of

$$-3375x^{12}+46x^9+630x^7-9x^4+6x^2-1,$$

whose domain is polynomials in x with integer coefficients.

Domains could be useful for run-time checks that mathematical expressions belong to some asserted domain when evaluated. Such "semantic" checking is not the same as the "syntax" checking that is performed on Meddle keyboard input. Domain information is also useful for guiding a MAN component to choose appropriate algebra servers for particular operations. For example, the AlgebraStructures package currently uses the SAC-2 package for polynomial GCD calculations but does its own integer GCD computations. The design of the algebra system using domains provides a convenient framework for organizing such choices.

The design of AlgebraStructures was influenced by VIEWS [Abdali86] and SCRATCHPAD [Jenks84], among others.

4.2. *Computation with algebra servers*

Algebraic computation with systems other than AlgebraStructures is accomplished by selecting an expression or subexpression in a CaminoReal viewer and sending it to the desired algebra server (COMP) for evaluation. CaminoReal's MAN first converts the expression to abstract syntax appropriate for that server, and then sends it to the server over the network. The result of the algebra system's evaluation returns to CaminoReal by the same steps in reverse. Currently, a new process on the remote machine is created for each such request.

Suppose we have the following integral in a CaminoReal tool:

$$\int \frac{1-2x^3}{(1+x^3)^2} \, dx$$

Since AlgebraStructures has no integration algorithms, its evaluator returns a value of:

$$\int \frac{-2x^3+1}{x^6+2x^3+1} \, dx$$

If we send the integral to Reduce for evaluation, after about ten seconds we get back:

$$\frac{x}{x^3+1}$$

in our CaminoReal viewer.

The abstract syntax into which CaminoReal converts the integral for transmission to Reduce is:

int(quotient(difference(1, times(2, expt(x, 3))), expt((plus(1, expt(x, 3))), 2)), x)

For transmission to SMP, the abstract syntax is:

Int[Div[Minus[1, Mult[2, Pow[x, 3]]], Pow[(Plus[1, Pow[x, 3]]), 2]], x]

Thus, CaminoReal allows the user to compute with different algebra systems without knowing the different command names and styles used in each. CaminoReal's style of interchange of mathematical expressions may be contrasted with the encoded directed-acyclic graphs of the Iris system [Leong86].

4.3. *Issues for future work on computation*

The ability to access multiple algebra systems through CaminoReal has raised several issues requiring future work. One is the synchronization of outstanding algebra requests with concurrent interactive editing. Because some algebra operations may take a considerable length of time, it is unreasonable to suspend editing completely during such an operation. Long running computations also raise the need for inquiries to the algebra system for status and progress reporting, as well as additional controls to suspend or abort computations.

It would be desirable to permit multiple concurrent algebra requests from CaminoReal. This raises two issues: (1) the multiplexing of algebra requests to a single server and (2) the definition of the computational state for each request. The simplest scheme would probably be to fork a separate process for each request, giving it a clean initial state, with a limit on the number of such processes active at any one time, and a queue for requests that arrive after the limit is reached.

Additional error-handling and error-reporting protocols are necessary for the full incorporation of algebra servers into the CaminoReal user interface. At present, the data and message streams are combined into one, making it difficult to identify errors returned by the server. The overhead and low bandwidth of communications between clients and servers may mandate compression and caching of conversations, facilities which are provided by Cedar's underlying communications software, but are not currently used in CaminoReal.

5. Computed documents

5.1. *Mathematical form letters*

CaminoReal's expression language supports an assignment statement. Also, expressions assigned to variables (by the evaluation of an assignment statement) are maintained in a symbol table that is global across all Tioga documents and all CaminoReal tool instances, and so constitutes an environment with respect to which evaluations are performed. Variables which have not been assigned values evaluate to themselves. Supporting utilities include the function $killAll[]$, which clears the environment, the notation ❡*expression*❡ (abstract syntax: quote[*expression*]), whose semantics are that $Eval[$❡*expression*❡$]$ returns *expression* unevaluated, and the function $killVariable[$❡t❡$]$, which removes the value of the variable t from the environment.

When CaminoReal's internal EvalBeforePaint switch is off (the default), math expressions in a Tioga document are painted just as they are stored. When EvalBeforePaint is on, they are evaluated before being painted. As might be expected, the order in which expressions are evaluated and painted in the latter case is left-to-right and top-to-bottom order in the Tioga document. A Cedar command is provided for toggling the EvalBeforePaint switch. References to previous expressions in the definitions of later expressions (via the symbol table), coupled with EvalBeforePaint on, make possible Tioga documents that are spreadsheets, "mathematical form letters," or, more generally, "computed documents." For example, here is the "definition level" (EvalBeforePaint off) of a sample form letter:

Let F be defined to be $F \leftarrow y^3 - 3xy + x^3$.
Let G be defined to be $G \leftarrow xy^2 - 15x^3y + 1$.
Let M be the Sylvester matrix of F and G:

$$M \leftarrow sylvesterMatrix[F,G]$$

Then the resultant is the determinant of M, that is

$$det[M]$$

The right sides of the first two assignment statements constitute the "input data" to the form letter, in the sense that the right sides of the last two assignment statements are functions of them. If we now turn EvalBeforePaint on, and simply repaint the document (on screen or printer), we get:

Let F be defined to be $y^3-3xy+x^3$.
Let G be defined to be xy^2-15x^3y+1.
Let M be the Sylvester matrix of F and G:

$$\begin{bmatrix} 1 & 0 & -3x & x^3 & 0 \\ 0 & 1 & 0 & -3x & x^3 \\ x & -15x^3 & 1 & 0 & 0 \\ 0 & x & -15x^3 & 1 & 0 \\ 0 & 0 & x & -15x^3 & 1 \end{bmatrix}$$

Then the resultant is the determinant of M, that is

$$3375x^{12}-44x^9-720x^7+9x^4+6x^2+1$$

Suppose now that we change the input data, for example, let us replace (at the definition level) the expression $F \leftarrow y^3-3xy+x^3$ by $F \leftarrow y^3-x^3$. Then by turning EvalBeforePaint on and repainting the document, we get the correctly updated matrix and determinant:

Let F be defined to be $-x^3+y^3$.
Let G be defined to be xy^2-15x^3y+1.
Let M be the Sylvester matrix of F and G:

$$\begin{bmatrix} 1 & 0 & 0 & -x^3 & 0 \\ 0 & 1 & 0 & 0 & -x^3 \\ x & -15x^3 & 1 & 0 & 0 \\ 0 & x & -15x^3 & 1 & 0 \\ 0 & 0 & x & -15x^3 & 1 \end{bmatrix}$$

Then the resultant is the determinant of M, that is

$$-3375x^{12}+x^9+45x^7+1$$

Having the math in a technical paper computed "on the fly" minimizes the introduction of typographical errors and thereby lightens the proofreading task.

5.2. *Future work on automated proofreading, spreadsheets, audit trails*

The example in the previous section showed the use of the expression environment and evaluation for generating documents. In the future, we expect to refine the use of these tools to provide more proofreading features. For example, suppose in the form letter above that we stored both the unevaluated and evaluated form of each expression. Then one need only do the (possibly expensive) evaluations occasionally, when one wishes to check and verify that the document is correct. The unevaluated expressions could thus be viewed as "assertions" about the actual expressions in the document, which can be checked by evaluating them and checking for equality with the evaluated form.

Because current spreadsheets may contain formulae and perform computations, it is natural to consider the extension of CaminoReal to provide such capabilities in Tioga documents. An interesting issue is how to provide a naming scheme for math equations and expressions that is equivalent to the cell-naming scheme of typical spreadsheets. CaminoReal's current use of a global symbol table presents some difficulties. A recent discussion of spreadsheets [Davis86] raises many of the issues of interest to CaminoReal.

Similarly, an audit trail of computations within a document is a natural extension of the ability to compute expressions. The audit trail would retain the dependency of subexpressions as well as the mathematical operations used to compute the results, so that when one expression was edited, all of the relevant changes elsewhere in the document would be computed and updated. Audit trails could be examined or edited to modify the derivation of new results.

Acknowledgments

Thanks to Michael Plass, Ken Pier, and Christian LeCocq for technical assistance. Thanks to those in the Computer Science Lab at PARC who have used CaminoReal for their documents and computations, and suggested improvements, particularly James Rauen. Thanks to Alan Perlis and Alan Demers for inspiration.

Dennis Arnon has been the chief architect and maintainer of CaminoReal and wrote AlgebraStructures. Carl Waldspurger wrote Meddle. Kevin McIsaac has handled the care and feeding of algebra servers and contributed performance improvements and design ideas. Rick Beach had the first vision of the system architecture, helped build the connections between Meddle and Tioga, and has provided continuous guidance and moral support.

References

[1] Abdali, K., Cherry, G. & Soiffer, N. (1986). An object-oriented approach to algebra system design. In *Proc. Symp. Symbolic and Algebraic Computation*, ed. B. Char, 24-30. New York, NY: ACM.

[2] Allen, T., Nix, R. & Perlis, A. (1981). PEN: a hierarchical document editor, *ACM SIGPLAN Notices*, 16, 6, 74-81.

[3] Arnon, D. (1987). Report of the workshop on environments for computational mathematics, *Request for Comments No. RFC1019*. Menlo Park, CA: ARPANET Information Center.

[4] Avitzur, R. (1987). MILO system [a MacIntosh program]. Palo Alto, CA.

[5] Becker, J. (1987). Arabic word processing, *Comm. ACM*, 30, 7, 600-610.

[6] Berman, R. & Kulp, J. (1979). A new environment for computational physics. In *Proc. MACSYMA Users Conf.*, ed. V. Ellen Lewis, 622-632. Cambridge, MA: Laboratory for Computer Science, MIT.

[7] Bloomberg, D. & Hogg, T. (1987). Engineering/scientific workstation project, Xerox Palo Alto Research Center, GSL-87-01.

[8] Bundy, A. (1985). Discovery and reasoning in mathematics. In *Proc. Int. Joint Conf. Artif. Intell.*, 1221-1230.

[9] Calmet, J. & Lugiez, D. (1987). A knowledge-based system for computer algebra, *ACM SIGSAM Bulletin*, 21, 1, 7-13.

[10] Clapp, L. & Kain, R.Y. (1963). A computer aid for symbolic mathematics, In *Proc. AFIPS Fall Joint Comp. Conf.*, 24, 509-517.

[11] Collins, G. (1980). ALDES and SAC-2 now available, *ACM SIGSAM Bulletin*, 14, 2, 19.

[12] Crecine, J. (1986). The next generation of personal computers, *Science*, 231, 4741, 935-943.

[13] Crowley T., Forsdick, H., Landau, M. & Travers, V. (1987). The Diamond multimedia editor. In *Proc. Unix Users Conf. (USENIX)*, 1-17.

[14] Davis, R. (1986). Knowledge-based systems, *Science*, 231, 4741, 957-963.

[15] Donahue, J. (1985). Integration mechanisms in Cedar, *ACM SIGPLAN Notices*, 20, 7.

[16] Engeler, E. (1985). Scientific computation: the integration of symbolic, numeric and graphic computation, *Lecture Notes in Computer Science*, 203, 185-200. New York, NY: Springer-Verlag.

[17] Fateman, R. (1987). T$_E$X output from MACSYMA-like systems. Dept. of Electrical Engineering and Computer Science, Univ. of CA, Berkeley, unpublished manuscript.

[18] Foderaro, J. (1979). Typesetting MACSYMA equations In *Proc. MACSYMA Users Conf.*, ed. V. Ellen Lewis, 345-361. Cambridge, MA: Laboratory for Computer Science, MIT.

[19] Foster, G. (1984). *DREAMS: display representation for algebraic manipulation systems*, Dept. of Electrical Engineering and Computer Science, Univ. of CA, Berkeley, CSD 84/193.

[20] Genesereth, M. (1977). An automated consultant for MACSYMA, *Proc. MACSYMA Users Conf.*, publication NASA CP-2012, 309-314. Washington DC: National Aeronautics and Space Administration.

[21] Griesmer, J. & Jenks, R. (1971). Scratchpad/I - an interactive facility for symbolic mathematics. In *Proc. Second Symp. Symbolic Algebraic Manip. (SIGSAM '71)*, ed. S. Petrick, 42-58. New York, NY: ACM.

[22] Hearn, A. (1980). The personal algebra machine, *Proc. IFIP '80*, 620-628. Amsterdam: North-Holland.

[23] Hearn, A. (1982). REDUCE - a case study in algebra system development, *Lecture Notes in Computer Science*, **144**, 263-272. New York, NY: Springer-Verlag.

[24] Jenks, R.D. (1984). A primer: 11 keys to new SCRATCHPAD, *Lecture Notes in Computer Science*, **174**, 123-147. New York, NY: Springer-Verlag.

[25] Katz, A. (1987). Issues in defining an equations representation standard, *ACM SIGSAM Bulletin*, **21**, 2, 19-24.

[26] Knuth, D.E. (1984). *The T_EXBook*, Reading, MA: Addison-Wesley.

[27] Koved L. & Shneidermann B. (1986). Embedded menus: selecting items in context, *Comm. ACM*, **29**, 4, 312-318.

[28] Leong, B. (1986). Iris: design of a user interface program for symbolic algebra. In *Proc. Symp. Symbolic and Algebraic Computation*, ed. B. Char, 1-6. New York, NY: ACM.

[29] Licklider, J. (1960). Man-computer symbiosis, *IRE Trans. on Human Factors in Electronics*, **HFE-1**, 4-11.

[30] Martin, W. (1967). *Symbolic Mathematical Laboratory (Ph.D. dissertation)*, Cambridge, MA: MIT.

[31] Martin, W. & Fateman, R. (1971). The MACSYMA system. In *Proc. Second Symp. Symbolic Algebraic Manip. (SIGSAM '71)*, ed. S. Petrick, 59-75. New York, NY: ACM.

[32] MathSoft Inc. (1987). MathCAD system. Cambridge, MA.

[33] McCarthy, J. (1962). Towards a mathematical theory of computation, *Proc. IFIP '62*, Amsterdam: North-Holland.

[34] Minsky, M. (1963). *MATHSCOPE, part I - a proposal for a mathematical manipulation-display system*, Artificial Intelligence Project, Project MAC, MIT, MAC-M-118.

[35] Morris, J. *et al.* (1986). Andrew: a distributed personal computing environment, *Comm. ACM* **29**, 3, 184-201.

[36] Ng, E. (1979). Symbolic-numeric interface: a review, *Lecture Notes in Computer Science*, **72**, 330-345. New York, NY: Springer-Verlag.

[37] Pier, K., Bier, E. & Stone, M. (1988). Gargoyle: an interactive illustration tool, *Proc. EP'88 Int'l Conf. on Electronic Publishing, Document Manipulation, and Typography*, Nice, France.

[38] Quint, V. (1983). An interactive system for mathematical text processing, *Technology and Science of Informatics*, **2**, 3, 169-179.

[39] Quint, V. (1984). Interactive editing of mathematics. In *Proc. First Intl. Conf. Text Processing Systems*, 55-68. Dublin, Ireland: Boole Press.

[40] Schelter, W.F. (1987). *INFOR display editor*. Department of Mathematics, Univ. of Texas-Austin, unpublished manuscript.

[41] Shneiderman, B. (1983). Direct manipulation: a step beyond programming languages, *IEEE Computer*, **16**, 8, 57-69.

[42] Smith, C. & Soiffer, N. (1986). MathScribe: a user Interface for computer algebra systems. In *Proc. Symp. Symbolic and Algebraic Computation*, ed. B. Char, 7-12. New York, NY: ACM.

[43] Spirkovska, L. (1986). MUFIE: MACSYMA's user friendly interactive executive, Dept. of Electrical Engineering and Computer Science, Univ. of CA, Berkeley, M.Sc. report.

[44] Sundblad, Y., (1974). Symbolic mathematical systems now and in the future, *ACM SIGSAM Bulletin,* **8**, 3, 1-8.

[45] Suppes, P. *et al.* (1987). *Applications of computer technology to pre-college calculus, first annual report.* Inst. for Math. Studies in the Social Sci., Stanford University, Psych. and Ed. Series TR #310.

[46] Swinehart, D., Zellweger, P., Beach, R. & Hagmann, R. (1986). A structural view of the Cedar programming environment, *ACM Trans. Prog. Lang. Systems,* **8**, 4, 419-490.

[47] Wactlar, H. & Barnett, M. (1964). Mechanization of tedious algebra — the e coefficients of theoretical chemistry, *Comm. ACM,* **7**, 12, 704-710.

[48] Wolfram, S. (1985). Symbolic mathematical computation, *Comm. ACM,* **28**, 4, 390-394.

[49] Xerox Corp. (1986). *Character code standard.* Xerox System Integration Standard XSIS 058605.

[50] Xerox Corp. (1986). Viewpoint Document Editor: Viewpoint Series Reference Library Version 1.1. El Segundo, CA.

[51] Zellweger, P., Terry, D. & Swinehart, D. (1988). An overview of the Etherphone system and its applications, *Proc. 2nd IEEE Conf. on Computer Workstations,* Santa Clara, CA.

[52] Zellweger, P. (1988). Active paths through multimedia documents, *Proc. EP'88 Int'l Conf. on Electronic Publishing, Document Manipulation, and Typography,* Nice, France.

ACTIVE PATHS THROUGH MULTIMEDIA DOCUMENTS

POLLE T. ZELLWEGER

Xerox Palo Alto Research Center

ABSTRACT
We have developed a scripting mechanism for creating active paths through a document or set of documents. Scripted multimedia documents can contain a combination of text, graphics, audio, and actions. Scripts can be used in a wide variety of ways, such as for formal demonstrations and audio-visual presentations, for informal interpersonal communications, and for organizing collections of information. Scripted documents are a dynamic form of hypermedia document whose additional structure can be layered on top of existing documents.

1. Introduction
The advent of workstations has enabled a new and qualitatively different kind of document: a dynamic one that can incorporate audio and video in addition to text and graphics, one that can present itself in different ways depending on the needs or wishes of a particular reader at a particular time, and one that can serve as the backbone of a variety of "computations" that a reader might wish to perform. A prototype system for investigating these new capabilities has been built in the Cedar programming environment [Swinehart86] at the Xerox Palo Alto Research Center using the capabilities of the Etherphone voice system [Zellweger88] and the Tioga text editor [Teitelman84, Beach85].

1.1. *Overview of scripted documents*
A *script* is an active directed path through one or more documents that need not follow the linear order of the documents. Each entry in a script consists of a document location, such as a contiguous sequence of characters in a text document, together with an associated action and timing. Sample actions might play back a previously-recorded voice annotation, send text to a text-to-speech synthesizer, open a new window, animate a picture, or query a database. Script specifications are stored in a shared database separately from the underlying documents. A single document can have multiple scripts traversing it for different purposes.

A script can be played back as a whole, in which case the first document in the script is displayed on the screen, positioned to show the first location. The location is highlighted to call attention to it, and its associated action is performed. After the associated timing, the system highlights the location of the next script entry, scrolling if needed, performs its action, and so on. The same document location can appear at multiple points in the script, with the same or different associated actions and timing.

Arbitrary actions at a scripted location allow scripted documents to perform a wide variety of tasks, including demonstrations, tutorials, and programming tools. Parameterized actions allow a script to be personalized, such as "Hello <username>," or to more accurately reflect the current state of affairs, such as "There are <currentNumber> entries in this category." Scripts can be very formal items that are carefully crafted for pedagogical reasons, such as a videotape or a presentation, or they can be informal, used to communicate from a single script writer to a single script reader (who might well be the same person).

1.2. *Related work*

The capabilities of electronic documents have been expanding rapidly in recent years. Multimedia document systems have extended the contents of documents from text and formatting to include bitmap images, geometric graphics, spreadsheets, attributes, and voice [Ades86, Crowley87, Luther87]. Hypertext systems allow users to link non-contiguous portions of documents to express the associations between them [Delisle86, Halasz86, Meyrowitz86, Conklin87]. Electronic books and encyclopedias combine multimedia (text, graphic illustrations, and sometimes video) and hypertext (to link related sections) and may also include interactive portions in which readers can run simulations or other experiments to improve their understanding [Feiner82, Weyer85, Yankelovich85]. Presentation tools make it possible for users to capture sequences of actions to create automatic demonstrations [Xerox85]. Other document systems have included animation [Fiume87], actions [Hogg84], or sequencing [Christodoulakis86]. These advanced capabilities have been provided in several ways: by example, by direct manipulation, or by some form of programming language. The scripted documents system described in this paper forms a unique combination of multimedia documents, hypertext links, sequencing, and actions that increases document functionality still further.

2. Key ideas of scripted documents

This section discusses some of the key aspects of scripted documents, emphasizing ways in which scripted documents differ from typical hypertext systems.

2.1. Directed paths versus browsing

Most hypertext systems have concentrated on providing links between related nodes, creating an information space that a user can browse at will. The related concept of a *directed path* through a set of documents allows authors or script writers to include more structure. This structure consists of timed sequences of information, unrelated to the ordering of the underlying documents, to help the user understand the material. Although a few hypertext systems allow a sequence of links to be combined to form a path [Conklin87], we have instead made paths our primitive mechanism in order to explore the applications of sequentiality in electronic documents (see Section 3). For example, a later path entry can rely upon the user having seen earlier entries to overlay or animate previously-seen images or to abbreviate explanations.

There is a conceptual continuum from the directed mode of following paths to the browsing mode of exploring links. For example, although standard usage of scripted documents is to experience a path automatically, users can single-step through a group of directed paths to approximate the more conventional browsing paradigm. A more interesting combination of directed paths and browsing is an *interactive path*, in which the user answers questions to construct his or her desired path through the information. In fact, a hypertext link can be expressed as a degenerate script containing two locations that have no corresponding actions.

2.2. Emphasis on voice

As a result of the efforts of the Etherphone project, recorded and synthesized voice are widely available in the Cedar environment. Documents prepared with the Tioga editor can contain formatted text, graphics, and an unlimited number of arbitrary-length voice annotations. A direct-manipulation voice editor allows easy editing at the phrase or sentence level.

Voice is a critical component of a script. It provides a unifying thread for presentations and interpersonal communication, and it provides an out-of-band way to organize and comment on written material. Finally, it is easy to collect and modify (but as yet hard to search, although speech recognition systems are rapidly improving).

2.3. Script information separate from underlying ordinary documents

Separating scripts from the underlying documents enables an interesting mixture of public and private scripts. Scripts can refer to public documents without modifying those documents, allowing a user to create a personally organized information space (such as during an authoring task) without copying information into a closed hypertext system. Separating scripts from the underlying documents also allows for a smooth integration of scripted documents with other documents: scripts can gradually be added to a set of documents that continue to be accessed as ordinary documents.

2.4. *Arbitrary actions accompany document locations*
Script actions are unconstrained – they can call upon the power of the surrounding computing environment to execute commands or program fragments. The following section illustrates the resulting flexibility and power of scripts.

3. Examples of scripts

Scripts have a wide variety of uses. Script writers can create formal teaching materials and documentation. Users can build scripts that organize information or perform repetitive tasks. In addition, programs can construct scripts to ease complex tasks.

Teaching tool. A language dialog can be represented both textually and as a simultaneous sequence of voice annotations to demonstrate correct pronunciation. The same dialog can include multiple scripts, one for each language desired. Each script visits the same sequence of locations, but has different associated voice annotations.

Interpersonal communication. To review a manuscript, each reviewer can prepare a script for the manuscript, including voice annotations as well as branches through other supporting documents. Each script can follow an arbitrary path through the manuscript to collect related points. This use provides much of the value of a face-to-face interaction between the reviewer and the author, in which the reviewer makes comments while flipping back and forth through the manuscript and other documents to substantiate those comments.

Personal information management. A user can create multiple scripts through a set of documents, each organizing a different topic. These scripts can be reordered as needed. The use of voice to annotate each location can be particularly helpful in early stages of idea exploration.

Audio-visual presentation. Voice, text, and graphics can be combined to simulate a "slide show" on a selected subject. Several versions of the slide show, including different or rearranged slides, can be constructed to accommodate different audiences or different time constraints.

User documentation and demonstration. Scripts can be used to explain how to use a complex program, such as a graphic illustrator. Actions can load and start the program, apply it to an example, visit noteworthy places in the user manuals, and explain some beginner's projects. Different scripts can be prepared for novice, intermediate, and expert users. Figure 1 shows the first few entries of such a script applied to the tutorial for the Gargoyle illustrator [Pier88].

"Bouncing ball" for songs or poems (looping actions). The text of a song or poem with a refrain can be successively highlighted with simultaneous audio, returning to the single copy of the text for the refrain as appropriate. Representing the song or poem in

this way emphasizes the identity of the refrain, so that the reader need not carefully compare repeated copies of a linear representation. Similarly, a presentation may repeatedly return to an overview slide to orient viewers or to emphasize important points.

Program-constructed scripts as history mechanisms. Programs can automatically construct scripts to act as history mechanisms for their users. For example, searching through annotations in a voice-annotated document can be tedious. An annotation system could automatically construct three scripts whenever voice annotations were added to a document. The first would connect all annotations to the document in document order. The second would connect all annotations to the document in the order that they were made. A third more ephemeral script would cross document boundaries to connect all annotations made during a single session in the order that they were made.

Scripts can also be used for collecting locations of interest rather than for their sequencing and/or action capabilities. Consider the following two examples.

Program debugging tool (repetitive actions). To provide an easy way of controlling a named group of breakpoints during program debugging, a collection of locations in several program files can be joined into a script with actions that set appropriate breakpoints: standard, conditional, profiling, tracing, etc. This script can be executed whenever a user wishes to activate those breakpoints. They can later be removed without disturbing other active breakpoints by overriding the script's stored actions with a separately-specified action that clears the breakpoint.

Program editing tool (empty actions). A compiler could build a script containing the locations of all the syntax errors in a group of files compiled together. The user could then single-step through the script, making corrections along the way. The script both makes it easy for the user to find the next error location and automatically manages the changing character positions as the user adds or removes characters to correct the errors.

4. Creating and playing back scripts

4.1. *Script creation and editing*

A script has two parts: the script entries, in which the script writer specifies scripted locations, actions, and timing; and the script header, in which the script writer specifies the script name and a simple program describing the sequencing of the entries. Separating the sequencing information allows the same script entry to appear in multiple scripts or multiple times in a single script.

A script tool is used to create and edit scripts. The prototype Script Tool is a form-based tool with a simple set of operations.

Figure 1a: *A sample user documentation script, part 1.*

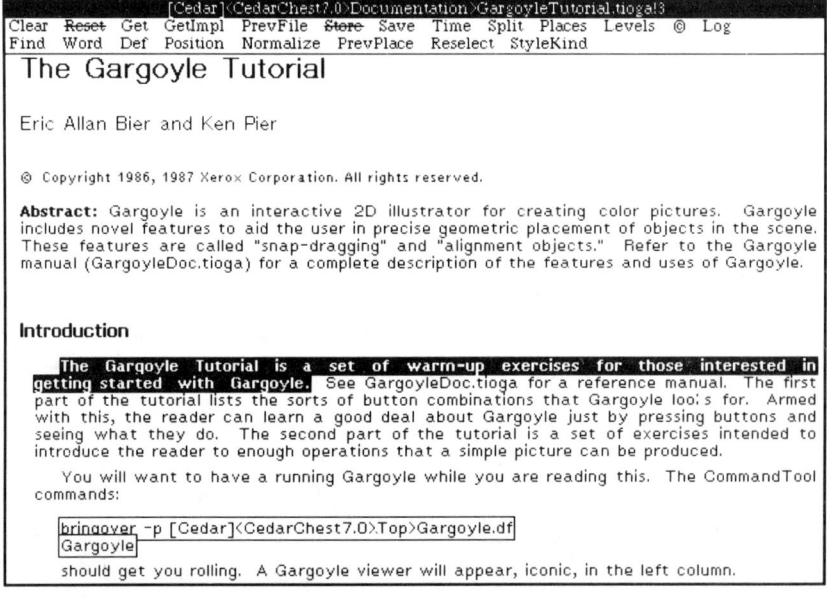

Sample script at the first entry. This action uses the text-to-speech synthesizer to greet the user by name, welcoming him or her to the Gargoyle tutorial.

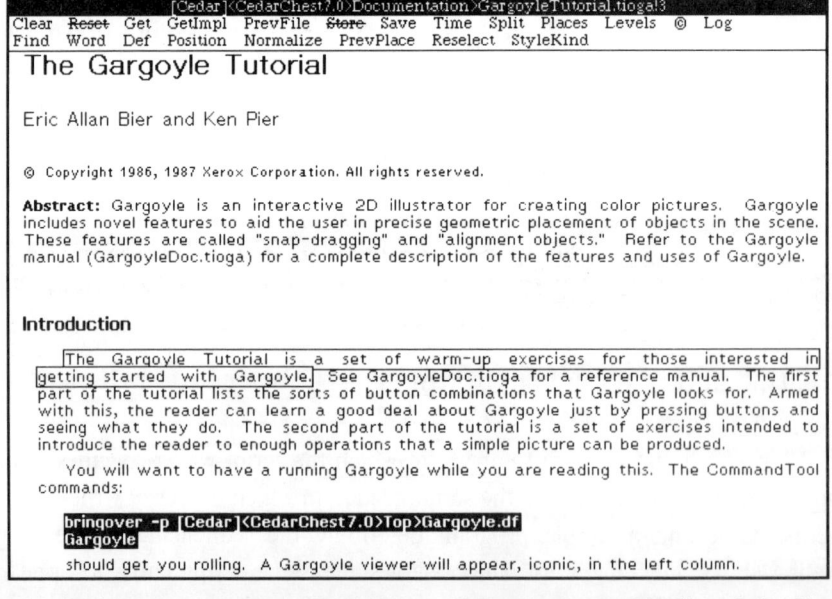

Sample script at the second entry. This action retrieves the executable files of the Gargoyle illustrator and starts the program (the same actions that the text is instructing the user to perform).

Figure 1b: *A sample user documentation script, part 2.*

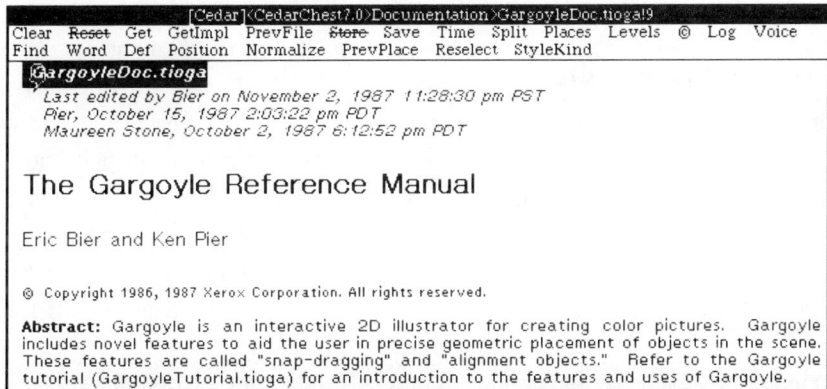

Sample script at the third entry. This is a different file. The action plays back the previously-recorded voice annotation on the first character of the scripted location (a tiny "word balloon" around the character G indicates the presence of voice). The voice annotation explains the difference between the Gargoyle tutorial and the Gargoyle reference manual.

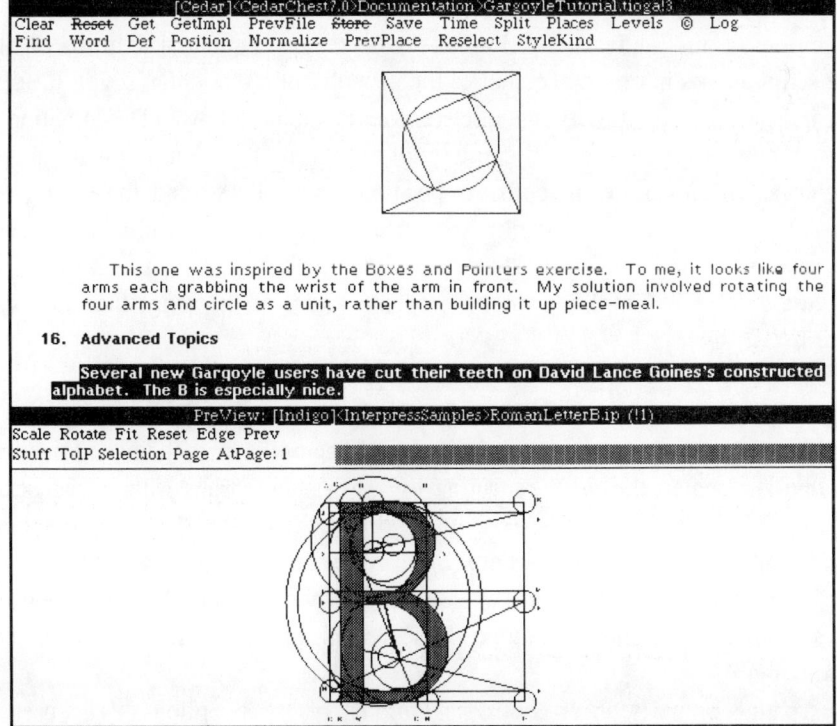

Sample script at the fourth entry. The script has returned to the tutorial document. The action displays on the screen an Interpress master for an image that was not included in the tutorial itself.

Script entries. To create or edit a script entry, the script writer specifies its action and timing fields by filling in the fields of a script entry form, sets its location by making a screen selection, and then saves the form. The user can name a script entry or provide keywords for later filtering, if desired. The system provides a unique identifier (id) for each script entry, records the creator and the create time, and writes the script entry to the script database. System defaults allow simple script entries to be created without forms: the default action is to play back all voice annotations at the location, if any, and the default timing is to continue when the action completes.

Action field. Any Cedar system command can appear in the action field of an annotation. Since system commands can invoke the Cedar language interpreter, arbitrary Cedar language statements can also be included.

Timing field. The script system continues to the next script entry when the specified duration has passed, regardless of whether the action has completed. The script writer can specify "*" to continue whenever the action completes or "~" to wait for user confirmation before continuing.

Script sequencing. The sequencing information for a script is specified separately from the script's entries. For a strictly sequential script, it consists of an ordered list of script entries (as unique ids). A script writer can create a sequential script by pointing to the script entries in order. To change the ordering of a sequential script, the script writer indicates the script entry that a selected entry should follow. (This situation can become a bit more complicated, because script entries can appear multiply in the same script, creating ambiguities in both the position being altered and the desired new position.) To create a more complex sequence, the script writer can edit the textual representation of the sequence to add loops, conditionals, or calls to other scripts.

Figure 2 shows a simplified internal representation of the script that appears in Figure 1.

4.2. *Script playback*

The Play command plays an entire script from the beginning, proceeding automatically from one location to the next, executing the associated actions with the associated timings. The user can pause an executing script at the end of the current action or abort the current action. A quiescent script can be continued or single-stepped. The user can also play a script backward or single-step backward from the current location. If the script contains branches or loops, the session history will be used to construct the backward path.

A separate property sheet controls additional playback options. The user can inhibit the actions associated with annotations (so as simply to traverse through the scripted locations), specify a single action to be executed at every scripted location, and increase or decrease the timing by some factor.

Figure 2: *Simplified internal representation of the script for Figure 1.*

Script header

script header id: 12345677 # PolleZ.pa
script name: Introduction to Gargoyle
file names:
   /cedar/documentation/GargoyleTutorial.tioga
   /cedar/documentation/GargoyleDoc.tioga
script sequence:
   12345678 # PolleZ.pa   12345679 # PolleZ.pa
   12345680 # PolleZ.pa   12345681 # PolleZ.pa

Script entries

script entry id: 12345678 # PolleZ.pa
filename: /cedar/documentation/GargoyleTutorial.tioga
class: Tioga text
location: 15..121
action: speak("Hello, ", UserCredentials.Get[].name,
   ". Get ready to blast off.")
time: 15 sec

script entry id: 12345679 # PolleZ.pa
filename: /cedar/documentation/GargoyleTutorial.tioga
class: Tioga text
location: 624..683
action: bringover -pm Gargoyle.df; Gargoyle
time: *

script entry id: 12345680 # PolleZ.pa
filename: /cedar/documentation/GargoyleDoc.tioga
class: Tioga text
location: 1..17
action: play(annotations)
time: 10 sec

script entry id: 12345681 # PolleZ.pa
filename: /cedar/documentation/GargoyleTutorial.tioga
class: Tioga text
location: 55417..55537
action: PreView RomanLetterB.interpress
time: *

4.3. *Script visualization and navigation*

Script visualization is a problem for both the script reader and the script writer, because script sequencing and script actions are not directly visible through examination of the document. The script reader must be able to tell that a document has associated scripts and which scripts are appropriate for him or her to play back. The script writer has the more difficult problem, in that he or she must also have tools for debugging faulty scripts.

The script reader is alerted to the presence of scripts in a document in two ways. First, when a document is displayed, a **Script** button appears in the document header if and only if the document has scripted locations. All script examination and playback operations are available from a popup menu generated by clicking the **Script** button. Second, each scripted location is distinctively marked. Textual scripted locations are marked with a surrounding rectangle; other scripted objects may be marked differently. The marker indicates the presence of one or more script entries at that location, which may appear at multiple places in multiple scripts. The user can view all script entries that include that scripted location or list the names of all scripts that include it. The reader can also ask what scripts have entries in a given document.

In addition, a user can browse the script database for script names, script entry names, keywords, or any other script field. Other navigation commands show the user the document location associated with a script entry, all scripts the entry belongs to, and all possible preceding or following entries in a given script.

5. Implementation

Scripted documents are implemented in the Cedar programming environment in the Computer Science Laboratory of the Xerox Palo Alto Research Center [Swinehart86]. The two systems that they rely upon most heavily are the Tioga editor and the Etherphone system. We describe each of these systems briefly, and then we describe the implementation of scripted documents.

5.1. *The Tioga editor*

The Tioga editor is a WYSIWYG "what you see is what you get" galley editor used for both program text and high-quality documents [Teitelman84, Beach85]. Tioga documents are tree-structured to express the organization of the document into sections, subsections, paragraphs, and so on. Tioga documents can be displayed at any level of detail, omitting nodes that are nested more deeply than the selected level.

Tioga documents can contain rich formatting and typography. Each node has an associated format, which specifies such parameters as its leading, margins, default typeface, and so on. A document as a whole has an associated style, which defines the meanings of all formats used in that document. Nodes can also have arbitrary named properties, added by the user or by programs. These properties are not directly visible when the document is viewed, but a separate Edit Tool can be used to examine their values. One use of node properties is to specify images, Interpress masters, and additional parameters to support illustrations embedded in Tioga documents.

Individual characters in a Tioga document can have looks, which specify special typeface parameters such as boldface, italic, subscript, and the like. Characters can also have arbitrary named properties. Tioga has search commands that allow rapid searching of documents for given node or character properties.

5.2. *The Etherphone system*

The experimental Etherphone system uses Ethernet communications to transmit digitized voice [Zellweger88]. The system consists of microprocessor-based electronic telephones, a centralized switching server, a voice file server, and workstation programs to support voice communications and voice recording services. From a workstation, a user can place and receive telephone calls, maintain private telephone directories, and manage a database of voice messages. A voice annotation package allows voice to be added to Tioga documents and provides a simple direct-manipulation interface for editing voice [Ades86]. Furthermore, a commercial text-to-speech synthesizer exists as a server in the Etherphone network. The synthesizer allows the system to "speak" text, initiated either by the user (perhaps by selecting the text in a viewer) or by a program (such as speaking an error message or proofreading a document).

This work on scripted documents began as a project to exploit the capabilities of the Etherphone system by creating narrated documents. Narrated documents are scripted Tioga documents with a single type of action: playing back previously-recorded voice annotations.

5.3. *Scripted documents*

The two parts of a script specification, the script entries and the script sequencing information, are stored separately from the underlying documents in a simple B-tree-indexed database [Terry88]. The database's ability to merge the results of queries to multiple databases allows users to simultaneously access private databases containing their private scripts and public databases containing public scripts.

5.3.1. *Tagged and absolute references to scripted locations*

An important goal of the scripting system was to allow script writers to create script entries that refer to any document they can access, including documents they cannot or do not wish to modify (hereafter called *read-only* documents). This capability is especially important when scripts are being used as an organizational tool, such as during an authoring task. Ideally, the owners of a scripted document would also be able to edit unscripted portions of the document without damaging the script.

Given our additional desire to use the existing version-based file system in our widely-distributed environment, we achieve reasonable functionality by allowing script entries to contain two different kinds of references to scripted locations. *Absolute references* refer to precise locations in documents, such as character or byte positions, while *tagged references* refer to uniquely tagged and hence movable objects within documents.

The initial prototype of the scripting system used only tagged references and stored each document's script entries within the document. However, the desire to script read-only documents suggested database storage for their script entries, and it proved more convenient in the later implementation to store all script entries together.

Absolute references are used to refer to items within read-only documents. The scripting system records the scripted location and the exact timestamp and version of the containing file. The file is considered immutable: if it is subsequently updated, the script will continue to refer to the older version. Note that many public documents, such as user documentation and reports, are likely to change less frequently than personal documents. We are exploring ways to handle such documents more robustly, such as also recording a signature containing the scripted location to permit the location to be found in the new version if it exists.

By contrast, creating a tagged reference to a scripted location modifies its containing file. The scripting system writes the unique id of the script entry in the scripted object. Tagged references allow other portions of the file to be edited without disturbing the scripted location, even when the scripting system is not running. However, editing the scripted location itself generally destroys its pointer to the script entry. These semantics are reasonable, because it is not clear that the new version of the scripted location is related to the old script entry. For example, consider scripting the word "reindeer" in a document to have an action that plays a bit of "Rudolph the Red-nosed Reindeer," and suppose that later edits change "reindeer" to "moose."

For either kind of reference, if a scripted location cannot be found during playback, the system displays an informational message and continues with the next script entry.

5.3.2. *Scripting different kinds of document content*

The design of the scripting system is object-oriented to permit scripting a variety of documents, such as Tioga documents and VLSI diagrams, and a variety of contents, such as text, bitmaps, and synthetic graphics. Each class of visual object must implement the following functions:

identify [object] -- *returns class and location, suitable for storing*

add [object, unique id] -- *tag object with unique id*

remove [object, unique id] -- *remove tag*

showWithHighlight [filename, filedate and version, location, unique id]
 -- *used to highlight the object when it is the script entry being executed*

The identify function takes a selected object, such as a sequence of text characters or a piece of a bitmap, and returns both the class of that object and its location (a persistent way of addressing it), suitable for storing in a script. For a sequence of text characters, it returns a character position and a length, while for a piece of a bitmap, it returns the coordinates of its bounding box. This function supports absolute references to scripted objects and provides a hint and a printable value for the location of a tagged object.

The add function supports tagged references to scripted objects by writing into the specified object a unique id that identifies a script entry. For example, for text in a Tioga file, the add function uses Tioga's ability to associate arbitrary property-value pairs with any character. The remove function is the inverse operation.

A class's showWithHighlight function finds an object in a file using either a filedate and location (for an absolute reference) or a unique id (for a tagged reference). This function positions the file so that the corresponding object is visible and highlights the object.

5.3.3. *Making scripted locations visible*

To avoid unknowingly destroying scripted locations, script writers and other document editors must be able to see them. To make tagged references visible, the scripted object's add procedure is responsible for adding the visible scripted location indicator to the object. Similarly, the remove procedure removes the indicator when it removes the script entry id. Making absolute references visible presents more of a challenge. The script system must consult the database whenever a new remote file is opened to see if absolute references to this file exist. If so, it constructs a view of the scripted read-only document with script indicators added.

6. Status and future work

The initial prototype of the scripting system was designed for creating narrated documents. Scripts performed a single action, namely playing back voice annotations, at each scripted location. Each script was constrained to refer to a single document, although a document could contain multiple scripts. Script entries were stored in the document header and contained their own sequencing information; tagged references referred to scripted locations throughout the document. A simple script tool allowed users to create, edit, play back, and navigate through scripts.

The current prototype separates sequencing information from the remainder of the script entry (to permit multiple scripts to share the same entry) and stores both in a database (to allow scripting read-only documents and to make it easier to refer to multiple documents in a single script). The system has been redesigned to permit scripting different classes of document content, but text is the only class that is currently handled. The language for describing complex sequencing is still in its infancy: the scripting system currently allows only sequential scripts, although they may visit the same location repeatedly. The implementation of the scripting system uses a variety of previously-existing Cedar packages: the Tioga text editor, the Etherphone telephone and voice management system, the LoganBerry database system, the Command Tool command interpreter (with its ability to execute Cedar language statements), and the FS version-based file system. Additional user interface features are still needed, as they have not progressed much from the earlier prototype. In particular, the more advanced user playback options, such as backward playback and variable playback timing control, have not yet been designed.

We are working on extending our prototype scripting tool to allow conditional and/or interactive scripts; better visualization of scripts for both script readers and writers, including browsing tools and visual displays of script sequencing; better control of screen and document layout at each script entry during script execution; and scripting other classes of documents, such as graphic illustrations or VLSI layouts.

7. Summary

The scripting concept unifies action, presentation, and hypermedia to form a useful and flexible mechanism for improving documents of the future. This novel mechanism allows writers to communicate additional information to readers. Scripted multimedia documents can contain any combination of text, graphics, audio, and action. Scripts need not follow the normal linear order of their associated documents. In addition, script writers can construct multiple viewing paths through documents for different readers and for different purposes.

The scripting mechanism can be widely applied to create electronic documents with increased capabilities. Scripted documents can orchestrate formal presentations, arrange informal communications, organize collections of information, and ease repetitive or complex tasks.

Acknowledgments

Dan Swinehart and Stephen Ades provided the initial impetus to create narrated documents. Jock Mackinlay suggested several improvements to the design of the later scripted documents system. While I would like to thank the many contributors to the Cedar programming environment as a group, I would also like to single out a few whose work has been particularly critical for the scripting system: Rick Beach and Michael Plass provided consultation on its interaction with Tioga, Doug Terry's LoganBerry database package supplied just the needed functionality, and Russ Atkinson's efforts on the Command Tool and Cedar interpreter were invaluable. Pavel Curtis, Subhana Menis, and Ken Pier helped to clarify the exposition of this paper.

References

[1] Ades, S. & Swinehart, D. (1986). Voice annotation and editing in a workstation environment, *Proc. AVIOS'86 American Voice Input Output Society Conf.*, Arlington, VA, 13-28. Also available as Xerox PARC Technical Report CSL-86-3.

[2] Beach, R. (1985). *Setting tables and illustrations with style*, Ph.D. thesis, U. of Waterloo, Canada. Also available as Xerox PARC Technical Report CSL-85-3.

[3] Christodoulakis, S., Ho, F. & Theodoridou, M. (1986). The multimedia object presentation manager of MINOS: a symmetric approach, *Proc. ACM SIGMOD'86 Conf.*, Washington, DC, 295-310.

[4] Conklin, J. (1987). Hypertext: an introduction and survey, *IEEE Computer*, 20, 9, 17-41.

[5] Crowley, T., Forsdick, H., Landau, M. & Travers, V. (1987). The Diamond multimedia editor, *Proc. USENIX Technical Conf.*, Phoenix, AZ, 1-18.

[6] Delisle, N. & Schwartz, M. (1986). Neptune: a hypertext system for CAD applications, *Proc. ACM SIGMOD'86 Conf.*, Washington, DC, 132-143.

[7] Feiner, S., Nagy, S. & van Dam, A. (1982). An experimental system for creating and presenting interactive graphical documents, *ACM Trans. Graphics*, 1, 1, 59-77.

[8] Fiume, E. & Tsichritzis, D. (1987). Multimedia objects, *IEEE Office Knowledge Engineering Newsletter*, 1, 1, 60-64.

[9] Halasz, F., Moran, T. & Trigg, R. (1987). NoteCards in a nutshell, *Proc. ACM CHI+GI'87 Human Factors in Computing Systems and Graphics Interface Conf.*, Toronto, Canada, 45-52.

[10] Hogg, J. & Gamvroulas, S. (1984). An active mail system, *Proc. ACM SIGMOD'84 Conf.*, Boston, MA, 215-222; also *SIGMOD Record*, 14, 2.

[11] Luther, W., Woelk, D. & Carter, M. (1987). MUSE: multimedia user sensory environment, *IEEE Office Knowledge Engineering Newsletter*, 1, 1, 49-59.

[12] Meyrowitz, N. (1986). Intermedia: The architecture and construction of an object-oriented hypermedia system and applications framework, *Proc. OOPSLA'86 Object-Oriented Programming Systems, Languages and Applications Conf.*, Portland, OR, 186-201; also *SIGPLAN Notices*, 21, 11.

[13] Meyrowitz, N. & van Dam, A. (1982). Interactive editing systems: part 1, *Computing Surveys*, 14, 3, 321-352.

[14] Pier, K., Bier, E. & Stone, M. (1988). Gargoyle: an interactive illustration tool, *Proc. EP'88 Int'l Conf. on Electronic Publishing, Document Manipulation, and Typography*, Nice, France.

[15] Swinehart, D., Zellweger, P., Beach, R. & Hagmann, R. (1986). A structural view of the

Cedar programming environment, *ACM Trans. Programming Languages and Systems,* **8**, 4, 419-490.

[16] Teitelman, W. (1984). A tour through Cedar, *IEEE Software,* **1**, 2, 44-73.

[17] Terry, D. & Swinehart, D. (1988). Managing stored voice in the Etherphone system, to appear in *ACM Trans. Computer Systems,* **6**, 1. An extended abstract appears in *Proc. of Eleventh ACM Symposium on Operating System Principles,* Austin, TX, 1987, 103-104.

[18] Weyer, S. & Borning, A. (1985). A prototype electronic encyclopedia, *ACM Trans. Office Information Systems,* **3**, 1, 63-88.

[19] Xerox Corporation. (1985). *ViewPoint 1.0 Demo Maker tool,* Xerox Corporation, P.O. Box 470065, Dallas, TX 75427.

[20] Yankelovich, N., Meyrowitz, N. & van Dam, A. (1985). Reading and writing the electronic book, *IEEE Computer,* **18**, 8, 15-30.

[21] Zellweger, P., Terry, D. & Swinehart, D. (1988). An overview of the Etherphone system and its applications, *Proc. 2nd IEEE Conf. on Computer Workstations,* Santa Clara, CA.

VISUAL STRUCTURE
AND THE TRANSMISSION OF MEANING

RICHARD SOUTHALL

Xerox PARC / Rank Xerox Cambridge EuroPARC

ABSTRACT
The visual structure perceived by the reader of an actual document derives from the physically measurable relationships between the properties of the marks on the substrate of the document. This visual structure provides an encoding of the structure of relationships between content objects that exists in the message the document carries. The paper discusses the characteristics of the encoding schemes that relate visual structure to content structure, and proposes a definition of the *text* of a document that takes into account the contribution made to the document's meaning by its visual structure.

Acknowledgements
The research reported on in this paper was carried out in the Intelligent Systems Laboratory at Xerox Palo Alto Research Center, and has been sponsored in part by the Nippon Telegraph and Telephone Corporation. It follows on from work described in a paper given at the INRIA winter school *Structures de/for documents* that was held in January 1987 at Aussois in France [Southall87]. This paper is referred to below as 'the Aussois paper'.

I am greatly indebted to colleagues in the Intelligent Systems Laboratory, and particularly to Rachel Hewson, David Levy and Susan Stucky, for discussions that helped to clarify the views on the relationships between actual documents and the messages they carry that are presented here.

1 The designer's problem

The system designer, beginning work on the conceptual design of a computer-based document production system, needs answers to two questions: 'What are the objects that the system should deal with?' and 'What properties and relationships do these objects have?'. The literatures of all the research areas the designer might refer to – computer science, typography, linguistics, psychology – contain answers to both of these questions; but the answers available from one area, even when they turn out to be of practical use to the designer, do not appear to have any relevance to the concerns of researchers in any of the other areas. It seems as if each specialism takes a completely different view of what documents are and what they contain: there is no comprehensive theory of documents that provides a coherent picture into which the detailed insights developed in the various fields of research could be fitted.

One approach to the problem of constructing such a theory is to explore ways of answering the question 'How do documents work?'; or, more precisely, 'What are the mechanisms by means of which documents convey to the reader the meaning of the messages they carry?'. In developing the ideas presented in this paper, I have started from what seems to me the indisputable fact that the actual documents that readers use are graphic objects, and that a reader's visual system provides the principal, if not the only, channel through which the reader and the document can interact. This implies that a consideration of the visual properties and relationships of the graphic objects of which an actual document is composed, and the kinds of relationships that exist between these objects and the content of the message the document carries, has to be a fundamental part of any study of the mechanisms by means of which documents achieve their function.

2 Kinds of documents

I use the phrase *actual documents* to denote the physical objects that readers see and use. If we accept the idea that the purpose of written documents is to provide a means by which authors can communicate with readers who are separated from them in space and time, then it becomes evident that the actual document that a reader sees is the only means the reader has of discerning the author's meaning. No part of an author's message that is not present in some form or other in an actual document will be conveyed to a reader of the document; equally, every perceptible feature of an actual document that *is* present, whether it is there by the author's intention or otherwise, plays some part in forming the reader's understanding of the meaning the document conveys.

An actual document is an assembly of *marks* on a *substrate*. The marks occur singly or in groups; each mark or group of marks forms a *graphic object* in the document. The substrate of the document may be *portable*, so that the document can be taken away from the device that produced it or the place where it was made; or it may be *fixed*, so that the reader has to come to the document in order to be able to read it. The most familiar portable document substrate is paper; perhaps the most common example of a fixed substrate at the present day is the display surface of an electronic display device.

Actual and virtual documents

Every mechanical system for producing documents contains at some stage in its operations a specification for the actual document the system is about to produce. This specification is a *virtual document*.

Inside the computer of a computer-based document production system, virtual documents exist as data structures constructed according to rules that depend on the way the system in question is conceived. The relationships between virtual documents of this kind and the actual documents that computer-based systems produce are discussed in detail in the Aussois paper. However, virtual documents can exist outside as well as inside computers. For the purposes of the present discussion, it makes a good deal of sense to regard as virtual documents the *printing surfaces* (whether formes of type, lithographic plates or photogravure cylinders) from which actual documents were produced in the traditional technologies of printing.

The fact that objects of this kind exist in their own right, rather than being transient patterns of voltage differences inside a machine whose existence (and, in a sense, purpose) is unaffected by their presence, does not seem to me to invalidate their status as virtual documents. The essential feature of a virtual document is that it is a specification, the instructions in which have to be interpreted by a marking device in order for an actual document to be produced. In the picture of traditional printing technology I am proposing here, the marking device is the printing press, and the instructions supplied by the printing surface concern the location and shape of the marks the press is to make on the paper that forms the document substrate. In this respect, the instructions in the printing surface are very much like those in the pixel array of a present-day electrographic marking device; and the marking processes of traditional printing technologies are non-ideal and non-deterministic in very much the same kinds of ways that electrographic marking processes are.

3 Graphic structure and visual structure

The graphic objects in an actual document are marks or groups of marks. These marks have *metric* and *graphic properties*.

The metric properties of marks are measurable physical properties of the marks themselves. They are such things as *calibre* or *stroke thickness*, that relate to dimensions of the marks. The graphic properties of marks are also measurable physical properties of the marks, though they may be less easy to measure than the marks' metric properties: they are such things as *edge-sharpness*, *reflection density* or *granularity*.

The document substrate also has measurable physical properties such as *size*, *hue* and *reflectance*.

The set of graphic objects in an actual document constitutes the *graphic content* of the document. The structure of relationships between the metric and graphic properties of the objects in the document, and between their positions on the document substrate, makes up the *graphic structure* of the document.

Because it is derived from properties of the marks in the document that are objectively measurable, at least in principle, the graphic structure of an actual document is itself an objective physical property of the document.

Criteria for resemblance between documents
In discussing the objects that document production systems produce, it is useful to have clear notions about what might be meant if two documents were said to be 'the same' (or, for that matter, 'different').

Clearly, every actual document that is written on a portable substrate is *distinct* from every other actual document, in the sense of being a separate physical object. Equally clearly, though, since actual documents are graphic objects, individual actual documents can resemble each other to a greater or lesser extent. We can erect criteria for judging such resemblances on a number of different bases.

One such basis is the ascertainable physical properties of the documents in question: the properties, that is, that give the documents their graphic structure. Considering such properties leads us to a definition of what we can call *graphic identity*: two actual documents are graphically identical if they have identical graphic structures.

Graphic identity is evidently a very severe criterion of resemblance. If we say that two objects are graphically identical, this implies that there are no measurable differences at all either between the properties of their substrates or between the graphic or metric properties or relationships of the marks on the substrates. Because of the non-deterministic nature of the marking processes used in both traditional and present-day systems for producing documents on portable substrates, it is difficult to imagine them ever giving rise to objects that had strict graphic identity. This is, nevertheless, the objective of all such systems, and if they fail to achieve it they usually manage to produce objects that resemble each other reasonably closely. To deal with such resemblances, we can relax the criterion of graphic identity a little, to produce a criterion of *effective identity*: two actual documents are effectively identical if the differences between their graphic structures lie within the normal range of variability for the process that produced them.

Graphic structure, visual structure and the reader
The visual structure of an actual document is the structure of relationships a reader perceives in the graphic structure of the document.

This is the definition of visual structure that was also proposed in the Aussois paper. The reason for making the distinction between visual and graphic structure is that readers' perceptions of the properties of the graphic objects in a document and the relationships between them often differ from the measured (or measurable) values of the properties and relationships themselves. Thus rectangular and circular marks of the same height usually appear to be different in size, strokes in character images that have the same slant often appear to be different in slope, and character images that are equal distances apart often appear to be unequally spaced [Carter37; Ryder79].

The graphic properties of objects, as well as their metric properties, often differ in their perceived and measured values. Marr [Marr82, pp. 251, 254] illustrates several situations in which the perceived relationships between the brightnesses of parts of monochrome figures differ from the relationships between their reflectances, and Albers [Albers75] gives many examples of analogous effects in colour perception. Thus the structure of relationships that a reader perceives between the graphic objects in a document, which is the visual structure the document presents to the reader, is often different from the objectively measurable structure of relationships between the marks on the document substrate that constitutes the document's graphic structure.

Albers' examples, which are to do with colour, raise an important issue. The marks in an actual document can be coloured. The colour of a mark is an objectively measurable graphic property of the mark; marks in a document can be similar or different in colour, in just the same way that they can be similar or different in height, or have similar or different stroke-widths. Thus the relationships between the colours of the marks in an actual document have equal status with the relationships between other properties of the marks as components of the document's graphic structure.

However, the perception of colour difference varies considerably between readers. Thus if some of the relationships between objects that go to make up the visual structure of a document are relationships of colour, different readers will perceive them differently. In particular, some readers will find it very difficult, in certain circumstances, to perceive differences between objects that other readers have no difficulty in telling apart.[1]

Since this is so, and different arrangements of visual relationships may be perceived by different readers in the same document, then an actual document's visual structure cannot be an objective property of the document itself in the same way that the document's graphic structure undoubtedly is. Instead, it becomes a consequence of the individual interactions between the document and each of its readers, and hence depends to a greater or lesser extent on the circumstances in which these interactions take place.

This does not mean, though, that there is no such thing as visual structure. Visual relationships between the graphic objects in an actual document do exist, and can be perceived by readers, and although these relationships are not invariable there will be a good deal of unanimity among readers about what many of them are. What readers perceive as being significant are the comparative relationships between objects in the document: relationships such as 'closer to', 'further away from', 'larger than', 'darker than' and so on. Although not every reader will perceive these relationships in the same way, and it may not be easy to describe the physiological mechanisms that underlie their perception, we can generally agree, in normal circumstances and

---

[1] Readers who have the common colour-vision defect that affects their perception of the difference between red and green light have more difficulty than normally-sighted readers do in seeing differences between yellow and green objects on cathode-ray tube displays. This is because colour-mixing on such displays is additive: yellow is made by mixing red and green. For readers in whom the defect is severe, red, green and yellow objects on the display all appear to be the same hue, with green and yellow distinguished only by a small difference in brightness.

as far as a given set of graphic objects is concerned, on the existence of the relationships themselves, and hence of the visual structure that they constitute.

4 Documents and their content

In this paper, actual documents are regarded as vehicles by means of which messages can be conveyed from an author to communities of readers who are separated from the author in space and time. This view implies that authors' messages have *content*.

For simplicity's sake, the discussion that follows is restricted to written documents – actual documents containing only graphic verbal language [Twyman79] – and the messages they carry. I shall take the view that the content of an author's message has *textuality*, in the sense in which de Beaugrande and Dressler [deBeaugrande81] use the term: I avoid adopting their definition of *text*, however, since I intend to propose a definition of my own later on. I shall also take the view that the content of an author's message is *structured*: that it is made up of *content objects* that have relationships with one another. The structure of relationships between the content objects in a message is the *content structure* of the message.

This paper is concerned with the graphic features of actual documents, and hence necessarily with what de Beaugrande and Dressler call the *surface text* [2] of the message a document carries.

Simple written documents are made up of groups of character images; these form *word images*, *word image rows* and *groups*, and *word image blocks* in the document. We now have to consider the relationship between these graphic objects and the content objects that make up an author's message.

Texts and documents

In the Aussois paper I stated that 'an actual document provides a visible realization of a text', and went on to define texts as collections of semantic objects. The views contained in both of these statements now seem to me to be considerably oversimplified. They suggest that texts are entities whose nature is purely semantic, and that they can exist independently of any realization in a document.

It seems clear that part of the content of an author's message can indeed be realized in ways that are independent of any particular written document. Before the invention of printing, books were produced by writing down the words of a reader as well as by copying directly from existing documents [Eisenstein79, pp. 12–16]. Writing down what we hear someone say allows us to reproduce the *verbal content* of the speaker's utterance: if the speaker is reading from a document, we can transcribe the verbal content of the message the document carries. In its everyday usage, the word *text*

---

[2] "...i.e. the actual words we *hear or see*" [deBeaugrande81, p. 3: my emphasis]. This confounding of spoken and written language seems to me to be typical of the approach adopted by conventional linguistics to the questions addressed in this paper.

refers to this verbal content. However, writing is more than a system for transcribing speech, and the verbal content of the message carried by an actual document is not normally the message's whole content.

Graphic verbal language is two-dimensional and persistent, in contrast to the linearity and temporality of spoken language. Written documents are made up of graphic objects whose properties remain fixed and observable during the time the document is in use, and these graphic objects instantiate content objects in the author's message. The relationships between the properties of the graphic objects in an actual document make up the graphic structure of the document: it is this structure of graphic relationships that can be preserved in copying from an existing document, and is likely to be lost in transcribing the document's verbal content.

Content structure, graphic structure and text
The relationships between graphic objects in an actual document can be exploited to realize the relationships between content objects that make up the structure of an author's message. Within a particular mark-making technology and over a period of time, conventions become established that dictate the graphic means used in written documents to instantiate content objects and the relationships between them in different kinds of message.[3] These conventions can come to delimit quite strictly the acceptable ranges of variation in the means used to realize objects and relationships in a message, and hence to define the immediately recognizable classes of communicative object that Waller calls 'genres' [Waller87; Norrish87, ch. 2]. Thus, once the appropriate conventions for its genre have become established, the graphic content and graphic structure of an actual document can provide a *graphic encoding* of the content and content structure of the message the document carries that is consistently interpretable within a particular cultural environment.

In present-day machine-written documents this encoding operates at four levels. The lowest of these is *verbal content encoding*. The conventionally-established sequence of word images in the document encodes the sequence of elementary objects in the verbal content of the author's message. The relationships between the word images and the content objects they encode are determined by the *orthography* of the language in which the document is written.

The next level of encoding in the document can be called, rather unsatisfactorily, *semantic attribute encoding*. Certain objects in the verbal content of the author's message may have attributes that differentiate them in some way from normal, 'unmarked' objects of the same kind. Perhaps the most common example of such an attribute is *emphasis*. Attributes of this kind are encoded in the actual document by differences between the graphic properties of the word images used to encode the

---

[3] New technologies begin by mimicking the conventions of existing technology, and take time to develop conventions of their own: *cf.* [Walker84].

differentiated objects in the message and those used to encode the undifferentiated objects.

Verbal content encoding and semantic attribute encoding both operate at the level of the word image in the actual document. The next level of encoding, which operates at the level of the word image group, can be called *syntactic structure encoding*. The 'surface' syntactic structures of the author's message – phrases, clauses and sentences – are encoded by word image groups in the document. The *rules of punctuation* for the document's language determine the identities or attributes of the character images that are used to delimit the word image groups that encode each type of structure.

The highest level of encoding in this hierarchy is *content structure encoding*. The relationships between content units that make up the content structure of the message are encoded by graphic relationships between the blocks of word images that realize the content units in the actual document.

The whole set of relationships between the content structure of the author's message and the graphic structure of the actual document that carries the message can be thought of as the *graphic encoding scheme* the document uses.

Certain features of this picture of the relationship between documents and the messages they carry are worth emphasizing. One point, that cannot be insisted on too strongly, is that the graphic encoding schemes used in machine-written documents are entirely arbitrary. The objects in such documents have no meaning of their own,[4] and the documents themselves have only graphic structure. The objects in the document, and the visual structure that their graphic relationships give rise to, are only meaningful when they have been interpreted by a reader; hence the reader's contribution to the interaction that takes place in the encounter between document and reader is as important for the document's communicative function as the contribution of the document itself.

Another point worth noting is the way in which the strictness of the conventions that dictate the relationships between content objects and graphic objects in a document varies from one level to another in the encoding hierarchy. At the first and third levels of the hierarchy, these relationships are governed by well-defined rules that change relatively slowly with the passage of time: the orthography and rules of punctuation of the language in which the document is written. Statements of these rules are easily available in works of reference, and a knowledge of them is usually supposed to be one of the components of 'literacy'. At the second and fourth levels, on the other hand, the conventions that determine the relationships between semantic and graphic content rest to a much greater extent on the prevailing visual culture, and on the capability of the system by means of which the document was produced, than on pedagogical prescription.

---

[4] I feel that this is not so much true of handwritten documents, in which the marks themselves can have considerable expressive quality.

Graphic capability
Every machine-written document is produced by a document production system of one kind or another, and each kind of system makes available to its users a different selection from the total resources of graphic verbal language. We can think of the nature and extent of this selection as constituting the *graphic capability* of the system in question.

The scheme used in a particular document to encode the content and structure of the message the document carries is necessarily built on the graphic capability of the system by which the document was produced. Transcribing a message that has already been realized in an actual document by means of a system that differs in capability from the system that produced the original document may require a quite different encoding scheme to be devised, if as much as possible of the content and structure of the message is to be preserved in the transcription.

This is a central problem for computer-based document production systems. One aspect of it, that of transferring authors' messages between systems of widely differing capability, was investigated as part of the research on the graphic translatability of text funded by the British Library at the University of Reading [Norrish84; Norrish87, ch. 4]. Not surprisingly, it was found necessary in this work to make very detailed studies of the content structures of different kinds of message, and of the graphic means used to encode them in documents [Norrish87, ch. 3].

The text of a document
I propose to define as the *text* of a document *the totality of information about the content of an author's message that the document carries.* Part of this information is the verbal content of the message: this, as we have seen, is independent of its realization in a particular document. All the rest of the information that the document contains is encoded in elements of the document's graphic structure, and conveyed to a reader by the visual structure the reader perceives in the graphic structure.

5 The invention of printing revisited

We can test these ideas by using them to reconstruct the traditional account of the effect of the invention of printing on the dissemination of texts. Graphically identical documents clearly carry identical texts, because both their graphic content and their graphic structure are identical. Documents that are effectively identical also carry identical texts, provided that the normal range of variation in the process that produces them does not affect either their graphic content or the relationships in their graphic structure.

This is why early printing had the advantage over the industrialized production of manuscripts for the publication of theological and scientific work, in which the consistency of a text between different realizations was important [Bühler60; Eisenstein79]. The graphic content and graphic structure of early (and later) printed books was mechanically determined by the specification contained in the formes of type from which the books were printed. This specification remained the same, in principle at any rate, for all the books printed from the same formes, and these therefore all carried the same text. On the other hand it was very difficult for a copyist, even when working from an existing document, to avoid making mistakes [Reynolds74, ch. 6]. The document that was being copied indeed played the role of a virtual document, in that it specified both content and structure for the document that was being produced. However, the connection between virtual and actual document was not a mechanical one, as it was in printing: hence the possibility of changes in content resulting from the copying process, that had the effect of changing the text carried by the new document, was not ruled out.

In writing from dictation, no physical realization of the original document's content structure was presented to the maker of the new document. The reader could *describe* structural features of the document that was being read from, and if the descriptions were sufficiently detailed there might well be some uniformity in the structures of the documents that were produced: but this uniformity depended very much on the establishment of a common understanding between reader and writers, and could not be guaranteed.

There is a striking analogy between this situation and the problem, mentioned in the previous section, of interchanging documents between computer-based systems with differing graphic capabilities. Indeed, if the ideas presented here have any immediate practical application it is in the field of document interchange. The fundamental objective of any document interchange system is to exchange authors' messages without losing any of their meaning: the actual documents the system produces, and the virtual documents that specify them, are in a sense incidental to this objective.

Present-day data transmission networks make it straightforward to transmit the verbal content of a document, and consequently the verbal content and syntactic structure of a message, over an interchange link to a remote location. Interchanging the components of the message's content that were encoded in the graphic structure of the original document involves the construction of an equivalent graphic encoding at the receiving end of the link. If the graphic capability of the production system at the receiving end is identical with that of the system by means of which the original document was produced, there is no difficulty: the receiving system simply produces a document which is effectively identical with the original. With systems of unequal capability, though, three things are necessary for the successful interchange of a message to take place. The first of these is an explicit understanding of the relationship between the original document's graphic encoding scheme and the objects and structures in the message it encodes. The second is a method of describing the content and structure of a message that is independent of the message's realization in any particular document; and the third is an understanding of the principles on which graphic encoding schemes as a whole are constructed.

The first of these is necessary in order for all the graphically-encoded components of the message's meaning to be extracted from their realizations in the graphic structure of the original document. The second is needed to provide a description of the content and structure of the message that can be sent over the interchange link, and the third so that an actual document can be constructed at the receiving end of the link whose graphic content and graphic structure fully realize the meaning of the original message.

It has to be said that in the present state of our knowledge about documents we are a long way from an adequate understanding of any of these issues.

References

[1] Albers, J. (1975). *Interaction of color*. New Haven, Connecticut: Yale University Press.

[2] de Beaugrande, R.-A. & Dressler, W. (1981). *Introduction to text linguistics*. London: Longman.

[3] Bühler, C. L. (1960). *The fifteenth-century book*. Philadelphia: University of Pennsylvania Press.

[4] Carter, H. G. (1937). The optical scale in typefounding. *Typography*, **4**, 2-6.

[5] Eisenstein, E. L. (1979). *The printing press as an agent of change*. Cambridge: Cambridge University Press.

[6] Marr, D. (1982). *Vision*. New York: Freeman.

[7] Norrish, P. (1984). Moving tables from paper to screen. *Visible language*, **18**, 2, 154-170.

[8] Norrish, P. (1987). *The graphic translatability of text* (British Library R & D report 5854). University of Reading, England: Department of Typography & Graphic Communication.

[9] Reynolds, L. D. & Wilson, N. G. (1974). *Scribes and scholars: a guide to the transmission of Greek and Latin literature*. Oxford: Clarendon Press.

[10] Ryder, J. (1979). *The case for legibility*. London: Bodley Head.

[11] Southall, R. (1987). Interfaces between the designer and the document. In *Structures de/for documents*, ed. J. André & V. Quint. Rocquencourt: INRIA.

[12] Twyman, M. L. (1979). A schema for the study of graphic language. In *Processing of visible language 1*, ed. P. A. Kolers, M. E. Wrolstad & H. Bouma. New York: Plenum.

[13] Waller, R. (1987). *The typographic contribution to language* (unpublished doctoral thesis). University of Reading, England: Department of Typography & Graphic Communication.

[14] Walker, S. F. (1984). How typewriters changed correspondence: an analysis of prescription and practice. *Visible language*, **18**, 2, 102-117.

AUTOMATIC RECOGNITION AND REPRESENTATION OF DOCUMENTS

LYNN D. WILCOX and A. LAWRENCE SPITZ

Xerox Palo Alto Research Center

ABSTRACT

Automatic recognition of the content of documents yields a form of compression for document transmission and archival, and provides a high-level representation with which to manipulate the document. The ease with which a document can be manipulated depends on the representation of the components of the document and on the ability of the recognition system to produce a set of meaningful components. Ideally, a document is segmented into component regions containing text, line drawing graphics and pictures. The text is converted to character codes and related text format information. The line drawing graphics are translated into graphics primitives, and pictures are optionally processed by half-tone screen detection and removal. These outputs are then translated into a document representation language, which also describes the layout structure of the document. In order to study issues in the design and use of document recognition systems, we are building a testbed system. It consists of a text/graphics segmenter, a structure analyzer which groups these segments into higher level concepts, the Kurzweil Discover (a multi-font character recognizer and format analyzer), and a module which translates these outputs into the document representation language, Maker Interchange Format (MIF), used by the Frame Maker publishing system.

1. Introduction

The task of a document recognition system is to convert the scanned image of a document into a representation language which models the original document as accurately and concisely as possible. Automatic recognition and representation of the contents of a document is an alternative to storing the document as a bitmap image. Not only does it greatly reduce the storage requirements, but it allows manipulation of the document in ways which would be impossible with only the image. Alterations of a bitmap document are limited to cut, paste and scale operations. To correct the spelling of a word would be difficult, particularly if the incorrect spelling had too few letters. On the other hand, a document which is described in a high-level language can be modified by editing text and graphics and by moving components to alter the layout. In addition, it allows automatic indexing for filing, storage and retrieval.

Document recognition comprises segmentation and classification of regions of text, line drawing graphics and pictures, and translation of this information into a document representation language. A segmenter classifies possibly overlapping rectangular regions of text and graphics, and a structure analyzer translates these regions into higher level descriptions such as columns of text and lines of text on graphics. Text is translated into its ASCII equivalent, and format characteristics such as font type and size, paragraph breaks, line spacing and centering are detected. Graphics recognition is performed to identify the graphics primitives [Henderson86]. Pictures are processed to detect possible half-tone screening, allowing data compression and optimal rendition on different output devices. These outputs are then translated into a document representation language. In this form, the document can be easily edited, stored or transmitted.

We currently limit ourselves to recognition of the layout structure of the document. That is, we attempt to recognize only the way the components of the document are placed on the page. We do not try to infer the meaning or the logical structure of the document from the set of recognized components. For instance, we do not try to interpret a line of text at the top of a document as a header or title, but simply declare it a line of text at a given location.

Commercial systems exist which provide subsets of the functionality required in a document recognition system. The Kurzweil Discover [Kurzweil87] can convert text to ASCII and recognize certain format characteristics, but cannot automatically handle mixed text and graphics or multi-column text. The GTX [GTX87] vectorization system can perform limited graphics recognition. The Frame Maker [FrameMaker87] publishing system can import text and bitmap graphics, and contains a set of tools for WYSIWYG editing. It also has a language for document representation, the Maker Interchange Format (MIF). However, none of these systems are capable of working together.

Several researchers are investigating aspects of the document recognition problem. A goal of the ESPRIT project HERODE [Meynieux86] is to test the adequacy of the proposed international standard document representation language ODA [Horak85] by using it as the target language for their document recognition system. Kida et al. [Kida86] describe a network-service document recognition system which allows users to edit a recognized file at their workstations, but no mention is made of structure recognition or document representation. A system described in Wong et al. [Wong82], discusses an interactive method for segmentation and character recognition. Srihari and Zack [Srihari86] discuss a method for the segmentation and labeling of document image components.

This paper discusses the current state in our development of a document recognition system. Our design methodology for this system is organized around a cycle of prototyping, experiment and theory development. Our prototype is a modular testbed which allows us to perform experiments while simultaneously working on the

Figure 1: *the original document (a), lines of text (b), and blocks of text, lines of text, and graphics (c)*

theoretical aspects of document recognition. We will describe the following components of our testbed: the segmentation algorithm which separates text and graphics, the structure analyzer which uses this information to infer a higher level description of the layout structure of the document, the integration of the Kurzweil character recognition system and format analyzer, the selection of a document representation language, and the procedure for translating the recognized components into the document representation language.

2. Segmentation and structural analysis
2.1. *Segmentation and classification*
The segmenter identifies rectangular regions of the document and classifies them as either a text line, a text block, or a graphics block. Our current system does not distinguish between line drawing graphics and pictures: all nontext regions are labeled graphics and treated as a bitmap image. A text block is defined as a set of equally spaced lines of text with left justification and approximately equal length. In order for the requirement of equal spacing to be meaningful, a text block must have at least three lines. A text line is an isolated line of text, or a line of text not meeting the text block criteria. The distinction is made between text lines and text blocks because a block of text can be treated as a single flow of text in which line breaks may be ignored, while line breaks in the text lines of a formula or figure label may be critical. The rectangular regions are allowed to overlap, so that text within graphics is supported.

The document is first described in terms of a list of marks (connected black regions). Individual marks are classified as text or graphics based on their size, complexity and classification of neighboring marks. The formation of text lines is based on the linear (horizontal) adjacency of individual marks which have been classified as text. Thus, with knowledge of the distribution of character widths, an inference is drawn about maximal inter-character spacing. In this manner, adjacent characters are clumped into words. Approximately collinear words with appropriate word-spacing are grouped into lines of text, provided there is no intervening graphic structure, such as a rule or grid. Figure 1 shows the lines of text of the document in (a), displayed as shaded rectangles in (b).

Text blocks are formed from lines of text by detecting periodicity in the line spacing. The autocorrelation of the absolute position of the base of each mark is used to estimate the vertical periodicity. Characters which rest on the baseline contain information on periodicity, while characters with descenders add noise to the information. The autocorrelation function is filtered to enhance peaks resulting from the baseline characters while suppressing noise from descenders. The first peak in the autocorrelation function as well as its expected harmonics are used to estimate the line spacing. Allowance is made for noise to corrupt a single isolated harmonic. Lines whose spacing agrees with the average spacing computed in this way are grouped to form a text block.

Graphics blocks are defined as minimal enclosing rectangles surrounding individual marks previously classified as graphics. If graphic blocks are adjacent or intersecting, they are merged to form a new graphics block and the enclosing rectangle is redefined. Figure 1(c) shows the text blocks of the document in Figure 1(a) as diagonally hatched rectangles, the remaining text lines as shaded rectangles and the graphics in its original form.

2.2. *Structural analysis*

The purpose of the structure analyzer is to infer a higher level structure of the document from the recognized components and their positions. While the position of individual text lines, text blocks and graphics blocks is sufficient to describe the layout structure of the document, a higher level description is preferable for integration with the rest of the system. For instance, the interface to the character recognition module is optimized by sending the maximum amount of text possible. In the case of intersecting text and graphics blocks, the concept of being above is important for layout. In our system, a bitmap drawn over text obscures the text, while the reverse is not true. Levy calls this the 2½ dimensionality of documents [Levy87].

The higher-level components of a document are thus columns of text and text on graphics. Columns of text provide the character recognition module with the maximum amount of text, subject to the constraint of single column data with no graphics. The text on graphics component implies that the text is superimposed on the graphics. The concept of text on graphics is also useful in the document representation language, since it allows later manipulation of the text and graphics as a unit.

Figure 2: *a segmentation tree: leaf nodes are text lines and graphics, intermediate nodes are text blocks, columns of text and text on graphics*

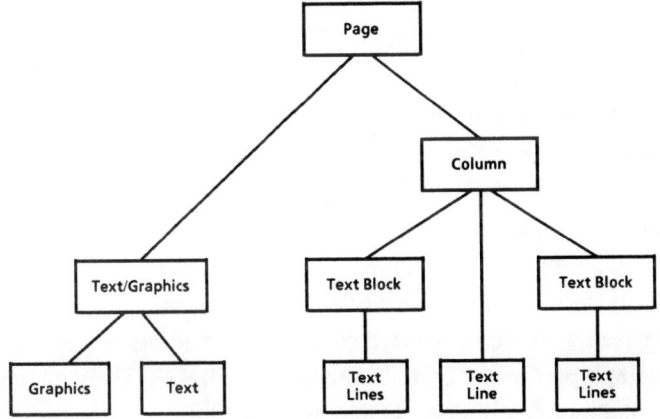

Figure 2 shows the hierarchical representation of a document page. The tree is built from the bottom up, with the segmenter supplying the text lines, text blocks and graphics. Columns of text are built by merging text blocks of approximately equal width (allowing for text set ragged right) that are vertically adjacent and that have no intervening graphics. Lines of text between text blocks, such as titles, should also be included in the column. Therefore, a line of text is redefined as a text block of arbitrary width, and the same rules for vertical adjacency and the exclusion of graphics are applied. Text on graphics is the union of all text blocks or text lines that intersect a given graphics block. The enclosing rectangle for the text on graphics component is redefined as the smallest rectangle enclosing all the text and graphics blocks.

3. Character recognition

The primary job of character recognition is to transform text portions of the scanned document image into their ASCII equivalents. For a system of this type, recognition should be font independent and should require little or no training by the user. By font independent, we mean that the system can recognize most fonts, except stylistic ones, produced by any output device ranging from a typewriter to a laser printer to a printing press. This is in contrast to certain systems, e.g., DEST [DEST87], which recognize only fixed pitch typewriter fonts. User-trained systems require the user to instruct the system as to the identity of each character it sees. Although this mode is useful for applications with large quantities of homogeneous text, we do not see this as practical in a system which expects many different types of documents.

For accurate reproduction of the document, it is also important to recognize the text format characteristics. This includes identification of paragraphs, recognition of font type and size, subscript and superscript detection, recognition of line centering and right justification, and estimation of line spacing and paragraph spacing. Font identification is a difficult task in that it requires examination of detailed characteristics of the text. In fact it is just this level of detail that an omni-font character recognizer wishes to ignore. However, an approximation can be made by recognizing whether the font has fixed or variable spacing.

Work on a font-independent character recognizer based on descriptive features [Spitz87] is in progress. In order to test other components of our system, we are currently using the Kurzweil Discover [Kurzweil87], a multi-font character recognition system which does not require any training by the user. The system performs character recognition and tags questionable and unrecognized characters for ease of later editing. A format analysis mode is available in which format descriptions in the form of escape codes are interspersed with the recognized characters. In addition, a file is generated which gives paragraph profiles for each distinct paragraph type. The paragraph profile file also includes the font descriptions. Our system uses the escape codes to recognize the start and the end of paragraphs, font changes, subscripts, and superscripts. The escape codes also indicate the actual line breaks of the original text and flag hyphens positioned at the ends of lines. We chose to ignore these line breaks in favor of those generated when reproducing the document from the representation language. However, the line break information is used in the translation procedure. The paragraph profiles define the font characteristics of all the fonts used in the paragraph, i.e., point size and whether the font is fixed or variable pitch. The profile also gives the line spacing, spacing above and below the paragraph, and whether the text is right justified or ragged.

4. Document representation language

After the document has been segmented and components of the document have been recognized, the outputs must be translated into the document representation language. This representation should describe the original document as closely as possible in a compressed form. This representation should be such that the document can be easily manipulated by arbitrary editing of text, graphics and layout. If the document is to be shared with other systems, a standard representation for storage and transmission is important.

An international standard for document representation such as ODA [Horak85] is highly attractive. ODA defines simultaneously the logical structure of the document, e.g., titles and paragraphs, and the layout structure of the document, or how it looks on paper [Joloboff86]. Unfortunately, a full implementation of the standard does not yet exist. Another possibility for document representation is SGML [International86], an international standard document description technique developed by IBM. SGML allows markups to be defined which suit the needs of the document, but does not describe how the definitions should be made.

Our current system uses the Maker Interchange Format (MIF) as the document representation language [FrameMaker87]. Although the Maker Interchange Format is not a standard, it is well documented and, as part of the Frame Maker publishing system, includes tools for WYSIWYG document editing, as well as graphics and bitmap manipulation capabilities. MIF allows the user to describe the layout structure of the document and provides for text formatting instructions. Except for the capability of tagging paragraphs and portions of text, it does not provide for description of the logical structure of a document. Maker also has a markup language, Maker Markup Language (MML) similar to SGML. However, it does not have all the capability of MIF. Our decision to use MIF was based on its documentation, its availability, the fact that it runs on Suns, and that it is relatively inexpensive.

The Maker Interchange Format (MIF) describes a document as a sequence of nested rectangular blocks. These blocks contain objects which comprise the document. Graphics objects include lines, arcs and rectangles. Pictures are objects defined by a rectangular bitmap and can be scaled arbitrarily. A text object is either a TextLine, a single line of text, or a TextRect, which is a rectangular column of text. Within a TextRect, text is separated into paragraphs. MIF provides a catalog facility for storing different types of paragraph definitions. Paragraphs are described by type and size of font, spacing before and after the paragraph, and centering. Paragraph definitions are indexed by a paragraph tag. In addition, format within a paragraph can be modified locally, so that, for example, font changes within a paragraph are possible. Groups of objects can be placed into an object called a frame, allowing the objects to be treated as a unit. Frames can be anchored to a location in the text flow or to an absolute location on the page.

Text is placed in the document with the TextFlow statements. TextFlow statements include the identity of the TextRect into which the text is to be placed. Para statements within TextFlow statements indicate either the paragraph tag or explicitly define paragraph characteristics. ParaLine statements within Para statements contain the actual text, as well as local font changes.

If the text in the TextFlow statement is too long for the TextRect, one of two things can happen. If the TextRect contains a pointer to the next TextRect, indicating the direction of the text flow, the text goes there. Examples of this are text flow between two columns of text, or text flow to the next page. In the absence of a next TextRect, the text is "hidden" and can be seen if the TextRect is enlarged, if the font size or line spacing is decreased, or if the next TextRect is added to the TextRect statement. A portion of the MIF code for the document in Figure 1, describing the placement of columns and the text "Abstract," is shown in Figure 3.

Figure 3: *Maker Interchange Format for part of the document in Figure 1a*

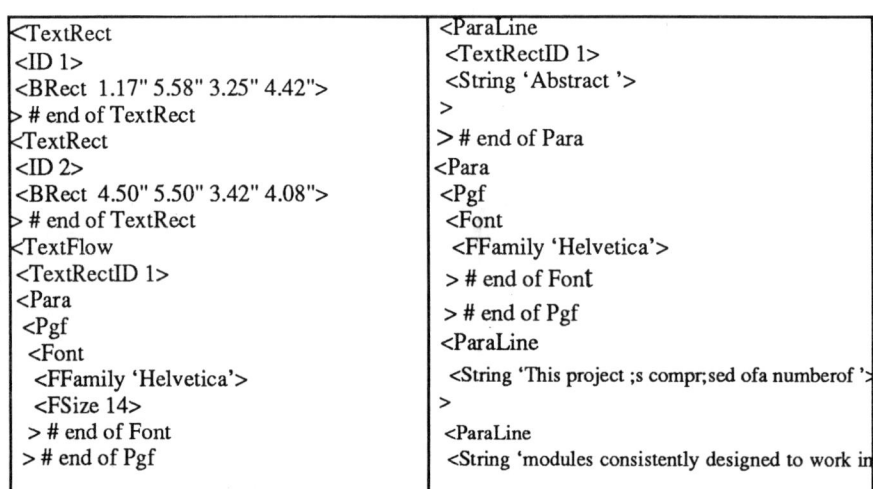

5. Implementation

The image is first scanned at 300 dpi and passed to the segmenter and structure analyzer. The output of these modules is a tree description of the document as shown in Figure 2. Each node describes a portion of the document by defining its type and its location. Types of nodes are page, column, text on graphics, text block, text line and graphics block. The location is given by the upper left corner, the width and the height of the rectangle enclosing the data for that node. The tree is traversed, and appropriate action is taken at each type of node. At a column node, the portion of the bitmap image corresponding to a column of text is passed to the character recognition module, and the recognized data and format information is returned. There is no need to pursue further branches from a column node. At a text in graphics node, the tree is traversed to each of the text branches, and the data from the character recognition is obtained. At a graphics block node, a new bitmap is cut from the old bitmap so that the new bitmap contains only the graphics within the bounding region.

To translate the components recognized above into the document representation language MIF, we again traverse the document description tree. For a column of text, the MIF TextRect structure is created at the appropriate position on the page. Then a table of font statements is made from the font information in the paragraph profile file from the character recognition format analysis. Next, the paragraph profiles are translated into MIF paragraph format descriptions, tagged, and placed in the paragraph catalog for later reference. Information given here includes line spacing within the paragraph, before the paragraph and after the paragraph, font information, justification and centering. Then, a TextFlow statement is generated to incorporate the actual text. The TextFlow statement first indicates into which TextRect the text should be placed, and then gives a sequence of Para statements. A new Para statement is generated when the escape code from the character recognition module indicates a new paragraph. The Para statements contain a tag indicating the correct paragraph description from the paragraph catalog, and a sequence of ParaLines. The ParaLines contain the actual ASCII text. A new ParaLine statement is generated for each line of text from the character recognition, although the actual line breaks will be determined when the document is formatted. Additional ParaLines are needed for format changes within a text line. Thus escape codes from the character recognition module indicating font change, or subscripts and superscripts, are translated by generating a new ParaLine statement. The font information is obtained by lookup in the font definition table.

Lines of text are placed into TextLines at the appropriate page location, with the appropriate font type and size. At a graphics node, an unanchored frame is created at the correct location, with a pointer to the bitmap graphics for that node. At a text on graphics node, a frame is first created to group the text and graphics. This allows the text and graphics to be manipulated as a unit. Within the frame, another frame is created for the graphics at the proper location with a pointer to the bitmap graphics. The text is then placed in TextLines or TextRects within the outer frame. In order for the text to appear on the graphics, Maker requires that the graphics be drawn before the text.

As mentioned before, the character recognition module cannot give the exact font type. Rather, it gives an estimate of the size of the font and whether is is fixed or variable pitch. Our system then uses the nearest point size available, and Helvetica for variable spaced text and Courier for fixed space text. This is one of the major problems with the system, since the recognized text rarely fits back into the original text block. If the text is too small for the original block, the result is obvious and can be corrected by either changing the font size or line spacing, or indicating the next block in the logical text flow. If the text is too large for the given block, a message is given to the user, since the "hidden" text may not be noticed without careful reading. Again, the user can correct the problem by changing font size or line spacing, setting the logical text flow direction, or by increasing the size of the text block.

Figure 4(a) shows again the original document in Figure 1. Figure 4(b) shows the results of the document recognition process. Several errors are present: "image acquisition" was detected as a single line of text, font changes such as the bold titles and italics in the abstract are missing, there are undetected errors in the character recognition, both in substitution and spacing, and the text does not completely fill the first column.

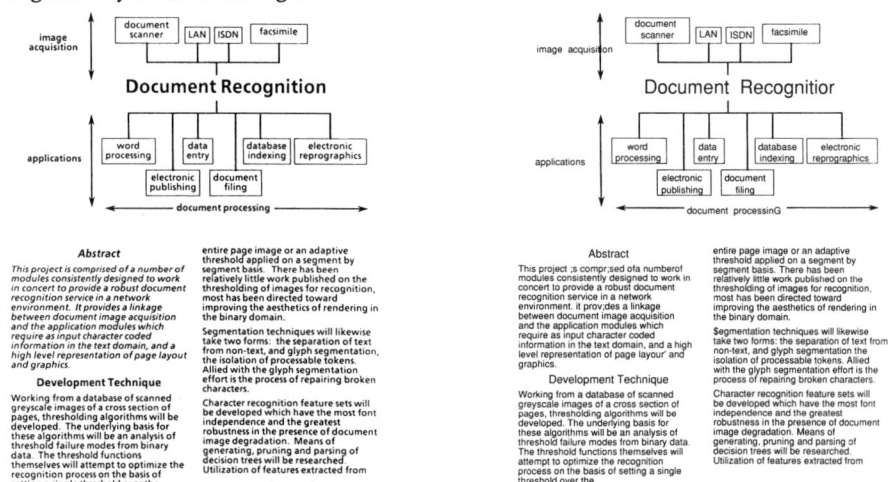

Figure 4: *(a) the original document, on the left; (b) the output of the document recognition system, on the right*

6. Conclusions

We have described our current document recognition system testbed. Much remains to be done in improving the existing components. For instance, errors in text/graphics segmentation are not provided for. In the case text is recognized as graphics, the document retains its appearance, but editing flexibility is lost. The more serious error is graphics recognized as text. This causes erroneous characters to be substituted for graphics. We need a mechanism by which poorly recognized characters could be reconsidered as graphics.

We have restricted ourselves to recognition of the layout structure of the document. There remains much to be done concerning the logical structure of the document. One example is the inference of reading order from the text block structure. Although in most cases one could assume a text flow from the bottom of the left column to the top of the right, a document with English on the left and a French translation on the right would be an exception. Other examples include recognition of a document abstract, author and title identification, location of running headers and footers, and footnote detection. This recognition would be made more robust by the inclusion of prior knowledge of a document. A model for including prior information about a document would specify different classes of documents, and assumptions consistent with the class of document could be made.

7. References

[1] DEST Series 400. (1987). DEST Corporation, Milpitas, CA.

[2] *Frame Maker 1.1 Reference Manual.* (1987). Frame Technology Corporation, San Jose, CA.

[3] GTX 5000. (1987). GTX Corporation, Phoenix, AZ.

[4] Henderson, L., Journey, M., & Osland, C. (1986). The computer graphics metafile, *IEEE Computer Graphics and Applications*, **6**, 8, 24-32.

[5] Horak, W. (1985). Office document architecture and office document interchange formats: current status of international standardization, *IEEE Computer*, **18**, 10, 50-60.

[6] International Organization for Standardization. (1986). *Standard Generalized Markup Language*. ISO DIS 8879.

[7] Joloboff, V. (1986). Trends and standards in document representation, *Proceedings of the Conference on Text Processing and Document Manipulation*, Nottingham, U.K., 107-124.

[8] Kida, H., Iwki, O., & Kawada, K. (1986). Document recognition system for office automation, *Proceedings of the Eighth International Conference on Pattern Recognition*, Paris, France, 446-448.

[9] *Kurzweil Discover TM7320 User Manual.* (1987). Kurzweil Computer Products, Cambridge, MA.

[10] Levy, D.M., Brotsky, D.C. & Olson, K.R. (1987). Formalizing the figural: aspects of a foundation for document manipulation, being submitted to *Electronic Publishing: Organization, Dissemination, and Design*.

[11] Meynieux, E., Seisen, S. & Tombre, K. (1986). Bilevel information recognition and coding in office paper documents, *Proceedings of the Eighth International Conference on Pattern Recognition*, Paris, France, 442-445.

[12] Nagy, G. & Seth, S. (1984). Hierarchical representation of optically scanned documents, *Proceedings of the Seventh International Conference on Pattern Recognition*, Montreal, Canada, **1**, 347-349.

[13] Spitz, A.L. & Wilcox, L.D. (1987). Classification techniques applied to the recognition of office documents, Conference of the International Federation of Classification Societies, *Proceedings of the 11th Annual Meeting of the German Classification Society*, Aachen, W. Germany.

[14] Srihari, S.N. & Zack, G.W. (1986). Document image analysis, *Proceedings of the Eighth International Conference on Pattern Recognition*, Paris, France, 434-436.

[15] Wong, K.Y., Casey, R.G. & Wahl, F.M. (1982). Document analysis system, *IBM Journal on Research and Development* **26**, 6, 647-656.

STRUCTURE RECOGNITION OF PRINTED DOCUMENTS

ROLF INGOLD, RENE-PIERRE BONVIN, GIOVANNI CORAY

Ecole Polytechnique Fédérale de Lausanne, CH-1015 Lausanne (Switzerland)

ABSTRACT
Optical document readers usually ignore information such as fonts, margins or relative positions on the printed layout. However, typographical indications of this nature can be useful for recognizing document content structure. This paper presents a model for logical and physical document structures. A two-pass recognition scheme, based on the typographical style description for a given class of documents, is described.

1. Intoduction

The purpose of optical reading is to acquire automatically texts printed on paper. A camera or a scanner captures a page of text in the form of an image, most often in black and white. The pixel grid thus obtained is then processed and analyzed by recognition software.

Optical reading has many aspects and various methods are used for it [Gaillat79]. The most studied area is certainly the optical reading of printed or typed texts [Holt76], [Kahan87], but more recently research has been done on recognition of the Arabic and Chinese alphabets, and of manuscripts [Suen80].

Up to now there has been very little work done on the recognition of text structures. Methods have been developed [Rastogi85] for detecting graphical figures and images, so that parts of a text can be isolated. In a few studies [Verges73], [Nagy85] a structured model based on the position of the characters is put forward, but in general there is no analysis of the typographical font, as present systems focus exclusively on character recognition.

Structure recognition has at least two advantages:
  - automatic retrieval of printed archives and recording of their databases;
  - integration of optical reading in a document production and handling system.

This article deals with the subject in the particular context of typeset documents belonging to a well-defined category. The analysis is based on the two dual structures of the document, i.e. physical (PS) and logical (LS). If it is assumed that a document is composed in accordance with a formatting function applied to its logical structure, the purpose of recognition is to evaluate the converse of this function. The conditions for this converse to exist, and for its uniqueness, must be studied, and a precise model of the problem is proposed for this.

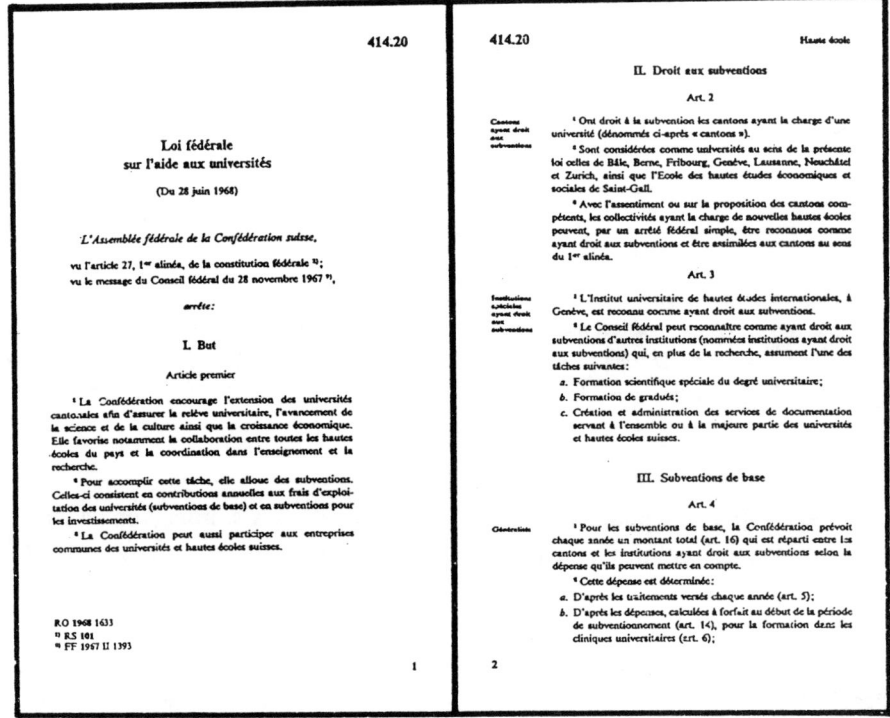

Figure 2.1: Example of a structured document.

The core of the article is divided into three parts. In section 2 a precise model of the document's structures is put forward and in section 3 the possible mechanisms for deducing the logical structure from the physical structure are described. Recognition algorithms for the physical structure are given in section 4.

2. Modeling of Documents

The idea of structuring documents to make it easier to process them by computer seems to be becoming widely accepted [Joloboff87]. However, the notion of structure is vague and depends essentially of the nature of the documents in question and the processes to be used.

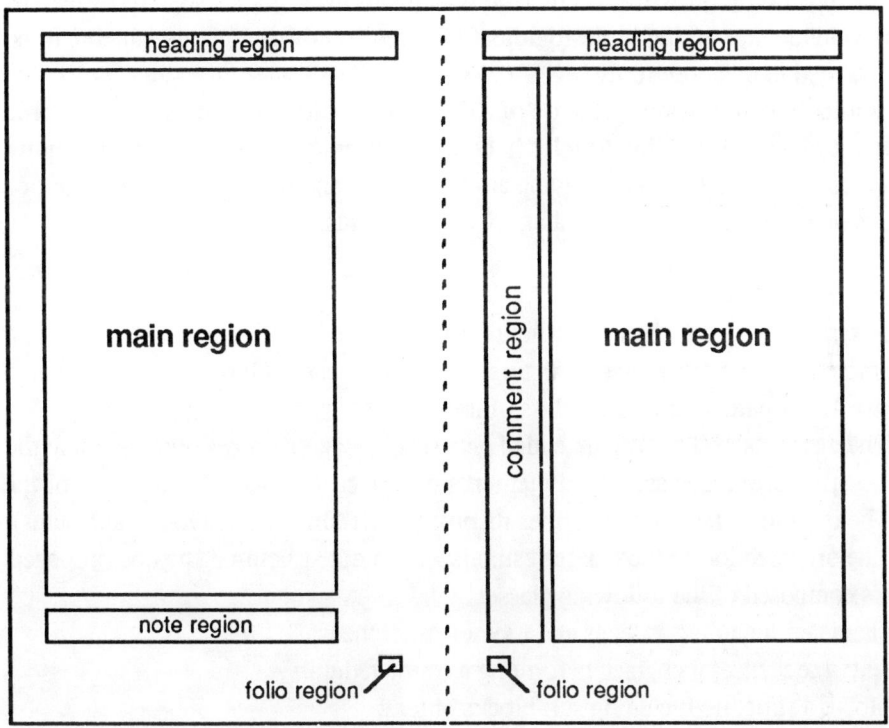

Figure 2.2: Division into regions for figure 2.1.

In this article a document is considered from the two opposite points of view of *content* and *shape*. Using Oda's method, two distinct structures are thus associated with a document: the *logical structure* (contents) and the *physical structure* (presentation).

2.1. Physical Structures
The presentation of a printed document can be described by separating it into several levels. Thus the physical structure can be expressed as:
- *geometric* structure (GS): this is not very detailed and describes the contents of each page of a document indicating the position and the characteristics of all basic shapes (a character and its font, for example);
- *typographic* structure (TS): more detailed than the geometric structure, this includes a series of pages and shows how the basic shapes are grouped; the characters are sorted into words, and the words into fragments (with a uniform font) and into lines; the lines are sorted pavements (whose division into lines

depends on the justification mode), which can overlap the page division. The pavements are divided into regions (a succession of pavements which can be arranged in one order only).

The particular typographic structure of a document therefore follows a typographic model (TM) which, in this article, is considered unique. However, typographic attributes which indicate page organization, margins and the justification mode of a pavement are specified for each category of documents.

2.2. Logical Structures

In the same way as the physical structure can be modeled, the logical structure of a document has a generic logical structure (GLS). This cannot however be considered universal, it is particular to each class of documents.

The elements of the GLS are called generic objects, or simply objects, while the logical structure nodes are called elements or object instances. Each object of the GLS belongs to a class which defines its properties (number and type of attributes).

The organization of the classes establishes a meta-structure. The one proposed here is composed of the following classes:
- character: including indexes and footnote references;
- text: a sequence of characters forming a formattedunit;
- block: a structure including sub-blocks or text;
- document: the unit to be analyzed, formed of a group of blocks.

On the basis of ideas developed in recent studies on the structuring of documents [Coray86], [Quint87] it will be assumed that the LS is a "family tree" (referred to here as tree) which reflects the structural hierarchy of a document. This tree is completed by references between its nodes.

The GLS of a class of documents can be described by a grammar. Context-free grammars in Chomsky's classification appear to be suitable for most of the applications, with an ad hoc interpretation for the references: however, the use of more specialized grammars (attribute or tree grammars) should be considered.

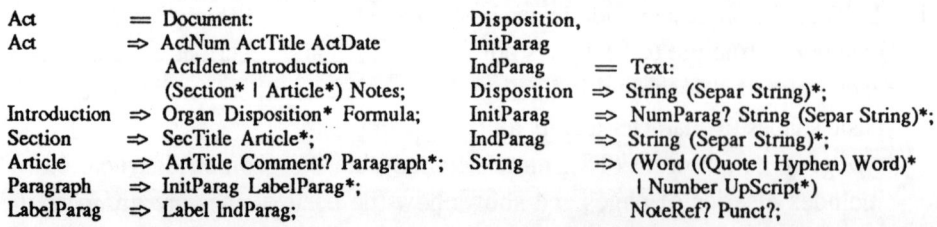

Figure 2.3: Grammar describing the GLS for the document in figure 2.1

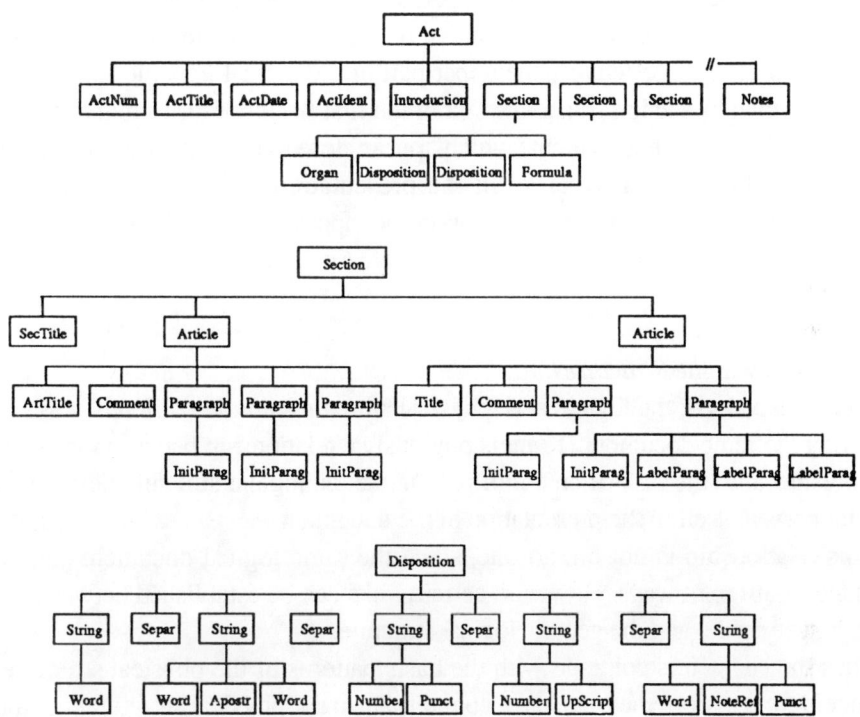

Figure 2.4: Logical structure of the document in figure 2.1

2.3. An Example

In this section the definitions given in sections 2.1 and 2.2 are illustrated by concrete examples t.

Figure 2.1 shows the two first pages of a printed law, taken from the Swiss "Recueil Systématique des Lois Fédérales", which is a typical extract from a structured document. It includes, in particular, a headline formed by a title, a date and an introduction, followed by the main text. The document has an obvious hierarchical structure including sections, articles and paragraphs. Figure 2.2 shows the division of these pages into regions

A part of the grammar which defines the generic logical structure of this document is given in Figure 2.3. The symbol "==" indicates that an object belongs to a class, while typesetting rules are expressed by "=>". In addition, the right-hand sides of these rules are usual expressions assuming the monadic operator "*" for iteration, "?" for options, and the binary operator "|" for alternatives.

The logical structure of a document itself is partly shown in Figure 2.4. The three trees represent respectively the upper part of the logical tree, the contents of the block formed by section II, and the text of the first layout of the introduction.

It should be noted that elements which appear close to each other in the logical structure are not necessarily close in the presentation. Thus, the act number (ActNum) and act identification (ActIdent) do not appear in the main region, but in that of the headline and of the note respectively. Another example of this are the comments in the margin.

2.4. Links between the Structures

As already explained, the logical and physical structures are two different ways of perceiving the same document. There is obviously a relationship between these two structures because the task of an editor is to make the logical structure defined by the author reveal itself in the presentation of the document.

This relationship is not one-to-one, since the same logical document can be presented in different ways. However, certain links can be established between the typographical model and the generic logical structure.

Thus the characters coincide with the basis patterns of the physical structure. Another logical notion, the text, has a counterpart in the physical structure, i.e. the pavement; finally, the document, in the logical sense of its content, corresponds to a succession of physically existing pages.

Physical notions such as a page or a line do not have logical equivalents, nor do page numbers and hyphens in divided words; these must be considered as artificial elements introduced during typesetting.

The most interesting links in optical recognition are those which show the characteristics of the physical presentation of a generic object: these are called presentation attributes. They determine both the choice of font and the position of the objects in relation to each other

3. Structure Recognition

As suggested in section 2, structure recognition has two aspects, physical and logical. The main objective of the applications is definitely the recognition of the logical structure of a document.

The importance of the physical structure must not be neglected, however, not only because it is an important piece of information for possible reformatting, but above all because it is a compulsory stage in the recognition of the logical structure.

In this section methods for recognizing the logical structure are considered as a way of parsing of the physical structure. Recognition of the latter, which is generally done by pattern recognition techniques, is dealt within section 4.

3.1. Hypotheses

A physically existing document, in the form of a series of page images, is considered: it is also assumed that the contents of this document correspond to a description of the generic logical structure and to the presentation attributes. The aim is to reconstitute the logical structure in accordance with the generic description, while respecting the relationship with the shapes and their typographical characteristics obtained by image analysis.

3.2. Breakdown of the Problem

In addition to the functional breakdown using the two-structure model, the recognition of a document can be divided according to a hierarchy of objects.

The recognition of paragraphs, including the identification of additional words and symbols, such as references to notes, can be a first stage in the analysis. The second will then be the recognition of blocks, and then the upper part of the logical tree can be constituted.

The order in which these operations are carried out requires comment. Two approches are possible:
- total recognition of a document, broken down into two passes: during the first the geometric structure of the document is completely recognized, and during the second the logical structure is established by a bottom-up analysis;
- stage-by-stage recognition of a document: during a first stage it is possible to construct the upper part of the tree on the basis of an image segmented into pavements; during subsequent stages their contents are recognized.

Each of these two approaches has advantages and disadvantages. With the first approach, more rigorous and more general, recognition of the physical structure is made independent of the objects of the logical structure. This of course means the recognition is somewhat cumbersome, since no simplifying hypothesis (for example restriction of the set of possible fonts) can be used.

Stage-by-stage recognition is the optimal use of the preceding algorithm, since additional information can be used for geometrical structure recognition. However, determining the characteristics of the intermediate shapes to be recognized, such as pavements, is a delicate problem. These characteristics will depend, at least in part, on the presentation attributes and will have to be adapted accordingly.

3.3. Methods of Analysis

An analysis of the physical elements, with their geometric and typographic characteristics, which lead to the construction of a tree of logical objects conforming to a generic description, can be compared with a parse. The logical structure to be built corresponds to the syntactic tree and the basic or complex shapes of the physical structure are to be related to the terminal alphabet, while the description of the logical generic structure defines the grammar.

The problems of syntax analysis have been widely studied in relation to programming languages and compilation. The algorithms can be divided into two classes: top-down analysis in which the tree is constructed starting with the roots, and the buttom-up parsing in which the tree is created starting with the leaves.

The latter approach is used for recognizing text structures. The first results seem to show that the methods are roughly equivalent for pavement recognition, in particular. However, the general nature of this approach, its possible limits, and the restrictions on the form of the grammars, must still be analyzed.

3.4. Special Cases

Irregularities in the physical structure introduced by formatting, in particular dividing into pages and into lines, must be treated in a special way, but using a method that is simple to apply. The idea is to create an image for the notions of region and line respectively.

The succession of homonymous regions through the pages can be reconstitued conceptually, replacing the page-end by a specially-marked line spacing interpreted by the block analyzer as an undetermined space.

In a similar way, the ends of lines are considered as ordinary spaces, insofar as the line does not end with a divided word. In that case the end of the line can be ignored. As for the possible deletion of the hyphen, this must be left to a semantic analysis of the document, for which a dictionary may be used.

4. Pattern Recognition

In this section some special methods for recognizing the specific physical structure of a document are described, with the emphasis on processes used in pattern recognition adapted as they are to the reading of printed texts.

4.1. Segmentation

In the first instance most of the applications require a segmentation phase for the analysis of a digital image. The purpose of this is to isolate the basic shapes before identifying them. Depending on the case, this analysis can supply additional information on the orientation, exact positioning or scale of the image portion concerned.

In optical reading of printed texts, segmentation also has a double purpose:
- to divide up all the pages and isolate the words from their context so an appropriate identification operator can be applied to them. Segmentation also supplies a vertical reference which estimates the relative positioning of a word in relation to the running baseline;
- to rearrange words and groups of words according to natural typographical links; for example a line, a pavement containing a paragraph, a region delimiting footnotes.

It should be noted that most optical reading systems produce a complete segmentation of the text up to the character level. This technique can be satisfactory in the large majority of cases; it poses problems, however, in the case of kerning and unevenly spaced letters. Segmentation errors unfortunately often lead to identification errors. This is why we have chosen a safer solution which uses a more sophisticated character identification algorithm (see 4.3).

The segmentation principle is based essentially on the detection of horizontal or vertical white strips. These are easily identifiable in the distribution of the projections as shown in Figure 4.1.

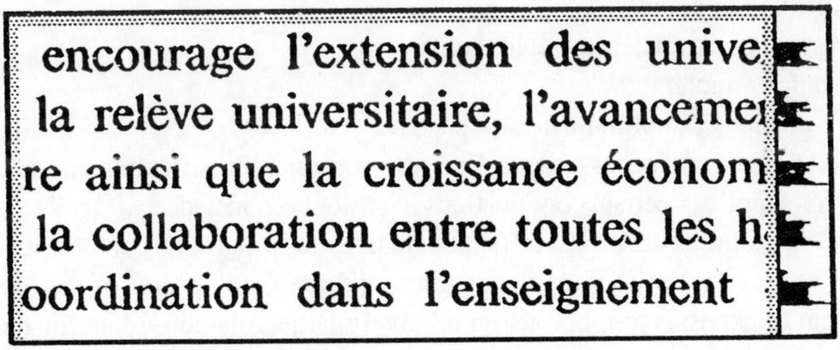

Figure 4.1: Vertical distribution for line segmentation.

Depending on the type of segmentation, external information may be required to locate the separation line more easily, or avoid incorrect segmentation. Thus the delimitation of the footnote region requires values for the admissible line spacing, for example.

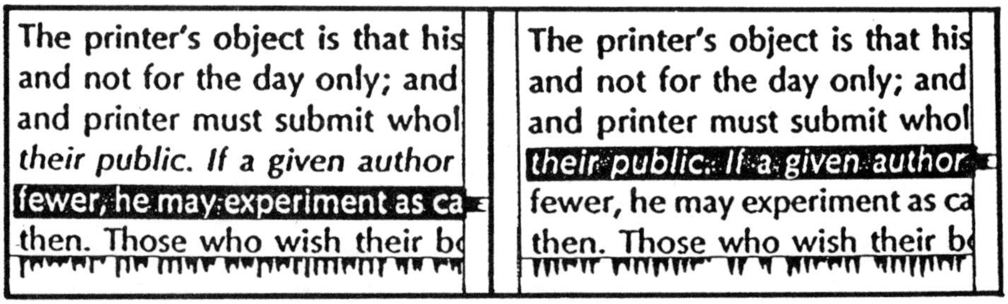

Figure 4.2: Horizontal distribution for font identification.

4.2. Font Recognition

Identification of the font may be required for recognizing structures; it constitutes a new element in optical reading algorithms.

The aim of our project is to identify the font from a relatively restricted catalogue containing all the fonts which could be found in a document. Our font identification system is based on an orthogonal classification using several criteria:
- family: Times, Clarendon, Helvetica, etc.
- size expressed in points
- thickness: light, normal, semi-bold, bold
- slope: italic or roman
- density: condensed, normal, widely-spaced.

This model does not necessarily reflect the rigorous classification used in typesetting: for simplicity certain combinations have not been included.

The family is definitely the most difficult parameter to recognize from the image of a text. It requires not only a very detailed description of the features of the font (serif, medium thickness, etc.), but also a relatively large volume of data for the analysis. Fortunately, it is customary in typesetting to have only a small number of different font families in a document: in most documents one family alone occurs.

The other characteristics are easier to estimate by a statistical analysis of a portion of the text. Without going into details, it should be pointed out that the estimates are to a large extent made using the projection distributions and, with the exception of some pathological cases, the size can be measured using the vertical distribution. The horizontal distribution of a (portion) of line is the first element needed for evaluating the other criteria (see Figure 4.2).

The typeface thickness can in fact be deduced from the average thickness in the horizontal distribution: the density can be measured using its spectrum, while the slope is determined by the variations in the first derivative of the distribution. It should be noted that certain criteria depend on one another, which leads to a hierarchy in the classification.

Finally, it should be pointed out that the technique can be improved insofar as the analysis produces probabilities to be used in the character identification algorithm, which will subsequently confirm or invalidate the choice of font.

4.3. Character Identification

Structure recognition, assuming font identification, has an effect on character identification. In fact, distinguishing between an italic character and its roman counterpart is an additional requirement for the identification algorithm.

Recent developments in optical reading have shown a tendency for character identification algorithms to make use of topological or structural methods. These certainly have the advantage of not being sensitive to small defects and ensuring reliability whatever font is used, but as a consequence they are unable to distinguish the fonts. Also criticism is made in the literature of the overall comparison pf a sample submitted for recognition with an imprint judged to be representative. This technique is considered too sensitive to the distortions, even slight ones.

In spite of this we have taken up this last idea and generalized the notion of imprint. In this new approach, the imprint calculated as a function of the characteristics of the retrieval peripheral contains several components which allow a more detailed and more accurate analysis to be made, mainly of differentiation between the fonts. This method can be used even when a character has not been completely removed from its context, it combines very well with the segmentation of the word into letters.

5. Conclusions

Structure recognition of a text was neglected for a long time in optical reading techniques. A preliminary study of this problem has been done, limited to good-quality printed texts. A document structure model covering its logical and physical perception has been developed. The model assumes that a document will be analyzed using a generic description of the logical structure and the presentation attributes.

Assume the physical structure has been recognized in a first stage. It includes the segmentation of pages, and the identification of both the characters and the font. Identification of the font is an improvement on usual OCR techniques, and is essential for recognizing logical structures in accordance with the proposed model.

The second stage, i.e. logical structure recognition based on the physical structure, is being developed. Syntactic analysis techniques seem to be promising in this connection. However, there are still a number of problems. The constraints imposed by the parsing method and their repercussions on the generic description of the documents must be analyzed more closely.

Another proposed area of study involves the hierarchical division of the recognition process. The isolation of characteristic blocks in the image before analyzing their contents is an interesting optimisation which should be studied. In practice this requires knowing more information peculiar to a class of documents, and this might be built up using a sophisticated learning process.

Finally, the two-level approach, i.e. physical and logical, to structuring, and the resulting duality between formatting and recognition, seem to be of general interest for document handling. We hope that the complementary nature of these two points of view will contribute to an integrated approach to the production and "consumption" of documents.

References

[1] G. Coray, R. Ingold & C. Vanoirbeek. Formatting Structured Documents: Batch versus Interactive? Proc. of EP86, Nottingham 1986, pp. 154-170.

[2] G. Gaillat & M. Berthod. Panorama des techniques d'extraction de traits caractéristiques en lecture optique de caractères. Revue Thomson-CSF, vol 11, no 4, December 1979.

[3] A.W. Holt. The Imapct of New Hardware on OCR Design. Pattern Recognition, vol 8, 1976, pp. 99-105.

[4] V. Joloboff. Représentation des documents: Etat de l'art, Recherche. Bigre+Globule no 53, May 1987, pp. 45-67.

[5] S. Kahan, T.Pavlidis & H.S. Baired: On the Recognition of Printed Characters of Any Font and Size. IEEE-PAMI-9, no 2, May 1987, pp 274-288.

[6] G. Nagy, S.C. Seth & S.D. Scoddard. Document Analysis with an Expert System. Pattern Recognition in Practice, Amsterdam 1985, pp 149-159.

[7] V. Quint. Une approche de l'édition structurée de documents. Thèse d'Etat, Université Scientifique, Technique et Médicale de Grenoble, may 1987.

[8] A. Rastogi & S.N. Srihari. Recognition Textual Blocks using the Hough Transform. TR 86-01, Dept. of CS, SUNY/Buffalo, 1986.

[9] C.Y. Suen, M. Berthod & S. Mori. Automatic Recognition of Handprinted Characters - The State of the Art. IEEE Proceedings 68, April 1980.

[10] J.-C. Verges-Escuin & J.-P. Verjus. Reconnaissance automatique des structures des textes en vue de l'édition. RAIRO, October 1973, pp.85-120.

HARD COPY RENDITION OF ODA-DOCUMENTS

J. BEHRMANN-POITIERS, H. KEIL, H. LOEBL

Philips Research Laboratory Hamburg

ABSTRACT
The standardization of the Office Document Architecture (ODA) of ISO DIS 8613 covers at present documents comprising text, raster graphics, and geometric graphics. Furthermore, ISO DIS 8613 defines the Office Document Interchange Format (ODIF) for the interchange of office documents between different host systems.
This paper describes the imaging process, which renders a document in a human perceptible form. It converts a document from ODIF into a printer dependent bitmap via a suitable internal document representation, which is based on the formal data definitions of the ODA standard. Such a conversion should be performed preferably in the printer controller.
In addition, a proposal will be discussed to extend the raster graphics content architecture by grey-scale and colour images. For this purpose the CEPT Videotex standard seems to be a suitable base.
The above mentioned solution for the rendition of ODA documents will be compared to an approach using PostScript, a procedural page description language, where the same internal document representation is converted to the corresponding PostScript format, which is subsequently transmitted to a PostScript printer.

1. Introduction

Desktop Publishing [1] is a relatively new field of electronic document processing. It is associated with the generation and rendition of complex and high quality documents. Unfortunately, it is seldom possible to exchange documents in electronic form between different document processing systems. The reason is that each processing system uses its own specific and therefore incompatible document architecture.

In order to solve this problem, ISO currently standardizes a so-called "Office Document Architecture" (ODA), which is defined in ISO DIS 8613 [2]. ODA is a collection of rules that allow the hierarchical composition of a document, either in logical or in layout form. Content types like character text, raster graphics, and geometric graphics are specified in so-called content architectures.

Besides a document architecture, ISO 8613 also defines an "Office Document Interchange Format" (ODIF) [3] which supports the electronic interchange of documents between different host systems. When documents are interchanged in ODIF form, three modes can be distinguished: the processable form, the formatted form and the formatted processable form. The processable form contains a logical document structure and content, which can be further edited by the receiver. The formatted form contains the layout document structure and content and can only be displayed or printed. Finally, the formatted processable form contains both the logical and the layout structure.

The various steps necessary to convert an ODIF document from its formatted form into a bitmap for hard copy rendition will be discussed in this paper.

General Aspects

The block diagram of figure 1 illustrates the flow of data from the host system to the printing engine. An ODIF byte-stream is analysed by the ODIF-Analyser,

Figure 1: Conversion of an ODIF Byte-Stream into a Bitmap

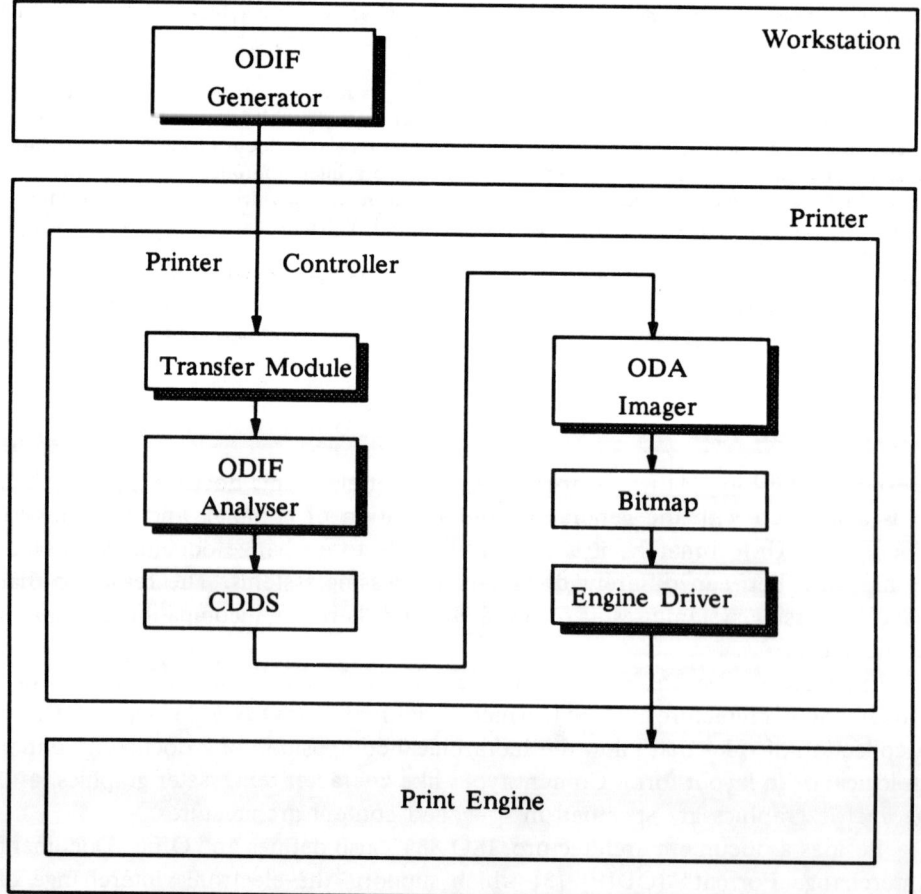

which generates a hierarchical tree structure, the so-called Common Document Data Structure (CDDS) and calls the rasterization process, also termed ODA-Imager. This process performs a transformation into a bitmap suitable for the rendition on a page printer. In order to relieve the host system from a time consuming task, the whole ODIF-to-bitmap conversion will be performed by the printer controller.

According to ISO 8613 part 5 data stream B is associated with the formatted form of an ODIF file and consists of one document profile descriptor and may contain the following interchange data units:
- layout object descriptor
- layout class descriptor
- presentation style descriptor
- text unit

A layout object descriptor contains all the information, i.e. attributes and references to subordinate objects, which define the layout of the corresponding specific object (page, frame, block) and its relationship to other specific layout objects. A layout class descriptor describes a generic layout object. A presentation style descriptor is a collection of attributes that define the presentation of a content portion within a basic object, i.e. a block. The content portions itself, like character text or graphics, are included in text units.

ODIF-Analyser

Because the ODIF form of a document is not well suited for its further processing, it is at first converted into an internal document representation by means of the ODIF-Analyser. The ODIF-Analyser is created by a generator program, which in turn is generated by means of the Unix software tools LEX and YACC by using the formal data definitions of ODIF in ISO DIS 8613 part 5. Since the standardization of ODA/ODIF is not yet completed and changes must be expected in the future, this approach has the advantage that a fast adaptation of the ODIF-Analyser to the latest version of ISO 8613 is feasible. A discussion of this generator program is outside the scope of this paper.

The internal representation of a document created by the ODIF-Analyser is a hierarchical tree structure. It is based on a so-called Common Document Data Structure (CDDS) which is implemented in the programming language C and was automatically derived by a suitable generator program from the formal data definitions of ISO 8613.

Figure 2 illustrates the tree structure of a layout structured document with composite objects like document as the root of the tree, page and frame. Blocks at the lowest level are basic objects of this tree. Content portions constitute the leaves and are connected to block nodes. All the various attributes can be found in the tree nodes and the associated data structures.

Figure 2: Data Structure (CDDS) of a Layout Structured Document

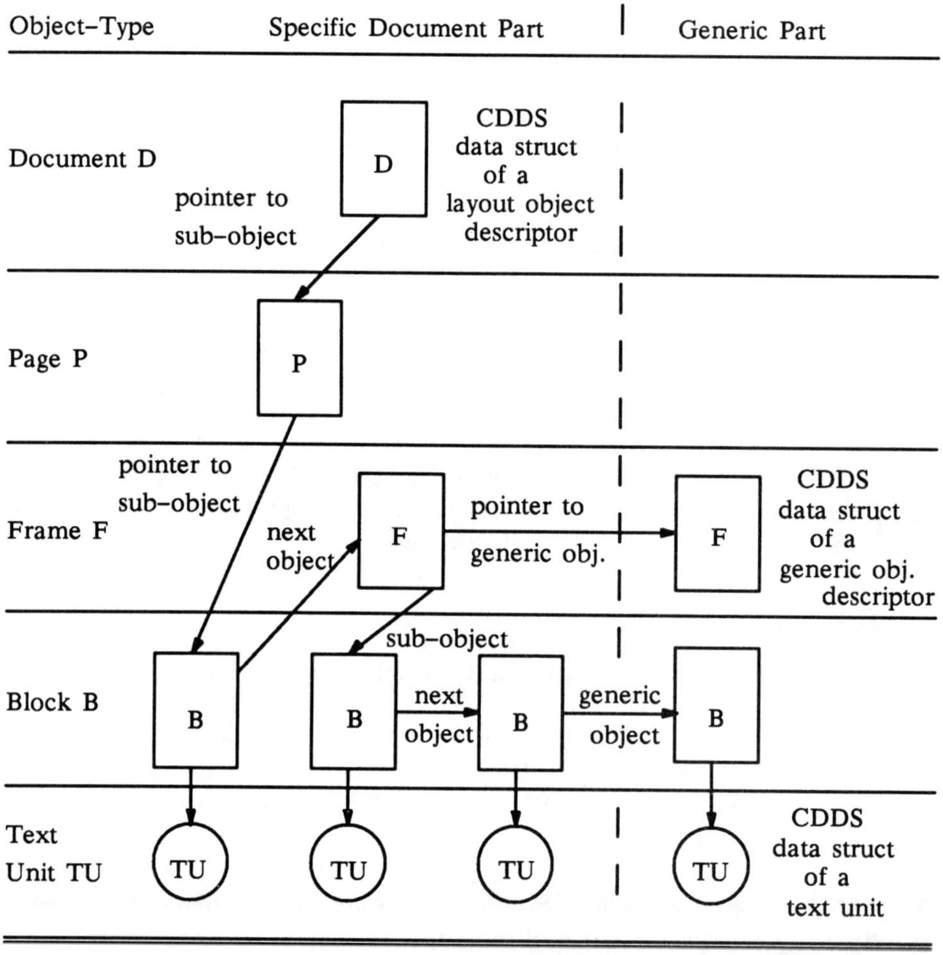

Object-Type	Specific Document Part	Generic Part
Document D	D — pointer to sub-object	CDDS data struct of a layout object descriptor
Page P	P	
Frame F	pointer to sub-object; next object; F — pointer to generic obj.	F — CDDS data struct of a generic obj. descriptor
Block B	B, B — next object — B — generic object — B	
Text Unit TU	TU, TU, TU, TU	CDDS data struct of a text unit

Figure 3 and figure 4 present the formal data definition of a layout object descriptor and its representation as a CDDS struct. The advantage of such an internal representation results from the fact that the access to the attributes (variables) and the subordinate or peer layout objects, generic objects and presentation styles is very convenient.

Figure 3: Formal Definition of a Layout–Object–Descriptor according to ISO 8613/5

```
Layout-Object-Descriptor          ::= SEQUENCE {
    object-type                   Layout-Object-Type OPTIONAL,
    descriptor-body               Layout-Object-Descriptor-Body
                                        OPTIONAL }


Layout-Object-Type                ::= INTEGER {
                                  document-layout-root (0), page-set (1),
                                  page (2), frame (3), block (4) }


Layout-Object-Descriptor-Body     ::= SET {
    object-identifier             Object-or-Class-Identifier OPTIONAL,
    subordinates                  [0] IMPLICIT SEQUENCE OF
                                        Numeric String OPTIONAL,
    . . .
    position                      [3] IMPLICIT Measure-Pair OPTIONAL,
    dimensions                    [4] IMPLICIT Measure-Pair OPTIONAL,
    . . .}
```

Figure 4: C–Data Representation of a layout–Object_Descriptor

```
struct layout_Object_Descriptor {              /* SEQUENCE */
    INTEGER                                    object_type;
    Layout_Object_Descriptor_Body*             descriptor_body; };

struct layout_Object_Descriptor_Body {         /* SET */
    PrintableString                            object_identifier;
    SEQUENCEOF_NumericString                   subordinates;
    . . .
    Measure_Pair*                              position;
    Measure_Pair*                              dimensions;
    . . .};
```

ODA-Imager

In the document processing model of ISO 8613, the following three processes are mentioned:
- the editing process : it handles the logical structure and content of a document
- the formatting process : it generates the layout structure of a document
- the imaging process : it renders the document in a human-perceptible form on a presentation medium.

The ODA-Imager corresponds to the imaging process of this model. It processes the specific layout structure of a document, the associated content portions, generic layout parts, and presentation styles and generates a format suitable for printing / displaying. Figure 5 presents a module structure of the ODA-Imager.

Figure 5: Module Structure of the ODA-Imager

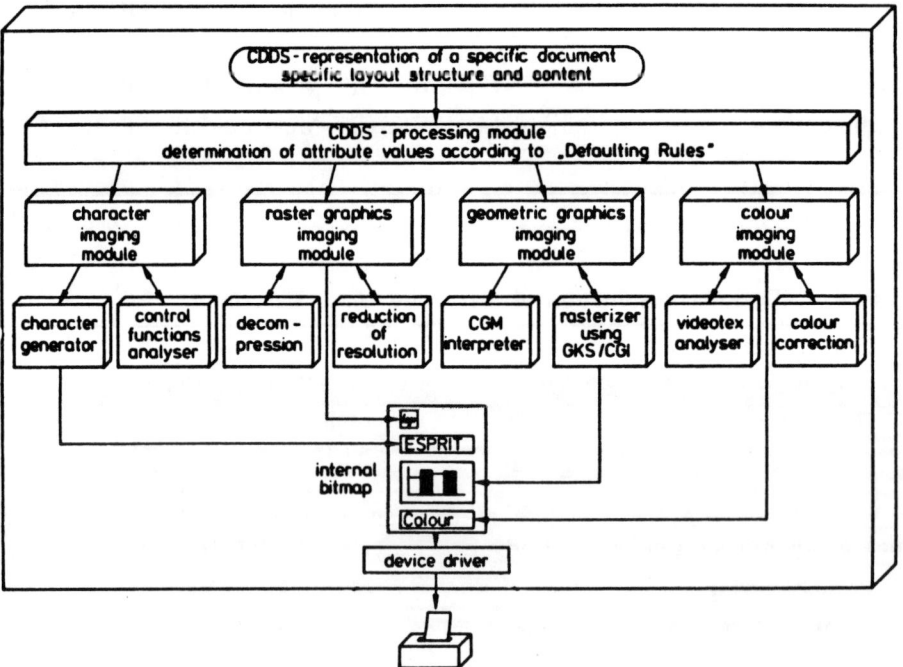

This module structure can be subdivided into the following parts:
- a layout structure processing part,
- separate content imaging parts,
- a device-adaptation part.

The main task of the layout structure processing module is the determination of attribute values by means of the imaging rules for documents as defined in ISO 8613. A central role plays the determination of attribute values, such as position, dimensions, and presentation attributes according to ODA's "Defaulting Rules". The value of an attribute may be specified in different parts of a document's layout structure:
- in the specific layout object directly
- in a presentation style, which is referenced by a pointer from the specific object
- in a generic layout object which is referenced from the specific object
- in a presentation style, which is referenced from a generic layout object, which in turn is referred to from the specific layout object
- in a default value list specified at a higher level of the hierarchical layout structure
- the default value defined by ISO 8613

An attribute takes the value delivered by the first of these rules which is applicable.

Further rules guide the positioning and dimensioning of the layout objects such as frames and blocks within a page. The origin of the orthogonal page coordinate system is the top left corner on the page. Position and dimensions are specified in "Basic Measurement Units" (BMU). Frames and blocks are positioned relative to the layout object to which they are immediately subordinate. Both objects may intersect partially or fully without restriction. The kind of intersectioning is ruled by the attribute "transparency". Its permissible values are 'transparent' and 'opaque'. Two cases may occur when a block is imaged :
- The block is 'opaque'; then any content of underlying objects is not imaged in the area of intersection.
- The block is 'transparent'; then the content of this block and any underlying content are combined.

When the structural part of a document has been analysed according to the above mentioned procedure the next imaging step is performed and the content imaging modules are called. The imaging of content is described by "Content Architectures", which are defined in ISO 8613/6-8. Three types of content are defined at present:
- text :   ASCII characters
- raster graphics :   pictorial information
- geometric graphics : geometric primitives

The character imaging module employs character bitmaps from a set of UNIX fonts. A probably better approach is the use of outline fonts, which reduces the amount of memory for font storage, but needs a fast processor for the generation of character bitmaps. Constant spaced fonts and proportional fonts are supported by the current definition of the character content architecture. There is a limitation to only four character orientations, namely 0°, 90°, 180°, and 270°, which may be too restrictive.

Raster graphics, i.e. monochrome pictorial information with a single bit per pixel is processed by the raster imaging module, which provides for decompression of compressed data according to the CCITT Recommendation T.6 [4] and for scaling of raster images.

The most complex content to deal with is geometric graphics, which is encoded according to ISO 8632 [6] as Computer Graphics Metafile (CGM). The latter is a four-part standard. Part one contains a functional specification of a set of elements which may occur in a CGM file. Parts two to four describe three different encodings, which serve for different needs:
- the character encoding :   minimum size of metafile
- the binary encoding :   minimum effort to read and generate
- the clear text encoding: human readable form

An appropriate approach to rasterize geometric graphics is based on the Computer Graphics Interface (CGI) [7]. CGI is a graphics standard which offers functions for rendering graphical information on output devices, setting attributes, etc. Using this functionality, a CGM metafile can be interpreted and the corresponding CGI calls can be issued. For the development of such a transformation program the UNIX tool YACC is employed. The generation of such a transformation program, also referred to as CGM-Imager, is illustrated in figure 6.

Input for the YACC is a file consisting of three sections :
- declarations of the tokens and necessary data type definitions,
- the formal grammar of the CGM metafile (as listed in part one of ISO 8632), extended by actions that make the appropriate CGI calls,
- miscellaneous programs like a scanner routine, parameter decoding routines and an error routine.

The YACC then generates the source of the aspired transformation program. After compiling it, any CGM metafile can be rendered on an output device which is equipped with a CGI interface. An appropriate manner to handle CGI-calls is the use of a hardware graphics processor that permits a fast transformation into the corresponding pixel data.

At the time of writing this paper the draft ODA standard does not contain provision for colour and grey-scale. It is, however, intended to include colour in all three existing content architectures in a similar manner.

We have considered part three of the CEPT Videotex standard T/CD 6-1 [8], which deals with photographic data, in order to derive a Videotex file for colour and grey-scale raster graphics. Such a file could be incorporated into an ODA document if colour or grey-scale images should be added.

The file format consists of a "Photographic Data Header Unit" and a "Photographic Data Transfer Unit". Both units are further subdivided into a Presentation Protocol Information (PPCI) part and a Presentation Protocol Data Unit (PPDU)

Fig. 6: Generation of the CGM-Imager

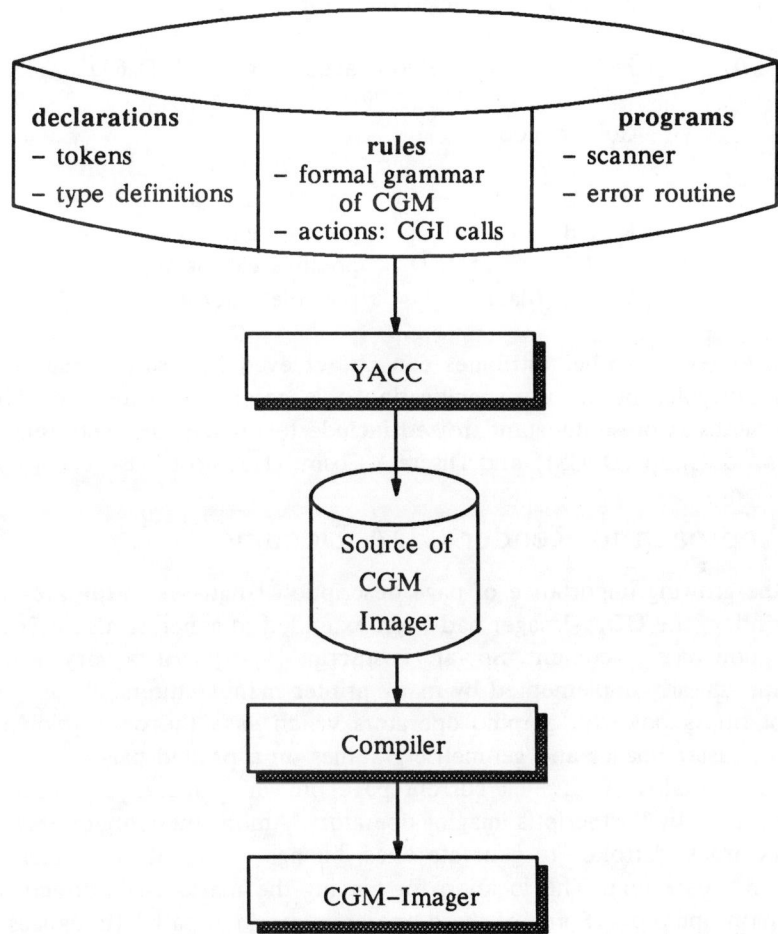

part. The PPCI part contains only control code, while the PPDU part of the header unit is a collection of all the relevant attributes and the PPDU part of the transfer unit contains the pictorial information according to the attributes specified in the header unit.

The attributes of the header PPDU are grouped into composition attributes and compression attributes. The following composition attributes are of special importance for hard copy rendition:
- COM :   specifies the colour model
- RES :   specifies the raster resolution
- BPC :   specifies the bits per colour component

Currently, the CEPT standard defines only attributes suitable for the display of images on a screen. It is, however, quite simple to extend the present standard towards additional functionalities. The following example shows a possible extension of the COM attribute: (values in hex-notation)

<COM> := 2/0   3/C   (definition according to T/CD 6-1)

3/C   Colour model

3/0	YL U* V*	standardized in T/CD 6-1
3/1	R G B	possible extension
3/2	Y M C	possible extension
3/3	Y M C Black	possible extension

An extension of the other attributes can be achieved in a similar manner. Compression attributes permit the specification of a compression method. The compression methods presently standardized include techniques like Differential Pulse Code Modulation (DPCM) and Discrete Cosine Transform (DCT).

Further Approach to Render ODA Documents

Because of the growing importance of page description languages in the area of document printing, the ODA-Imager had been extended to generate also a PostScript description of a document. So far, PostScript [9,10] is in a very widespread use and already implemented by many printer manufacturers.

PostScript offers powerful graphic operators which ease the description of character text, raster images and geometric graphics on a printed page.

PostScript maintains an implicit current page on which marks are placed. These marks are set by PostScript's imaging operators. Among these operators are "fill" to mark areas, "stroke" to generate lines, "image" to paint raster images and "show" to create text. The location for placing the marks is described by PostScript's path operators. Some of these operators are "newpath" (initializes a new path), "moveto" (specifies the starting point), "rmoveto" (relative movement from the previous point), and "lineto" (connects the path with a straight line). Other PostScript operators allow to set attributes like font, line width, fill colour, etc.

The concept of outline fonts permits the choice of arbitrary character orientations and character sizes, limited only by the printer's raster resolution.

The transformation program from CDDS to PostScript is structured in the same way as the ODA-Imager. The modules for the processing of the hierarchical CDDS representation and the determination of the attribute values according to the "Defaulting Rules" are totally the same. Only the content imaging parts had to be replaced by modules which generate the appropriate PostScript commands and write them to an external file. Finally, that file contains the page descriptions of the document and is sent to a PostScript printer where the hard copy is produced.

In this case the whole transformation is performed on the host system and not in the printer controller.

Conclusions

It has been shown how a document in ODIF form can be transformed into a bitmap for rendition on a hard copy device. One possibility is the rasterization of the ODIF document by the printer controller, which relieves the host system from a time consuming task.

A second approach with PostScript, a page description language, was discussed. Although the transformation from ODIF to PostScript must be performed by the host system, this approach has the advantage that there is variety of PostScript printers with high print quality already commercially available. PostScript is able to express all the features of an ODA document and has even capabilities beyond those of ODA, e.g. arbitrary character orientations and character sizes.

ODA still lacks further important features like colour or grey-scale content and cannot represent data types like tables and mathematical or chemical symbols. However, with respect to colour and grey-scale a preliminary concept is already in discussion. In this paper we have proposed the inclusion of colour and grey-scale raster graphics according to the CEPT Videotex Recommendation T/CD 6-1 for photographic content .

The work described was sponsored by the German Federal Ministry for Research and Technology (grant number ITM 8501 A) and the Commission of European Communities (ESPRIT project 295). Only the authors are responsible for the contents of this publication.

References

[1] The Seybold Report on Publishing Systems
Vol. 16, No. 2, September 22, 1986

[2] ISO DIS 8613, 1987-07-16, part 1-8
Information Processing - Text and Office Systems -
Office Document Architecture (ODA) and
Interchange Format

[3] ISO DIS 8613-5.2, 1987-07-16, part 5
Office Document Interchange Format (ODIF)

[4] CCITT Recommendation T. 6 : Facsimile Coding Schemes
and Coding Control Functions for Group 4 Facsimile
Apparatus

[5] P. Stucki : Advances in Digital Image Processing,
Plenum Press, New York, 1979, pp. 201-218

[6] ISO 8632 : Information Processing Systems - Computer
Graphics - Metafile for the Storage and Transfer of Picture
Description Information

[7] ISO TC97/SC21 N1179 (CGI Working Draft), Information
Processing, Computer Graphics, Interface Techniques for
Dialogues with Graphical Devices, May 1986

[8] CEPT Recommendation T/CD 6-1 :
Videotex Presentation Layer Data Syntax

[9] PostScript Language Reference Manual,
Addison-Wesley Publishing Company of Reading, Mass.

[10] PostScript Language Tutorial and Cookbook,
Addison-Wesley Publishing Company of Reading, Mass.

WELL-ESTABLISHED DOCUMENT INTERCHANGE FORMATS

JEAN-MARIE DE LA BEAUJARDIÈRE

Xerox Palo Alto Research Center

ABSTRACT

A number of standards exist to facilitate the interchange of electronic documents between different computer systems. Though they each have their place and have proved very useful, none has reached the level of generality and completeness required to ensure an exchange of information without loss, especially in round-trip interchange. This paper takes a look at four well-known interchange formats (DIF, DCA, SGML and ODA) and compares the ways they handle the same sample document.

1. Introduction

The technology of document interchange between incompatible computer systems is still in its infancy, especially in the case of round-trip interchange. Both sides of the interchange, the sending side and the receiving side, are too weak to perform a completely useful exchange:

- On the sending side, there is not yet a fully defined interchange format which captures and describes the complexity of composite documents. The contents and structure of electronic documents may vary from simple text with limited typographical variations, to data-driven graphics, color images, voice recordings and other elaborate objects. No language exists today to describe all these objects in a consistent way. The most recent proposal, ODA [1], is much talked about, but so far there has been more talk than solid implementations.
- On the receiving side, it is not clear how a system should handle a document object which it does not support. Were a fully complete interchange language to exist, what would a lowly PC do when presented with a voice recording or a complex chemical equation? Today's solution is to discard the embarrassing object or some of its attributes. This cannot be the long-term solution.

Figure 1: a composite (text & graphics) document to interchange

1. **The Beginning.**

   John "Le Naïf" Léger paced the room, reading and rereading the <u>incredible</u> offer that came in the mail this morning.

   It was too good to be true...

2. **The Middle.**

   ... They went to see that "land" they bought in Florida ...

3. **The End.**

   ... Jane said: "I will come back as soon as chicken start growing teeth." She left the room, leaving John holding the mortgage.

Defining a general interchange format and specifying the proper behavior of systems that do not implement its full generality are difficult problems. Quite a number of systems have successfully provided solutions to a subset of the problems, limiting themselves to the interchange, for instance, of structured graphics or simple text and its logical structure. This paper takes a look at several interchange formats and compares the way they handle a small example, shown in Figure 1. An interesting comparison of two of the products discussed here, SGML and ODA, can be found in [Joloboff86].

2. DIF

DIF stands for Document Interchange Format. It is an encoding developed at the behest of the Department of the Navy by the National Bureau of Standards and a group of software manufacturers [Knoerdel84]. It is used to exchange text, not graphics or complex structures, and formatting instructions across a wide variety of word processors and publishing systems.

A DIF document is a linear stream of 7-bit ASCII bytes. Control codes, prefixed by an Escape character, are interspersed with the text. Thirteen DIF functions are actually codes already defined in other standards ([ANSI79], [ANSI83] and [ISO83]). Twenty-nine additional functions are encoded according to the escape sequence mechanism provided by [ANSI79].

Figure 2 represents a DIF encoding of Figure 1. The conversion program had no choice but to discard the graphics (the three faces). It replaced the proportionally-spaced typeface by an undefined fixed-pitch font of the closest size (the only choices being 12- and 10-pitch). Finally, it dropped the accents

Figure 2: legible representation of DIF encoding of Figure 1

ESC [1$K	start document
ESC [0 SP K	10-pitch
ESC [1$J	start page
ESC [1m	emphasis on

1.HTThe Beginning.

ESC [22m	emphasis off
ESC E	end paragraph
ESC [14$F	temporary left margin

John "Le Naif" Leger paced the room, reading and rereading the

ESC [4m	underscore on

incredible

ESC [24m	underscore off

offer that came in the mail this morning.

ESC E	end paragraph
ESC [14$F	temporary left margin

It was too good to be true...

ESC E	end paragraph
ESC [1m	emphasis on

2. HT The Middle.

ESC [22m	emphasis off
ESC E	end paragraph
ESC [14$F	temporary left margin

... They went to see that "land" they bought in Florida ...

ESC E	end paragraph
ESC [1m	emphasis on

3. HT The End.

ESC [22m	emphasis off
ESC E	end paragraph
ESC [14$F	temporary left margin

... Jane said: "I will come back as soon as chicken start growing teeth." She left the room, leaving John holding the mortgage.

ESC [0$J	end page
ESC [0$K	end document

over accented letters and replaced the opening and closing quotes by neutral quotes, because of the limitations of the 7-bit ASCII code set.

3. DCA

DCA stands for Document Content Architecture. It is an encoding promoted by IBM as a common document format for its word processors. Since a large number of software companies jumped onto the band-wagon and provided document conversion from and to DCA, that format became a *de facto* interchange standard. DCA comes in two flavors: Final-Form-Text DCA [IBM85], not amenable to editing and not discussed further here, and Revisable-Form-Text DCA [IBM83], encoding documents which may be edited.

The DCA document model is typewriter-oriented. Ever present is the image of a printing assembly moving horizontally and vertically over a sheet of paper. Superscripting, for instance, is seen as an instruction to the printing assembly to "move up a fraction of a line," rather than being a property attached to a character. Consistent with the typewriter model, a DCA document contains character text only; it does not contain images, structured graphics, bar charts, tables (except primitive ones), equations, etc.

A DCA document is internally represented as a stream of EBCDIC bytes. The stream is divided into *Structures*, some containing the document text intermingled with control information, and some containing pure control information governing the appearance of the document. There are structures subdivided into *Self-Identifying Parameters* which act like buckets to collect a set of related control information. The text itself may be interspersed with *One-byte Controls* and *Multibyte Controls*, some of which may contain Self-Identifying Parameters. In light of the paucity of features of DCA, it is not clear what is gained by encoding the control information in five different ways: fixed structures, parameterized structures, fixed multibyte controls, parameterized multibyte controls, and one-byte controls.

As in DIF's case, a program converting the sample document into DCA has no choice but to discard the graphics. It has to map the typeface into one of the typefaces registered by IBM (with the attending problem of font substitution). The accented letters are correctly mapped since they have a code in the EBCDIC character set 337. The opening and closing quotes are replaced by left angle and right angle quotes, rather than neutral quotation marks. Figure 3 represents the Revisable Form stream corresponding to the sample document. For brevity's sake, a number of DCA codes have been dropped and, for legibility, the remaining ones have been replaced by explanatory text.

4. SGML

SGML stands for Standard Generalized Markup Language. An outgrowth of IBM's Generalized Markup Language, SGML is an international standard developed by ANSI and ISO [ISO86a]. SGML has a very different approach to document interchange. It divides the world of makers of documents into authors, who know the meaning of their writings, and publishers, who know how to layout and present documents. (Obviously, SGML was invented before the advent of desktop publishing).

Figure 3: DCA Revisable-Form encoding of Figure 1
(DCA codes replaced by legible text and comments)

Structure FUP (5 bytes)	format unit prefix
Structure DP (26 bytes)	document parameters
Structure FUP (5 bytes)	format unit prefix
Structure PMF (61 bytes)	primary master format
Structure PIP (19 bytes)	page image parameters
Structure LP (30 bytes)	line parameters
Structure TP (7 bytes)	tab parameters
Structure TUP (11 bytes)	text unit prefix
Structure BT (694 bytes)	body text
Multibyte SFG (7 bytes)	set font attributes
Multibyte BES (3 bytes)	begin emphasis
1.HTThe Beginning.RCR	
Multibyte EES (2 bytes)	end emphasis
ITJohn «Le Naïf» Léger paced the room, readingCRE and rereading the	
Multibyte BUS (4 bytes)	begin underline
incredible	
Multibyte EUS (2 bytes)	end underline
offer that came in CRE the mail this morning.RCR	
ITIt was too good to be true...RCR	
Multibyte BES (3)	begin emphasis
2.HTThe Middle.RCR	
Multibyte EES (2 bytes)	end emphasis
IT ... They went to see that «land» they bought inCRE Florida ...RCR	
Multibyte BES (3)	begin emphasis
3.HT The End.RCR	
Multibyte EES (2 bytes)	end emphasis
IT... Jane said: «I will come back as soon asCRE chicken start growing teeth.» She left the room, CRE leaving John holding the mortgage.	
PE	page end
Structure EUP (5 bytes)	end unit prefix
Structure BT (6 bytes)	body text
PE	page end

Authors know which portion of text is dependent on another, which fragments should be emphasized, what is a quote and what is a qualifier. Authors know the different meanings they attach to the quotes in the strings: "Le Naïf" (nickname), "land" (irony) and "I will come back..." (verbatim). SGML allows authors to note such differences of intent. On the other hand, since authors are not publishers, SGML does not allow them to specify the rendering of these differences.

Publishers know how to make the ink on paper look good: what typeface is appropriate for the document's contents, how much space is adequate around each paragraph, where to place pictures and footnotes, etc.

Publishers receive SGML files from authors, of course. The files contain the authors' text, the markups made by authors to annotate the logical structure of the text, and some "meta-language instructions" which describe the markups themselves (defining, for instance, the actual characters used in the file to enclose the markup strings). The meta-language instructions enable the publishers' programs to verify the coherence of the authors' markups.

Publishers also receive from authors verbal or written instructions (that is, non-standard and non-computerized instructions) on the meaning of the markups. Aye, there's the rub when it comes to document interchange with SGML. Authors can attach meaning in many different ways to their text: publishers cannot know and SGML cannot standardize these ways in advance.

Consider, for instance, the three types of quotes in the sample document. They could be encoded in SGML as

John <n>Le Naïf</n> Léger

that <i>land</i> they bought

<v>I will come back as soon as chicken start growing teeth</v>

The author must explain to the publisher the intent behind the markups <n>, <i> and <v>, so that the publisher can decide how to render them in print. Having so decided, the publisher calls in an SGML application programmer, who writes a program to process the <n>s, <i>s and <v>s according to the publisher's instructions. A new SGML application must be developed for every new type of document. Figure 4 is an acceptable SGML input to produce Figure 1.

The lines beginning with ENTITY or ELEMENT up to the closing angle bracket are the SGML declarations. Assume that we are typing the document on a terminal without accented letters; the ENTITY declarations give a symbolic name to the accented letters used in the text and contain a comment to help the publisher understand the meaning of the declaration. The line numbered 1 declares that the document is made up of objects labelled h, each containing one or more objects labelled p and zero or one object labelled pict. A pict, if present, appears after or before the p's; the string "- -" means that the markups <h> and </h> are required. Line 2 declares that a p consists of characters or e's or n's or i's or v's, in any number and combination. Line 3 says that the contents of a pict is not to be found in the SGML stream; all that

Figure 4: SGML markup for Figure 1

```
<!ENTITY      eacute      SDATA        "-- e, acute--">
<!ENTITY      idier       SDATA        "-- i, dieresis--">
<ELEMENT
1   h      - -    (p+|pict)                       --header--
2   p      - O    (#CDATA|e|n|i|v)+               --paragraph--
3   pict   - O    NONE                            --picture--
                  name             CHARS  REQUIRED
4   e      - O    (#CDATA)                        --emphasis--
5   n      - O    (#CDATA)                        --nickname--
6   i      - O    (#CDATA)                        --irony--
7   v      - O    (#CDATA)                        --verbatim--
>
<h>The Beginning.
<pict name="SmilingFace">
<p>John <n>Le Na&idier;f</n> L&eacute;ger paced the room,
reading and rereading the <e>incredible</e> offer that came in
the mail this morning.<p>It was too good to be true...</h>
<h>The Middle.
<pict name="SadFace">
<p>... They went to see that <i>land</i> they bought in Florida
...</h>
<h>The End.
<pict name="AngryFace">
<p>... Jane said: <v>I will come back as soon as chicken start
growing teeth</v>. She left the room, leaving John holding the
mortgage.</h>
```

appears with a pict object is a required character string spelled name; we will come back to this in a minute. The strings "- O" in lines 2 through 7 mean that the beginning markups must be present, but the end markups may be omitted when implied by the context (e.g. </p> isn't necessary before <h> or <p>).

As we have just seen, the contents of the pictures come from somewhere else. Each picture might be shipped to the publisher in a file with a name matching the name attribute of the pict element, or the pictures might exist only on paper and need to be pasted in manually. The author, the publisher and the SGML application programmer will agree among themselves on how to manage this process and make everything fall in place. The vagueness of the procedure is one of the reasons why SGML is looking toward ODA ([ISO86a], discussed below) as a kind of packaging tool to transport all the data pertaining to a composite document together.

5. ODA

ODA (Office Document Architecture) and ODIF (Office Document Interchange Format) are a standard developed by ISO to facilitate the interchange of documents [ISO86a]. ODA describes the concepts embodied in the standard in English prose and illustrations, while ODIF describes the bits and bytes of the actual encoding format.

Three aspects of ODA documents are discussed here: *layout structure, logical structure* and *content*.

5.1. Layout Structure

The layout structure tells application programs where to place the document elements on the presentation surface. The layout structure is a hierarchy of objects with a *document layout root* at the top, then *page sets*, *pages*, multiple levels of rectangular *frames*, and one level of rectangular *blocks* at the bottom. Page sets and frames are optional; the minimum layout structure consists of a root, a page and a block. Frames may overlap on the page; blocks within the same frame may not. Blocks point to content portions of a single type (such as text or raster graphics) with which they are filled. Layout objects have attributes. A block, for instance, beside its identifier and type, has two coordinates, two dimensions and a list of content portion identifiers.

A possible layout structure for our sample document is represented in Figure 5: a set of rectangular blocks owned by a page owned by the document layout root. There are no intermediate frames, but this is purely arbitrary; another ODA application might decide to place a frame around the paragraphs under each title in our example. ODIF assigns the identifier *1* to the layout root, and tracks objects by their owner's identifier and a suffix starting from *0*; hence the numbering scheme shown.

5.2. Logical Structure

The logical structure is a hierarchy of objects with a *document logical root* at the top, intermediate levels of *composite logical objects*, and one bottom level of *basic logical objects*. Composite logical objects are optional; the simplest logical stucture consists of the logical root and a basic logical object. Like layout blocks, basic logical objects point to content portions of a single type.

ODA, like SGML, does not attach a meaning to the logical objects. It does not say, for instance, that the top composite logical object represents a chapter and the bottom basic logical object a paragraph or a figure. Particular ODA applications might choose to attach a meaning to logical objects, perhaps for

Figure 5: ODA Layout Structure of Figure 1

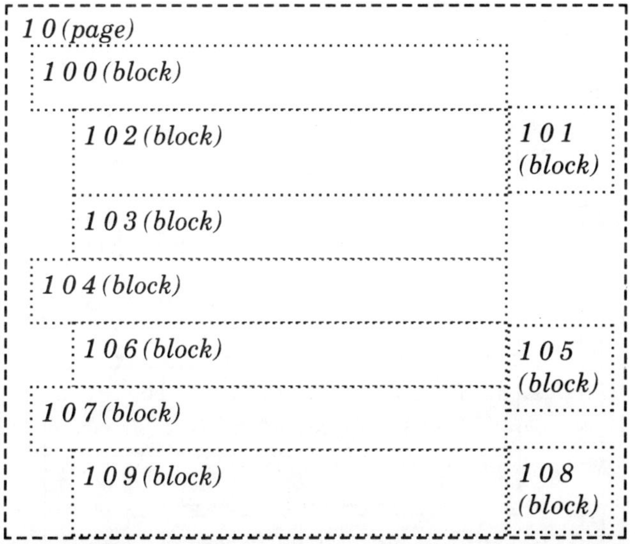

```
1 0 (page)
  1 0 0 (block)
     1 0 2 (block)        1 0 1 (block)
     1 0 3 (block)
  1 0 4 (block)
     1 0 6 (block)        1 0 5 (block)
  1 0 7 (block)
     1 0 9 (block)        1 0 8 (block)
```

the benefit of the user interface, but that meaning cannot be understood by other ODA applications because it is not standardized.

A logical structure for the sample document might be the following. At the top is the document logical root, to which ODIF assigns the identifier *3*. The next level level are composite logical objects, identified as *3 0*, *3 1* and *3 2*. We could call each a "Section", to take advantage of the optional *user visible name* attribute, which may be used in the user interface of an ODA application. The last level is made up of basic logical objects; let's give them the name "Paragraph" when they contain text and "Illustration" otherwise. Figure 6 represents the logical structure and attributes just described.

5.3. *Content*

Document content means characters, raster graphics, geometric graphics, and other data types to be introduced at a later date. These data types are or will be described in *Content Architectures*, separate sections of the standard which generally refer back to other standards. The Geometric Graphics Content Architecture, for instance, is based on the Computer Graphics Metafile Standard [ISO86b].

In the ODIF stream, the content is parcelled out in portions with a logical identifier or a layout identifier or both. These identifiers are present when there is a layout block or a basic logical object pointing to the content portion.

Figure 6: Logical Structure of Figure 1

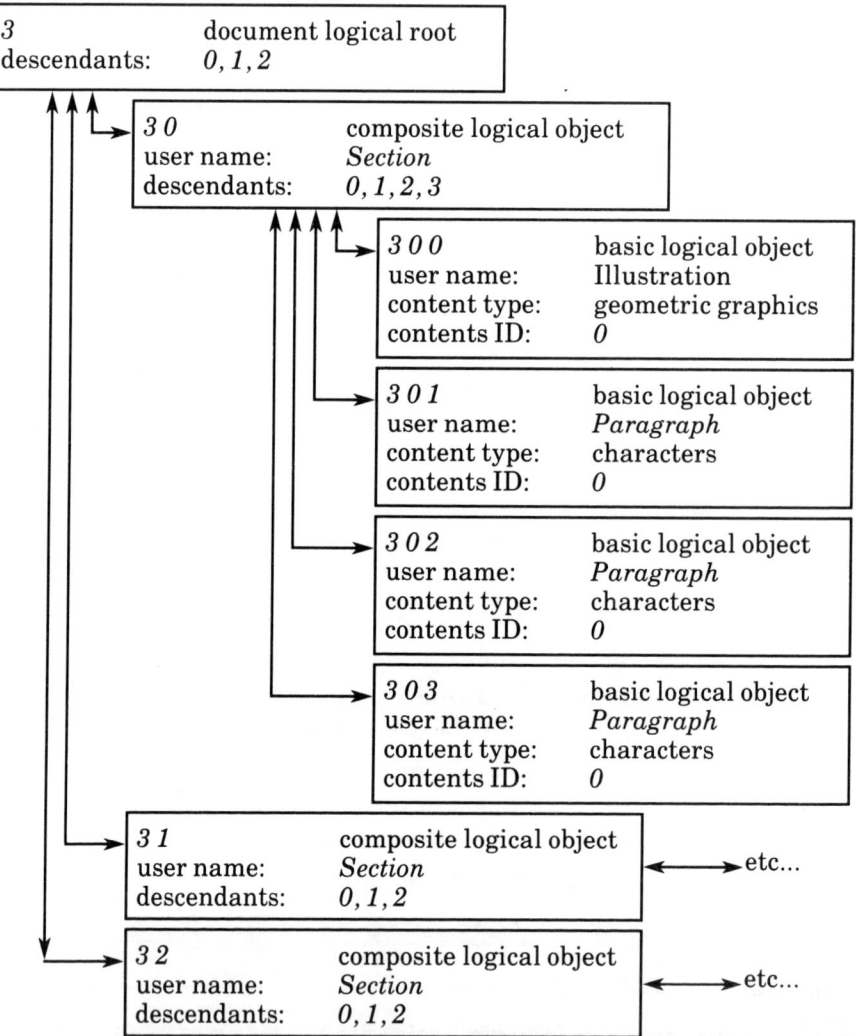

Figure 7 gives a legible representation of the encoding of the content portions of the sample document.

Within each type of content, there are additional structures to govern both the layout and the logical organization of the content's elements. For instance, character text has codes to specify typeface changes, superscripts, hyphenation points and the like. Readers of the standard will note that the part on character content architecture reverts back to the typewriter model of DIF and DCA: it is replete with Partial Line Up, Line Feed, Backspace, Reverse Presentation Direction, etc.

Figure 7: Content Portions of Figure 1 (legible representation)

logical content identifier:	*3 0 0 0*
layout content identifier:	*1 0 1 0*
coding:	geometric graphics
content value:	sequence of VDM instructions for the smiling face picture

logical content identifier:	*3 0 1 0*
layout content identifier:	*1 0 0 0*
coding:	character text
content value:	text *1. The Beginning.* intermingled with control codes for typeface, margins, etc.

logical content identifier:	*3 0 2 0*
layout content identifier:	*1 0 2 0*
coding:	character text
content value:	text *John ... this morning.* & codes

logical content identifier:	*3 0 3 0*
layout content identifier:	*1 0 9 0*
coding:	character text
content value:	text *It was too good to be true....* & codes

etc...

logical content identifier:	*3 2 2 0*
layout content identifier:	*1 0 9 0*
coding:	character text
content value:	text *... Jane said.... mortgage.* & codes

5.4. *Assessment*

The above section does not discuss many other aspects of ODA, such as generic and specific structures, document and application profiles, styles, objects and document classes. ODA appears to be a heavy standard (lengthy and difficult to understand), but is it heavy-duty? This will not be known until there are enough implementations to test it in the real world.

6. Conclusion

In the matter of document interchange format, much work remains to be done on two fronts. First, we need a complete interchange standard. Existing products like DIF, DCA and SGML have already rendered numerous services, within the constraints for which they were designed. But some of the existing products cannot interchange composite documents, others require a team of programmers at the receiving end, and the jury is still out in the case of ODA.

Second, we need a clear understanding of what application programs should do with objects and structures they do not support. Discarding the information is not the solution. There can be no complete interchange until we insure round-trip exchange without loss.

References

[1] American National Standards Institute (1979). *Additional Controls for Use with American National Standard Code for Information Interchange.* ANSI X3.64.
[2] American National Standards Institute (1983). *Text Information Interchange in Page Image Format (PIF).* ANSI X3.98.
[3] IBM (1983). *Document Content Architecture: Revisable-Form-Text Reference.* SC23-0758.
[4] IBM (1985). *Document Content Architecture: Final-Form-Text Reference.* SC23-0757.
[5] International Organization for Standardization (1983). *Additional Control Functions for Character Imaging Devices.* ISO IS 6429.
[6] International Organization for Standardization (1986). *Standard Generalized Markup Language.* ISO DIS 8879.
[7] International Organization for Standardization (1986). *Computer Graphics Metafile.* ISO IS 8632.
[8] International Organization for Standardization (1987). *Office Document Architecture.* ISO DIS 8613.
[9] Joloboff, V. (1986). *Trends and Standards in Document Representation.* Proceedings of the Conference on Text Processing and Document Manipulation, Nottingham, U.K..
[10]Knoerdel, J. & Ward Watkins, S. (1984). *Document Interchange Format.* National Bureau of Standards, NBSIR 84-2836.

THE FORMAL SPECIFICATION OF THE DOCUMENT STRUCTURES OF THE ODA STANDARD

WOLFGANG APPELT*   RICHARD CARR**   GERNOT RICHTER*

* *Gesellschaft für Mathematik und Datenverarbeitung, Sankt Augustin, FRG*
** *National Computing Centre, Manchester, UK*

Abstract:
The Office Document Architecture (ODA) is an International Standard, currently developed by TC 97/ SC 18 of the International Organization for Standardization (ISO). This paper describes the current state of a formal specification of the ODA document structures by mathematical means.

1. Introduction
For several years major efforts concerning the development of standards in the field of document processing have taken place within the International Organization for Standardization (ISO). As a result of this work an "*Office Document Architecture (ODA) and Interchange Format*" was developed which will become an International Standard in the near future [ISO8613]. The purpose of the standard is to facilitate the interchange of office documents, such as reports, invoices, letters etc., where the interchange is by electronic means, e.g., by electronic mail. The standard is divided into several parts, including "*Document structures*", "*Document processing reference model*", "*Office Document interchange format*", "*Character content architecture*" and "*Geometric graphics architecture*", consisting of several hundred pages of text. As it is usually the case with such standards, the means of expression by which the standard is defined, is natural English. The publication of the standard is expected for 1988.

In spring 1985 a special working group within ISO started to develop a formal specification of the ODA Standard [Appelt, Carr, Richter, 87]. The work was concentrated mainly on part 2 of [ISO8613], called "*Document structures*", since this part plays a central role: The *document structures* can be regarded as the skeleton of the whole standard, supporting the other parts, e.g., the different content types of a document as *character contents*, *geometric graphics* or *raster graphics*. Furthermore, because of the complexity of this part of the standard, a formal specification was considered to be very useful. It is expected that after the usual balloting procedures among the ISO member bodies the formal specification will become an addendum to the ODA Standard.

2. Aims of the formal specification

The formal specification of the ODA Standard has been developed with the aims of providing
— an unambiguous and consistent interpretation of the standard,
— a reference point for examining effects of revisions to the standard,
— a basis for implementations of the standard and
— a basis for the verification of systems conforming to the standard.

One of the major advantages of applying a formal specification technique in addition to a natural language text is that it provides a single interpretation of that text during the specification, implementation and utilisation process. It avoids different views of its information structures, functions and processes and hence different interpretations of the natural language text.

The formal specification can also be used as a basis for further developments since the specification can provide an ideal model for accurately and economically predicting the effects of changes and extensions to the standard.

A further advantage of formalising the standard is that potential implementors will be provided with a more precise specification with which they can work. By considering the formal specification rather than relying entirely on the natural language text readers can reason more thoroughly and gain better insights into the standard. This will greatly reduce the risk of producing non-conforming implementations.

Testing conformance to the standard involves the development of test tools that determine whether a system can correctly transmit and receive conforming data streams. In the development of such tools, the formal specification is expected to ensure that the testing software is evaluating the system against the valid interpretation of the standard.

A side-effect of the work on the formal specification was the detection of a number of inconsistencies and ambiguities in the natural language text. Corresponding comments were produced and submitted to the working group responsible for the development of the natural English version of the ODA Standard.

3. Method of the formal specification

An appropriate method for a formal specification of ODA document structures should have several, partially conflicting properties:

- To provide a rigorous and unambiguous specification the method must rely on a formal language, based on well defined syntactical and semantical constructs.
- Such a language should be especially appropriate for the constructs and cross relationships found within ODA documents.
- The language should be easy to learn; it should not prerequisite a specific knowledge, that cannot be expected from the average reader/implementor of the ODA Standard.
- The formal specification should be as close as possible to the natural language standard; relationships between specific clauses of the natural language text and its formal counterpart should be obvious.

The formal approach that was chosen after reviewing several alternatives is based on an information model developed by *Durchholz* and *Richter*, called "*Information Modelling by Composition*" (IMC) [Richter, Durchholz, 88]. An associated formal language, called *IMC-language* or *IMCL*, whose principles will be illustrated in the next section, is also available. (An earlier version is applied in [Richter, Durchholz, 82].) This language has its mathematical foundations in elementary set theory and first-order predicate logic. The relevant part of the language is described in a short self-contained annex to the formal specification of the Standard and a reader with an education in computer sciences or mathematics should be able to understand the language and following this the formal specification itself. One of the main reasons for choosing compositional information modelling was that it meets in particular the second and the fourth of the above mentioned requirements and, not less than comparable formalisms, the third one. The first criterion is exspected to be met by any sound formalism.

Using IMCL the complete formal specification of ODA document structures yields about 150 so-called *definitions* (first-order formulae), where each definition usually describes a specific property or relation in a rigorous, formal way (see section 6). Furthermore, each definition has an associated semi-formal English explanation. Though these semi-formal English text clauses do not belong to the formal specification, they provide links to the natural language text of the ODA Standard by referencing explicitly those clauses in the standard that are under definition. This gives some indirect confirmation about the completeness of the specification. Furthermore, the formal specification is structured to provide a high level of decomposition which aids the implementor by revealing just those parts of the standard under consideration at any time.

4. Survey of IMCL

Though a complete description of IMCL is not possible within this paper a short survey of the basic principles shall be given within this section.
The "world" of IMCL consists of
— the *universe* which in turn consists of abstract elements called *entities*; an *entity* may be a *construct*, a *spot* or a *spotset* (i.e., a set of *spots*),
— *predicates* on *entities* of the *universe* and
— *operators* on *entities* of the *universe*.

A *construct* is either
— an *atomic construct* or
— a *composite construct* (a *composite construct* may be a *collection*, a *catenation* or a *nomination*).

A *collection* is a set of constructs in the sense of mathematical set theory. A *catenation* can be regarded as a sequence of constructs where each construct has a preceding construct (except the first one) and a succeeding construct (except the last one). A *nomination* can be regarded as a set of pairs (*name,construct*) where each *name* (usually an atomic construct) is unique within the *nomination*. As a consequence, within a *nomination* each element can be addressed by its *name*.

Atomic constructs are either numbers or atoms without built-in semantics. They are syntactically denoted as character strings, e.g.,

$$314 \quad \text{'a'} \quad \text{'data'}$$

Note the single quotes enclosing a character or character string to denote an *atomic construct* without built-in semantics. *Composite constructs* are denoted by brackets and their component terms are separated by semicolons (in the case of *collections* or *nominations*) or by arrows (in the case of *catenations*), e.g.,

[314; 'a'; 'data'] [→'d'→'a'→'t'→'a'→] ['pi':314; 'std':'ODA']

The first expression denotes the collection of the three atomic constructs 314, 'a' and 'data'. The second expression denotes a catenation consisting of the atomic constructs 'd', 'a' and 't'. Notice the difference between the atomic construct 'data' and the composite construct [→'d'→'a'→'t'→'a'→]. The third expression denotes a nomination with two components, one having the name 'pi' with the associated component construct 314, the other one having the name 'std' with the associated component construct 'ODA'. A name and its associated component construct are syntactically separated by

a colon. The empty collection, catenation or nomination is denoted by [],
[→] or [:], respectively. Of course, more complicated composite constructs
may be formed by nesting collections, catenations and nominations, e.g.,

[314; [→'d'→'a'→'t'→'a'→]; ['pi':314; 'std':[→'O'→'D'→'A'→]]]

Using collections, catenations and nominations, rather complex structures
and especially many of the structures which are encountered in the modelling
of information in computer sciences can be built-up. To allow the decomposition of composite constructs or to address a specific construct within a
composite construct the concept of a *spot* has been introduced. For example, the component constructs of the catenation [→'d'→'a'→'t'→'a'→]
are 'a', 'd' and 't'. Whereas the atomic constructs 'd' and 't' appear
at one *spot* only, the atomic construct 'a' appears at two *spots*, namely
at the second and at the fourth position counted from the front end. So,
[→'d'→'a'→'t'→'a'→] has four component *spots*, but only three component *constructs*. If a construct is considered outside of any context, it is said
to be at its *ownspot*.

At a first glance, constructs might appear to play the central role in information modelling. However, it is the spots that are the primary objects
of manipulation and therefore they are often more prominent in actual applications of information handling than the constructs themselves. Usually
they are selected by selection criteria. A selection criterion need not give a
single spot: in many cases applying a selection criterion on some construct
will return a set of spots, called a *spotset*. Thus, the objects most naturally
dealt with are not even spots, but rather *spotsets*. So in IMCL, the emphasis
is on *spotsets* rather than on spots. If a spotset contains only one spot, it is
called a *singleton spotset*.

Several unary and binary *predicates* with built-in semantics are defined
in IMCL. A *predicate* is either True or False. For example,

$t_1 = t_2$ is True, iff (if and only if) the entities t_1 and t_2 are identical;

$t_1 \in t_2$ is True, iff the entity t_1 is a member of the collection t_2;

$t_1 \hat{\in} t_2$ is True, iff the entity t_1 is a singleton spotset and a subset of the spotset t_2;

$t_1 \subset t_2$ is True, iff t_1 is a subset of t_2 and t_1 and t_2 are both collections or spotsets, respectively;

IsAtom(t) is True, iff t is an atomic construct;

IsNumber(t) is True, iff t is a number;

IsCol(t) is True, iff t is a collection;

IsCat(t) is True, iff t is a catenation;

IsNom(t) is True, iff t is a nomination;

IsSpotset(t) is True, iff t is a spotset;
IsSingle(t) is True, iff t is a singleton spotset.

IMCL also includes several *operators* with built-in semantics. For example, for entities being numbers the usual arithmetical operations $+ - */$ are defined. For collections or spotsets the usual set theoretical operations $\cup \cap \setminus$ (union, intersection, set difference) are defined. Some additional IMCL operators are, for example:

^t If t denotes a construct, ^t denotes the singleton spotset whose element is the ownspot of the construct given by t (read "ownspot of").

t. If t denotes a spotset without atomic spots, t. denotes the set of all spots which are immediately inward the spots given by t (read "next inward").

C t If t denotes a singleton spotset, C t denotes the component construct at the spot given by t.

N t If t denotes a set of exactly one spot immediately inward a nomination spot, N t denotes the name at the spot given by t.

CARD t If t denotes a collection or a spotset, CARD t returns its cardinality, i.e., the number of component constructs or spots within it.

t FIRST If t denotes a spotset whose spots are immediate component spots of catenations, t FIRST denotes the set of those spots of t whose position from the front end is 1.

Since IMCL is a first-order language based on predicate logic the usual logical quantifiers $\forall$ (for all) and $\exists$ (exists) are part of the language as well as the logical connections *not*, *and*, *or*, *iff* and *impl* (implies). For successive quantification the usual notational simplification is used, i.e.,

$\exists x (x \in m$ *and* formula)   may be abbreviated as: $\exists x \in m$ (formula)
$\forall x (x \in m$ *impl* formula)   may be abbreviated as: $\forall x \in m$ (formula)

Some simple examples may illustrate the use of the predicates and operators. For t being the construct

$$[[\to \text{'d'} \to \text{'a'} \to \text{'t'} \to \text{'a'} \to]; \text{'ODA'}]$$

IsCol(t) is True whereas IsAtom(t) or IsCat(t) are False. CARD t returns the number 2 since t contains the two constructs $[\to \text{'d'} \to \text{'a'} \to \text{'t'} \to \text{'a'} \to]$ (a catenation) and 'ODA' (an atomic construct).

^t denotes the singleton spotset containing as the only element the ownspot of $[[\to \text{'d'} \to \text{'a'} \to \text{'t'} \to \text{'a'} \to]; \text{'ODA'}]$. Consequently, ^$t$. denotes the spotset containing the two component spots with the constructs $[\to \text{'d'} \to \text{'a'} \to \text{'t'} \to \text{'a'} \to]$ and 'ODA'. Starting from the ownspot of $[\to \text{'d'} \to \text{'a'} \to \text{'t'} \to \text{'a'} \to]$ the expression

$$\hat{}[\to\text{'d'}\to\text{'a'}\to\text{'t'}\to\text{'a'}\to] . \text{FIRST}$$

returns the singleton spotset with the spot of 'd', and the expression

$$\text{CARD}\ (\hat{}[\to\text{'d'}\to\text{'a'}\to\text{'t'}\to\text{'a'}\to]).$$

returns the number 4 (four component spots).

5. Document models in ODA and their specification

ODA provides two kinds of abstraction in its architecture. The *structural model* is used to model the logical and layout objects found in a document while the *descriptive representation* provides a collection of data structures, called *constituents*, which hold information on these objects, as shown in figure 1.

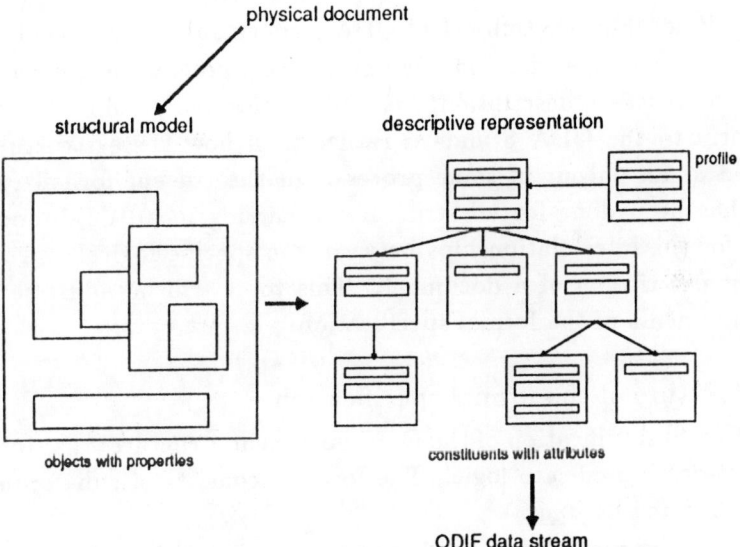

Figure 1: Structural model and descriptive representation in ODA

The abbreviation *ODIF* stands for "Office Document Interchange Format" which is described in part 5 of [ISO8613]. ODIF defines the binary coding format of the descriptive representation of an ODA document and is based on the Abstract Syntax Notation One (ASN.1). ODA does not require that an implementation uses the ODIF format for the internal representation of its documents; other formats might be more suitable for a specific implementation. For interchange purposes, however, ODIF is the format proposed in the standard.

The objects in the *structural model* are represented in the *descriptive representation* by *constituents* with *attributes*. That is, in the descriptive representation, a *constituent* is a *set of attributes* used to describe an object and its properties in the structural model. For example, a *constituent* 'page' has attributes describing its *dimensions*, the *content type* it contains (e.g., character contents or raster graphics), the *subordinate objects* it has, etc.

The full descriptive representation of an ODA document is a *set of constituents* as shown in figure 2 on the next page. It contains a constituent called the *document profile* together with the constituents that form the *document body*. The body, in turn, comprises the subsets of constituents called the *generic part*, the *specific part* and the *style part*.

The *formal specification* of the ODA document structures is concerned with the *descriptive representations* of documents since constituents and their attributes are the basis of the interchange stream and their make-up and relationships the subject of ODA conformance requirements.

The formal specification pursues a *purely declarative approach* to information structure description, i.e., it specifies the possible structures that conform to the ODA Standard rather than how these structures are obtained as an output of some process. In the current formal specification this has been done for all structures occurring in an ODA document except for the interrelationships between the specific logical and the specific layout description of a document. This topic will be addressed in future enhancements of the formal specification.

6. Structure of the formal specification

The formal specification of the ODA document structures is a single formula in first-order predicate logic. The formula consists of sub-formulae which are connected by *and*:

$$\text{formula}_1 \underline{\text{ and }} \text{formula}_2 \underline{\text{ and }} \text{formula}_3 \underline{\text{ and }} \ldots \text{formula}_n$$

A formula is also called a *definition* since it either defines a *concept* used in the natural English description of the ODA Standard, or a so-called *subsidiary predicate* or *subsidiary function* which has been introduced for the sake of readability.

To make the formal specification more readable and to provide an easy link to the natural English text the definitions are presented in four groups. The first group, having about 35 definitions, contains all formulae defining the *sets of constituents* as, e.g., a whole document, a *document body*, a *generic part* or a *generic logical description* (see figure 2).

The second group, having also about 35 definitions, contains the formulae defining the *constituents* as, e.g., a *logical object class description*, a *logical object description*, a *content portion description*, a *layout style* or a

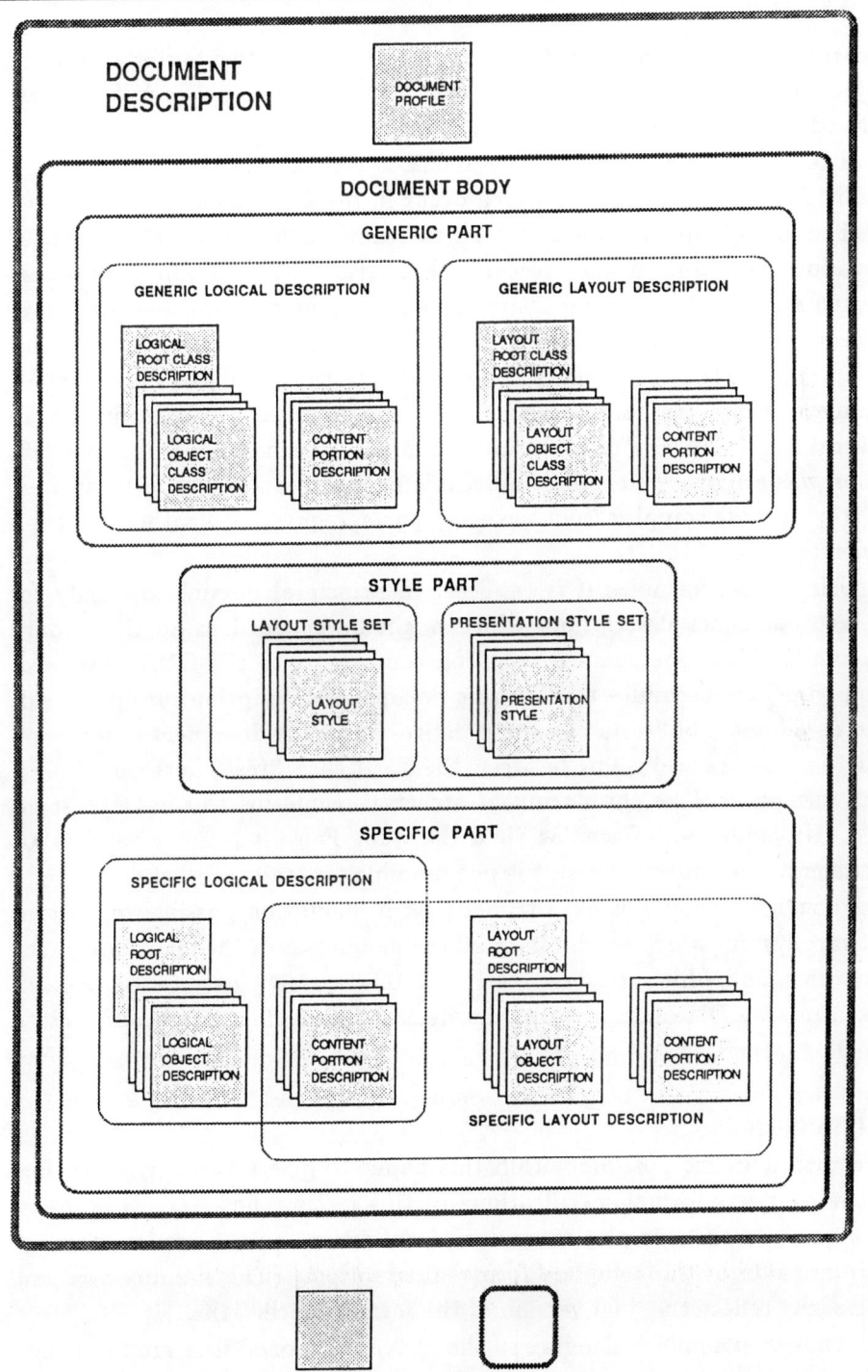

Figure 2: Descriptive representation of a document

presentation style (see figure 2 again). Also the constituents concerning the objects of ODA's layout structure such as 'page', 'frame' and 'block' are defined within this group.

The third group with currently about 40 definitions contains all the formulae defining the *attributes* which occur in the *constituents*.

The last group contains about 35 *subsidiary definitions* which are used in various definitions in the preceding three groups. For example, some constituents of an ODA document are embedded in *hierarchical tree structures* with complicated cross relationships which are rigorously defined within this group. These structures belong, by the way, to the those parts of the ODA Standard which are hard to understand and where a precise definition in natural English is very difficult. By the formal specification a rigorous definition was achieved but, admittedly, this part of the formal specification is a little bit more complex than the other parts, requesting a rather thorough understanding of IMCL.

Using these formulae it is (at least in principle) possible to verify for a given document description, which might be encoded as an ODIF data stream, if it is a document description conforming to the ODA Standard. "Applying" the formulae to a specific document description can be considered as a bundle of "tests" on the constituents of the document description and the cross relationships between them. If each "test" succeeds, i.e., if each formula is True the document structure conforms to the ODA standard. If one or more formulae yield the value False it is not a valid ODA document. An undefined result is not possible for logical reasons.

Though it might not be a trivial task it should be possible to write a software system which has built-in all the definitions of the ODA document structures, and which, reading a given ODA document description, e.g., in the form an ODIF data stream, can decide if that document conforms to the ODA Standard.

7. Examples

Of course it is not possible within this paper to give a thorough overview on the complete formal specification. In this section, however, we want to show some (rather simple) examples of *definitions* so the reader may get an impression of the complete formal description. (The examples do not necessarily reflect the final version of the formal specification.)

The first example, belonging to the above mentioned first group of definitions, is definition 1 in the formal specification (see figure 2). It reads as follows:

Definition 1

1 $\forall doc$
2 $(_0 \text{IsDocument}(doc)$ _iff_
3 $\exists prof$
4 $(_1 \text{IsDocumentProfile}^{35}(prof)$ _and_
5 $(_2 doc = [prof]$ _or_
6 $\exists doby$
7 $(_3 \text{IsDocumentBody}^2(doby)$ _and_ $doc = [prof] \cup doby$ _and_
8 $(doby)\text{IsConsistentWith}^{117}(prof)_3)_2)_1)_0$

The superscripts refer to the numbers of the definitions, where the predicates and operators used within a definition are defined, e.g., the predicate IsDocumentProfile is defined in definition 35. The subscripts attached to some of the parentheses are used to indicate the balancing. These numbers do not belong to the formal description itself but they are, especially in more complicated definitions, to help the readers and, of course, the developers of the formal specification.

The semi–formal explanation of the formula reads as follows:

> Predicate "is a document"
> An entity *doc* is a document or, more precisely, a document description if it is a collection of constituents consisting either of a single document profile *prof* (4, 5) or of a document profile *prof* along with other constituents which constitute a document body *doby* (4, 6, 7). In the latter case the document body has to be consistent with the document profile (8).

The next example, also from the first group of definitions, is definition 2 in the formal specification. It steps down one level and describes the entities which are contained within a document body (see again figure 2). Furthermore, it defines several relations which must hold between those entities. These relationships are not visible in figure 2, but they are described in the natural English specification of the ODA Standard. The definition reads as follows:

Definition 2

1 $\forall doby$
2 $(_0 \text{IsDocumentBody}(doby)$ _iff_
3 $\exists glogct, slogct, glayct, slayct, laystys, prestys$
4 $(_1 \text{IsGenericLogicalStructure}^{22}(glogct)$ _and_
5 $\text{IsSpecificLogicalStructure}^{29}(slogct)$ _and_
6 $\text{IsGenericLayoutStructure}^{25}(glayct)$ _and_
7 $\text{IsSpecificLayoutStructure}^{30}(slayct)$ _and_
8 $\text{IsLayoutStyleSet}^{33}(laystys)$ _and_

```
9      IsPresentationStyleSet³⁴(prestys) and
10     (slogct ⊆ doby or slayct ⊆ doby) and
11     doby ⊆ glogct ∪ slogct ∪ glayct ∪ slayct ∪ laystys ∪ prestys and
12     (laystys ⊆ doby impl glogct ⊆ doby or slogct ⊆ doby) and
13     (slogct ∪ glayct ⊆ doby impl IsRootedGenericLayoutStructure²⁶(glayct)) and
14     (₂glogct ⊆ doby and IsRootedGenericLogicalStructure²³(glogct) impl
15        (slogct)IsCompletelyAssociatedWith³¹(glogct)₂) and
16     (₃glayct ⊆ doby and IsRootedGenericLayoutStructure²⁶(glayct) impl
17        (slayct)IsCompletelyAssociatedWith³¹(glayct)₃) and
18     (₄slogct ∪ slayct ⊆ doby impl
19        (slayct)IsLayoutOfLogicalPartIn¹¹⁸(doby)₄) and
20     (₅laystys ∪ glayct ⊆ doby impl
21        ∀ a ê ˜laystys . . 'layout object class'
22        (∃ g ∈ glayct (C ˜g . 'object class identifier' = C a))₅)
23     /* further cross relationships */ ₁)₀)
```

Since the definition is a bit more complicated than in the first example the semi–formal explanation is a bit longer now:

> Predicate "is a document body"
> An entity *doby* is a document body if it is a collection of constituents which includes at least (10) a specific logical structure *slogct* (5) or a specific layout structure *slayct* (7). It may additionally include (11) a generic logical structure *glogct* (4), a generic layout structure *glayct* (6), a layout style set *laystys* (8) and a presentation style set *prestys* (9). A layout style set may be part of the document body only together with a generic or a specific logical structure (12). If a specific logical and a generic layout structure belong to the document body, the generic layout structure is a so–called rooted generic structure (13). If a generic structure is part of the document body and is rooted, the corresponding specific structure is completely associated with the generic structure (14–17). If the document body includes both a specific logical and a specific layout structure, the latter has to be the result of a layout process on the logical part of the document body (18, 19). If a layout style set *laystys* and a generic layout structure *glayct* form part of the document body, all references 'layout object class' from *laystys* to *glayct* are satisfied (20–22)."*

The next example, belonging to the third group of definitions, shows how the formal specification of ODA document structures helped detecting errors or ambiguities in the natural language specification. The draft version of the ODA standard, submitted for voting among the ISO member bodies in

---

* In the meantime, the term *structure* in the above sense has been replaced by the term *description* (see figure 2).

autumn 1986, contained the following clause which describes the attribute 'separation' used during the layout process of an ODA document. (Parts of the text which are of no relevance here, are omitted and indicated by "...".)

> The attribute 'separation' ... "specifies minimum amounts of separation between the block used to present the content of this logical object and the nearest adjacent block immediately subordinate to the same immediate superior layout object.
> Separation may be specified for one or more of:
> a)   the 'leading edge';
> b)   the 'trailing edge';
> c)   the 'centre separation';
> The 'leading edge' specifies the minimum separation from the ...
> The 'trailing edge' specifies the minimum separation from the ...
> The 'centre separation' specifies the minimum distance between ...
> The value of this attribute is one or more integers which specify the amount of separation in Basic Measurement Units."

This natural language specification is unclear. For example, if there are three integers specified for the attribute, the standard does not explicitly say, that the first one is associated with the 'leading edge', the second one with the 'trailing edge' and the third one with the 'centre separation'. Although this might be the intuitive interpretation, implementors of the standard might have different views on this point. The standard also allows the specification of less than three integers. But if, e.g., only one integer is specified for the attribute, it could not be determined which edge this integer is associated with.

When trying to formalize this clause of the natural English specification of ODA these difficulties were identified immediately. The resulting definition which was later on also used for the natural English specification, reads as follows:

$$\boxed{\text{Definition 85}}$$

1   $\forall v$
2   $(_0 \text{IsSeparationValue}(v)$ <u>iff</u>
3   $(_1 \text{IsNeNom}^{133}(v)$ <u>and</u>
4   $\forall a \,\hat{\in}\, \hat{\;} v \bullet$
5   $(_2 \text{N}\ a \in [\text{'leading edge'}; \text{'trailing edge'}; \text{'center separation'}]$ <u>and</u>
6   $\text{IsNumber}(\text{C}\ a)_2)_1)_0$

The predicate $\text{IsNeNom}(v)$ (read "is non–empty nomination") used within this definition is True iff v is a nomination and v is not empty, i.e., $v \neq [:]$. The semi–formal explanation of this formula is:

Predicate "is a separation value"
The value of the attribute 'separation' is a non-empty nomination, i.e., a non-empty set of pairs (*name, value*). The *name* is an element of the set ['leading edge'; 'trailing edge'; 'center separation']; the *value* is a number.

By using the construct of a *nomination* the ambiguity in the natural language specification was removed.

8. Conclusions

A formal specification technique based on rigorous syntactical and semantical constructs can and should be used to describe information structures when standardizing document processing systems. Especially for complex structures, as in ODA documents, such an approach seems superior to a mere natural language description where, due to the lack of precision in any natural language, ambiguities and even inconsistencies are likely to remain, even when the authors make their best efforts to avoid these.

Although the final form of a standard will still be published in natural English following established regulations of ISO, an accompanying effort for a formal specification will surely improve the standard in various ways and provide a definitive reference document for all questions arising in its interpretation.

9. References

[1] Appelt, W.; Carr, R.; Richter, G. (1987). *Formal Specification of ODA Document Structures.* Draft proposal for an Addendum to IS 8613, Part 2; International Organization for Standardization.

[2] Richter, G; Durchholz, R. (1982). IML-Inscribed High-Level Petri Nets. in: *Information Systems Design Methodologies*; Ed.: Olle, T. W.; Sol, H. G.; Verrijn-Stuart; North-Holland.

[3] Richter, G; Durchholz, R. (1988). *Information Modelling by Composition — The IMC/IMCL Reference Manual.* Technical Report, GMD, Sankt Augustin.

[4] ISO8613. *Office Document Architecture (ODA) and Interchange Format* (1988). International Standard IS 8613, International Organization for Standardization.

Specifying Structured Document Transformations

Richard Furuta* and P. David Stotts[†]

University of Maryland[‡]

ABSTRACT

A major issue when representing a document as a grammatically-defined collection of composite objects is how changes to the context-free grammar specification can be translated into corresponding changes to document instances generated from the specification. We present a mechanism to represent the transformation between versions of the grammar, and describe how this representation can be used to convert a document instance from the old grammar G to one from the new grammar G'. The method is based on associating unique labels both with the right hand sides of grammar productions and with the corresponding nodes in the tree representing the instance. A manually-specified partial expansion of G', termed TG, showing the correspondence between elements removed from G and relocated in G', is used to generate the new instance. While the notation for a transformation is explicitly specified here, it could also serve as the target for heuristically-defined schemes to automatically generate transformations.

1. The Problem and the Approach

Recent research on interactive document preparation systems has focused on document representations that present the document as a collection of composite objects. In such a representation the document itself is an object composed from more primitive objects. For example, in describing a paper divided into sections, the document might be formed from a sequence of paragraphs and sections. Each section would be formed from a sequence of paragraphs and subsections. The composition would continue until each object was specified in terms of the most primitive, atomic objects—perhaps strings of characters.

Such documents are commonly called "structured documents."[1] Since more primitive objects are combined into higher-level objects, the document's overall structure is a tree. Grammatical specifications of the interrelationships between the document elements guide and constrain the formation of the tree.

---

*Internet address: furuta@mimsy.umd.edu. This work was supported in part by a grant from the General Research Board of the University of Maryland.

[†]Internet address: pds@leviathan.cs.umd.edu.

[‡]Affiliations of the authors: Department of Computer Science and the University of Maryland Institute for Advanced Computer Studies. Mailing address: Department of Computer Science, University of Maryland, College Park, MD 20742, U.S.A.

[1]See [AFQ88] for more discussion of issues associated with structured documents.

Much of the work into such document representations has concentrated on the interactive displays and operations for their creation and manipulation.[2] While such interactive interfaces are beginning to be understood [FQA88], problems remain to be solved before such systems can be incorporated completely into document preparation environments. Among the most important of these problems is to determine how composite document objects may be converted from one structure to another—in general due to alterations in the grammatical description that specifies the relationships among document components. Such conversions may result in the addition, deletion, or reordering of component objects. Levels of nesting may be added or removed. Reparsing the component objects with the new target production may not succeed because the desired ordering of the primitive components may have been changed and because the specifications generally are ambiguous. Simple redistribution schemes, such as those incorporated into some syntax-directed editors for programming languages, also will not necessarily provide correct results.

We have decided first to focus on the means for expressing the relationships between two different grammatical descriptions of a collection of document objects. To this end, we employ ideas from the theory of *hierarchical graphs*, or *h-graphs*, developed by T. W. Pratt of the University of Virginia.[3] Sets of h-graphs can be described by context-free grammars, just as can sets of strings (languages). The ability to label the graph nodes in the productions of h-graph grammars, however, gives them context-sensitive aspects. This extra power over context-freedom is the primary means by which we solve the document transformation problem.

In summary, a statement of the problem we seek to solve is: "There exist several document instances which are described by a single generic document, *i.e.*, a single context-free grammar. How can these instances be altered, without parsing, to reflect an alteration to the generic document structure?" The solution is provided in the form of answers to two questions. First, how can a transformation from one generic document into another best be specified? Second, given a transformation specification, how can an instance of the old generic document be transformed into an instance of the new one?

In the following section we present an overview of the notation used for document description. Section 3 describes the specification of transforma-

---

[2] See, for example, the several projects reported at EP86 [vV86].

[3] H-graph theory was first used to define programming language semantics. The theory was later extended to describe the transformation of data states during procedure executions in both sequential and parallel software systems [Pra83, Sto85].

tions through four extended examples. Section 4 explains the method of actually transforming instances once a specification is done. The concluding section discusses the automatability of these techniques.

2. Specification of the Document Class

A document *class* serves to group together documents with similar structures. Examples of classes that might be defined include letters, technical reports, and books. The permissible relationships between elements within a class are defined by a *generic logical structure*. Individual documents are *instances* of this generic logical structure.

The generic logical structure is defined and constrained by a context-free grammar. The syntax of the grammar's productions is modified from the BNF notation [Fur86b]. To understand the examples given in this paper, it is only necessary to employ nonterminals, distinguished by enclosure in angle brackets (`<document>`), terminal symbols whose content is to be provided by the document's author, shown in plain type (`text-block`), and terminal symbols representing constant and literal information, shown in double quotes (`"ABSTRACT:"`).

The right-hand side of a grammar production may contain an unnested grouping of grammar elements—syntactically a sequence of grammar elements is surrounded by parentheses and the sequence is treated as a single element with respect to the right-hand side of the production. Individual elements or grouped elements can be separated by the "|" operator, specifying the occurrence of one and only one of the connected elements. The elements of the production may be flagged with "?", meaning the element appears zero or one times, with "*", meaning the element appears zero or more times, or with "+", meaning the element appears one or more times. A final restriction is that a given name must appear on the left-hand side of exactly one of the grammar's productions.

The additions and restrictions in the form of the grammar were made to support a prototype system that automatically guided the preparation of document instances from the grammatical specification [Fur86a, Fur86b] and refinements to the form subsequently were made based on that experience. Interestingly, the syntax of the grammar associated with the ISO SGML standard [ISO86] is a superset of the one that we use. We believe that our results will easily be translatable into the SGML domain.

Figure 1: Commuting diagram for sequence of transformations

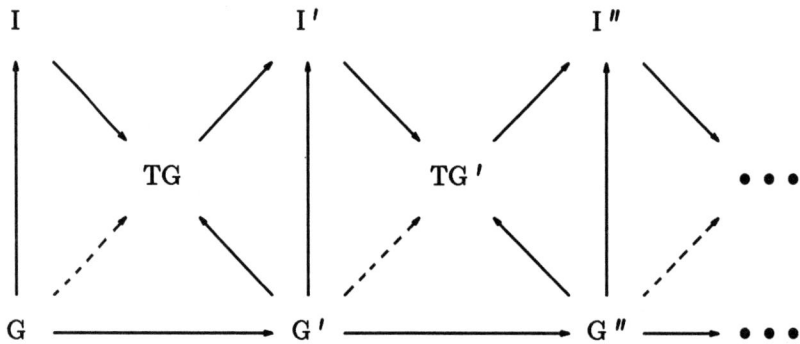

3. Specifying Transformations

A generic document transformation is specified with a pair of grammars, G and G'. Given an existing document grammar G, a new generic document is created by constructing an altered grammar G'. The user implicitly defines G' by describing the changes between productions in G and G'.[4] These new productions may consist of altered forms of the G productions, additional productions, or deletions of G productions. Any productions not altered in the transformation specification carry over from G to G'.

All terminal and nonterminal symbols on the right-hand sides of the productions of G and G' are assumed to be uniquely and permanently labeled, an assumption that can be enforced automatically by a software tool. These labels provide the context-sensitive aspects of h-graphs to the document grammars. These unique identifiers for elements of G are produced by an editing tool as the grammar is constructed. When a transformation is specified, the productions already in G that are altered retain the original labels on their unchanged symbols. Any newly added symbols, including all those in newly added productions, get new labels automatically. Thus all symbols in the productions of G' are labeled as well.

After G' is constructed from G, we need to know how to use such a transformation specification. We employ a third grammar, TG, or *transformation grammar*, to effect the conversion of existing instances of G into new instances of G'. TG is actually a restriction of G', along with notation using the labels in G and G' to specify relationships between the structure of G instances and the structure of G' instances. TG is formed by expanding,

---

[4]Throughout this paper, we assume that the modification of the generic logical structure is accomplished with a set of editing tools. A person creating such modifications is termed the *user*. An *author* creates specific instances of a generic logical structure.

via the rules of grammatical derivation, the specified new productions of G', thereby restricting the particular instances that TG can describe.

Figure 1 illustrates the relationships among the various grammars and document instances created by a transformation. In summary, the system's user first transforms grammar G to be grammar G' and then expands portions of the productions in G' to yield TG. Instance I has been specified by an author, based on the definitions given in G. The system employs grammar TG and some element mapping information to convert instance I to a new instance I', corresponding to to a derivation under G'. We will present the grammar transformation specifications using G, G', and TG by example, and then consider the conversion from instance I to I'.

Below are example specifications for several kinds of transformation. The notation we use is an "internal" one that would not be appropriate for a user interface. We assume that an editing tool of some kind would allow the user to construct specifications as they are illustrated below.

The CR is a "coat rack," which holds a sequence of elements in temporary form. It is used to preserve grammar symbols after deletion for possible later reinsertion. Several operators are defined for use in converting productions in G into productions in G' and TG:

DELETE	remove grammar symbol
ADD	create new grammar symbol
NEWPROD	create new production
Rewrite	expand production in G' to TG
MAP	attach CR elements to new symbols
Invoke	make productions available for use

These operations exhibit the following behaviors:

ADD: The newly created item is assumed empty unless it is a system-defined symbol or a literal.

Rewrite: Only certain rewritings are permissible.[5] If the source is empty, then both results are considered empty. If source is not empty, then only one of results is empty and the non-empty one must be able to contain all of the pre-existing elements.

MAP: The target of the map must be empty. All terminal symbols in the CR must be mapped directly or indirectly (*i.e.*, MAP of a subtree covers all

---

[5] For example, one such rewrite rule might be that "a+" may be rewritten as "a a*" for any element "a".

its elements). The special reserved target NULL may be used to discard information by MAPing to it.

Each production is labeled on the left side with a production number. On the right hand side, a sequence number and a unique label for each grammar symbol is enclosed in brackets, *e.g.*, [5,M]. When the unique letter label is not needed, the number alone is written, *e.g.*, [5]. Also, other notations occasionally appear in the brackets:

    (e)   empty subtree node
    (x:nn)   node is expansion of symbol with unique label **nn**
    (m)   node has been successfully mapped

Operators use the sequence number $[n]$ for addressing right side grammar symbols. The unique label of a symbol is carried from the grammar into an instance when one is created, thereby identifying the portion of the grammar from which each subtree originates.

Example 1: Element deletion and relocation. The first illustration involves deletion of a portion of a document. Part of this portion's contents are deleted and the rest is reclassified. The initial grammar G contains productions

```
p1:  <document> = [1,A]title [2,B]author [3,C]<abstract>?
                  [4,F]( [4.1,D]<section> | [4.2,E]<paragraph> )+
p2:  <abstract> = [1,G]"ABSTRACT" [2,H]<paragraph>+

CR: empty initially.
```

Consider, then, the following transformation specification:

```
>DELETE p1[3]
>rewrite p1[3] ==> [3.2(e)]+ [3]+
>invoke CR[1]
>MAP CR:p2[1] ==> NULL
>MAP CR:p2[2] ==> p1[3]
```

The intent here is that the sequence of paragraphs contained within the portion of the original generic document should become simply the first sequence of paragraphs of the new generic document, without a header. To effect this transformation correctly, This context-sensitive information is accurately captured in the grammatical notation by expressing the structures described by both the source and target productions, and labeling nodes in each to indicate the coinciding portions.

For a more detailed understanding, consider the effect of each command on the productions of G:

```
>DELETE p1[3]
    p1: <document> = [1,A]title [2,B]author
                [3,F]( [3.1,D]<section> | [3.2,E]<paragraph> )+
    CR: [1,C]<abstract>?
```

(Note that is now unreachable.)

```
>rewrite p1[3] ==> [3.2(e)]+ [3]+
    p1: <document> = [1,A]title [2,B]author [3(e,x:F),E]<paragraph>+
                [4,F]( [4.1,D]<section> | [4.2,E]<paragraph> )+
    CR: [1,C]<abstract>?

>invoke CR[1]
    CR: [1,C]<abstract>?
    CR:p2: <abstract> = [1,G]"ABSTRACT" [2,H]<paragraph>+

>MAP CR:p2[1] ==> NULL
    CR: [1,C]<abstract>?
    CR:p2: <abstract> = [1(m),G]"ABSTRACT" [2,H]<paragraph>+
```

(Note that CR:p2[2] is still not mapped.)

```
>MAP CR:p2[2] ==> p1[3]
    CR: [1(m),C]<abstract>?
    CR:p2: <abstract> = [1(m),G]"ABSTRACT" [2(m),H]<paragraph>+
```

After the transformation specification is completed, the grammar G' contains the unaltered productions of G and the production p1 as shown above after the DELETE command. The grammar TG contains the unaltered productions of G and p1 as shown above after the Rewrite command.

Example 2: Element addition. The second example shows the transformation specification for adding a new grammar element to a production. Let the initial grammar G contain a production p2:

```
    p2: <abstract> = [1,H]<paragraph>+
```

Consider, then, this transformation specification:

```
    >ADD p2[1] "ABSTRACT"
```

Here, a new literal string is being added as the first element of . The new grammar G' contains the unaltered productions of G, as well as this new version of p2:

```
    p2: <abstract> = [1,M]"ABSTRACT" [2,H]<paragraph>+
```

Note that "ABSTRACT" is not marked as empty because it is a literal. The transformation grammar TG is the same as G', because the addition operation is purely synthetic, and causes no rearrangement.

Example 3: Element reclassification. This illustration involves substitution of a different grammar element for an existing grammar element. Let the initial grammar G contain a production

```
p1: <document> = [1,A]title [2,B]author [3,C]<abstract>? [4,D]<body>
```

Consider, then, this transformation specification:

```
>DELETE p1[2]
>NEWPROD <author-list> = author+
>ADD p1[2] <author-list>
>invoke p1[2]
>rewrite p1:p2[1] author author*
>MAP CR[1] ==> p1:p2[1]
```

This transformation is essentially reclassifying an existing document element into another type, here converting **author** to **<author-list>**. The name of the original author becomes the first element of the new **<author-list>**. For a more detailed understanding, consider the productions of the grammars after each operation of the specification:

```
>DELETE p1[2]
    p1: <document> = [1,A]title [2,C]<abstract>? [3,D]<body>
    CR: [1,B]author

>NEWPROD <author-list> = author+
    p1: <document> = [1,A]title [2,C]<abstract>? [3,D]<body>
    p2: <author-list> = [1,Q]author+
    CR: [1,B]author

>ADD p1[2] <author-list>
    p1: <document> = [1,A]title [2(e),R]<author-list>
                     [3,C]<abstract>? [4,D]<body>
    p2: <author-list> = [1,Q]author+
    CR: [1,B]author

>invoke p1[2]
    p1: <document> = [1,A]title [2(e),R]<author-list>
                     [3,C]<abstract>? [4,D]<body>
    p1:p2: <author-list> = [1(e),Q]author+
    p2: <author-list> = [1,Q]author+
    CR: [1,B]author

>rewrite p1:p2[1] ==> author author*
    p1: <document> = [1,A]title [2(e),R]<author-list>
                     [3,C]<abstract>? [4,D]<body>
    p1:p2: <author-list> = [1(e,x:R)]author [2(e)]author*
    p2: <author-list> = [1,Q]author+
    CR: [1,B]author
```

```
>MAP CR[1] ==> p1:p2[1]
    p1: <document> = [1,A]title [2(e),R]<author-list>
                                [3,C]<abstract>? [4,D]<body>
    p1:p2: <author-list> = [1(x:R),Q]author [2(e),Q]author+
    p2: <author-list> = [1,Q]author+
    CR: [1(m),B]author
```

Example 4: Element transposition. The following transformation illustrates the transposition of two document elements, *i.e.*, swapping the order of the bibliography and the indices. We treat this operation as a sequence of deletion following by addition. Let the initial grammar G contain a production p1:

```
    p1: <document> = [1,A]title [2,B]author [3,C]<body>
                                [4,D]<bibliography> [5,E]<indices>
```

Consider, then, this sequence of commands:

```
>DELETE p1[4]
>ADD p1[4] <bibliography>
>MAP CR[1] ==> p1[4]
```

The altered productions of G' and TG are shown with a more detailed examination of each operation:

```
>DELETE p1[4] (we could just as well have deleted <indices>)
    p1: <document> = [1,A]title [2,B]author [3,C]<body> [4,E]<indices>
    CR: [1,D]<bibliography>

>ADD p1[4] <bibliography>
    p1: <document> = [1,A]title [2,B]author [3,C]<body>
                                [4(e),T]<bibliography> [5,E]<indices>
    CR: [1,D]<bibliography>

>MAP CR[1] ==> p1[4]
    p1: <document> = [1,A]title [2,B]author [3,C]<body>
                                [4,T]<bibliography> [5,E]<indices>
    CR: [1(m),D]<bibliography>
```

4. Implementing a Transformation Specification

We have the initial grammar G, and an instance I in $L(G)$, the language of G. We obtain G' from G with the operations ADD, DELETE, NEWPROD, Invoke, and MAP. we also obtain TG from G' by operation Rewrite. We now wish to transform I into an instance I' in $L(G')$. We note that: I' is in $L(TG)$ implies that I' is in $L(G')$. Alternately stated, $L(TG)$ is a subset of $L(G')$. Informally, the statement follows from the fact that the Rewrite operation restricts the language of some productions of G' while adding no extra generative power to them. Thus, we can produce I' in $L(TG)$ to obtain our transformation goal.

A document instance is presumed to exist in tree form, having been constructed by a structured editing tool. The nodes of the tree are all tagged with the grammar symbol labels from G, preserving information about which productions produced each subtree of the document instance's structure.

A new tree may then be constructed to represent the new instance. This is done by executing a post-order traversal of the original instance, with alterations at appropriate nodes as guided by TG. Any node that is not the left-side nonterminal of the main G transformation production is not the site of a transformation, and it gets placed directly into I' at the same location as it occupies in I.

A node corresponding to the site of a transformation is the root of a subtree that may need to be rearranged. Rearrangement of a subtree is achieved by regenerating it based on the grammatical template provided by TG, and employing some of the same components present in the original subtree. This activity is equivalent to deriving the tree according to the rules of the grammar TG, with decisions about expansions (?, *, +) and selections (|) being guided by the labels on the nodes of the old tree. As the derivation proceeds, when a TG production is applied, the grammar symbols are scanned left-to-right.

As each operation is executed in the transformation specification, an analogous operation is performed to contribute elements to I'. For DELETE, the specified subtree of elements from I is placed on the CR; nothing is done in I'. For ADD, a new target subtree is identified in I'; it is initially empty, i.e., grammatically unexpanded. For NEWPROD, nothing happens to either instance. For Rewrite, a new target subtree is identified in I' for an element that may already have contents. For MAP, the indicated elements from CR are placed under the indicated (empty) subtree roots in I'. For Invoke, the target location is moved downward in the new subtree, generating new empty nodes as necessary.

Handling operators in the grammar is the final concern. If the transformation calls for changing a single element or an element operated on by "?" into the same element operated on by "*" or "+", no problems arise since the new instance of that element is a special case of the old. However, if an old element operated on by "*" or "+" is being changed into the same element either with no operator or with the "?" operator, then something has to be done with the extra nodes in I that may be hanging off the subtree for the element. To handle this, we include a reserved target CAT that concatenates strings from these elements on the CR. The resulting string is placed back on the CR and may then be MAPped into I'.

The operator "|" requires special handling. For a production with a sequence of alternatives, that is, a list of "|" separated elements, we assume that transformations are performed for one alternative at a time. This requires enforcement during transformation specification, but creates no extra restrictions during instance transformation. The order of elements in I is maintained correctly in I' by the postorder traversal used to transform I.

5. Discussion and Conclusions

We have suggested that the transformation from G to G' and the expansion of G' to generate TG are aided and directed by specialized tools. The functions provided by the tool that permits specification of G' from G are straightforward—the tool must permit user specification of the DELETE, ADD, and NEWPROD commands and must generate a unique label when a new element is added to the right-hand side of a production. To permit the generation of TG fro G', the tool must permit specification of the Rewrite, Invoke, and MAP commands.

Although we have presented the creation of TG as an action requiring intervention by the system's user, the usefulness of the framework we have presented is not limited to expressing manually defined transformation specifications. The framework defines a notation for expressing the transformations—a notation that could be employed as a target for describing transformations derived automatically through heuristic means on examination of G and G'. Identification of such heuristics is clearly an important topic for further research.

Another issue of importance in manipulation of structured documents are developing the mechanisms that permit transformation from one document type into another within the *same* grammar (for example, transforming an itemized list into an enumerated list). In short, the task here is to manipulate a sequence of objects in an instance that correspond to the right hand side of one particular production so that they correspond instead to the right hand side of a different production. We believe that our techniques are applicable in this domain as well and such application is a further topic for additional research.

We have noted that our technique incorporates ideas from h-graphs. H-graphs are defined grammatically and are based on a directed graph data structure. We believe that the mechanisms we have developed for use with grammars describing tree structures can be applied to the fully general h-graph grammars as well. Thus the work described here seems to be extensible beyond the domain of structured documents, into applications of graph-related text organizations like hypertext. An interesting future project will be to further examine these ideas. Indeed, the ability to extend our techniques to handle graph-oriented structures will be useful in the document domain as well—particularly when encountering document description specifications that require maintenance of secondary relationships among the document objects (such as cross references) in addition to the primary tree relationship.

References

[AFQ88] Jacques André, Richard Furuta, and Vincent Quint, editors. *Structured Documents*. Cambridge University Press, 1988. To appear.

[FQA88] Richard Furuta, Vincent Quint, and Jacques André. Editing structured documents. 1988. Accepted for publication in *Electronic Publishing—Origination, Dissemination, and Design*.

[Fur86a] Richard Furuta. *An Integrated, but not Exact-Representation, Editor/Formatter*. In J. C. van Vliet, editor, *Text Processing and Document Manipulation*, pages 246–259, Cambridge University Press, April 1986. Proceedings of the international conference, University of Nottingham, 14–16 April 1986.

[Fur86b] Richard Furuta. *An Integrated, but not Exact-Representation, Editor/Formatter*. Ph.D. dissertation, University of Washington, Department of Computer Science, Seattle, WA, 1986. Also available as Technical Report No. 86-09-08, Department of Computer Science, University of Washington (August 1986).

[ISO86] *Text and Office Systems—Standard Generalized Markup Language*. ISO, October 1986. Document Number: ISO 8879-1986(E).

[Pra83] T. W. Pratt. Formal specification of software using H-Graph semantics. In H. Ehrig, M. Nagl, and G. Rozenberg, editors, *Lecture Notes in Computer Science number 153: Graph Grammars and Their Application to Computer Science*, pages 314–332, Springer-Verlag, 1983.

[Sto85] P. D. Stotts, Jr. *A Hierarchical Graph Model of Concurrent Real-Time Software Systems*. Ph.D. dissertation, University of Virginia, Department of Computer Science, Charlottesville, Virginia, August 1985.

[vV86] J. C. van Vliet, editor. *Text Processing and Document Manipulation*. Cambridge University Press, April 1986. Proceedings of the international conference, University of Nottingham, 14–16 April 1986.

DEFINING DOCUMENT STYLES FOR WYSIWYG PROCESSING

DONALD D. CHAMBERLIN, HELMUT F. HASSELMEIER, AND
DIETER P. PARIS

IBM Almaden Research Center

ABSTRACT

Recent years have shown two distinct but converging trends in document processing: the trend toward direct manipulation, or "WYSIWYG" systems, and the trend toward high-level generic markup. The Quill project at IBM Research is an attempt to combine the flexibility and ease of use of a WYSIWYG interface with the formatting power of the international standard SGML markup language. The Quill system will present a WYSIWYG user interface but will format documents under control of an external Document Design that specifies the degree of user control over document appearance. Quill includes a tool called the Designer's Workbench that enables a Document Designer to specify the syntax and semantics of a given type of document. Each element in the document type is defined by a "look" consisting of a property sheet and an optional semantic routine. The semantic routines are written in a high-level programming language and can call a set of system-provided utility functions that are designed, according to rules described in this paper, to be suitable for WYSIWYG processing.

1. Introduction

Over the last decade, the field of computer-based document processing has encompassed two different types of systems, originating from different sources and serving different requirements, and following distinct but converging evolutionary paths. The first type of system, which we will label with Ben Schneiderman's term "direct manipulation" [Schn83], is based on providing the user with a set of tools for directly controlling the physical appearance of documents. The first direct manipulation systems were simple word processors, based on a typewriter-like document model, which allowed users to manipulate text on a display screen using monospaced fonts and fixed line spacing. Powerful microprocessors, bit-mapped displays, and inexpensive laser printers made possible a new generation of direct manipulation systems: the WYSIWYG, or "what you see is what you get", systems, which provide the user with an accurate display of formatted pages with multiple fonts and sizes, often including graphics as well as text. WYSIWYG systems such as Interleaf [INT86] allow the user to specify the appearance of objects on the page by means of pop-up "property sheets" that control various properties such as fonts and justification. Some WYSIWYG systems allow users to give names to certain sets of properties and to invoke these names at various places in the document to create objects with uniform appearance. WYSIWYG systems combine editing with formatting in an interactive interface that immediately applies each editing change to the document. The WYSIWYG approach to document creation is characterized by simplicity, flexibility, and ease of use; it is typically applied to the "office" world of small and medium-size documents but is evolving toward larger and more complex documents and more sophisticated typographic features.

The other principal approach to document creation, which we will refer to as the "markup" approach, originated with the idea that processing commands could be imbedded in the text of a document and used to control the process of compiling the document into a form suitable for printing. The "compilation" process typically applies to a whole document at a time and takes place without user intervention. The first markup systems were based on procedural commands that directed the machine to take specific actions such as "skip a line" or "change fonts". More recent systems are based on the concept of "generic markup" pioneered by Brian Reid's Scribe system [Reid80], in which logical elements of a document such as lists, examples, and footnotes are identified by descriptive "tags", and their physical appearance is controlled by a "style definition" external to the document. The concept of generic markup, as exemplified by the Standard Generalized Markup Language (SGML) [ISO86], offers many advantages including device independence, enforcement of style standards, and use of a marked-up document for multiple purposes. Since generic-markup systems process documents according to an external style definition, the style definition can perform complex functions such as automatic numbering of figures, resolving of references, and generation of a table of contents. Therefore, markup-based systems tend to be characterized by sophisticated functions that often require more than one formatting pass over the document, and are typically used in the "publishing" world of relatively long and complex documents. Recent developments in markup-based systems point toward greater interactivity, including soft-copy preview facilities that provide a display of the formatted document before printing, and systems such as ICEF2 (formerly called Janus) [Cham87a] that provide a means for a user to edit and reformat individual pages without processing the entire document.

Viewing the two classes of document creation systems in a historical perspective, it seems clear that they are evolving along converging paths. We believe that a need exists for a new generation of systems that combines the ease of use and flexibility of WYSIWYG systems with the formatting power and generic processing capability of markup-based systems. The Quill project at IBM's Almaden Research Center is an attempt to build an experimental prototype of such a system.

Any attempt to combine WYSIWYG processing with generic markup must confront the central question of who is "in charge" of document appearance, since traditionally WYSIWYG and markup-based systems have taken opposite approaches to this question. In Quill, the extent of user control over appearance becomes a policy decision rather than a built-in characteristic of the document processing system. The Quill user is provided with a WYSIWYG display of the formatted document. To insert a new object into a document, the user invokes the generic name of the object (e.g., "footnote"), which causes the object to be created according to an external style definition. However, the external definition (called the "look") of any given object can be as rigorous or as flexible as desired by the Document Designer, who is simply a user of a Quill facility called the Designer's Workbench. A Document Designer might choose to specify all the properties of an object completely, leaving the user no options other than to invoke the object by its name. Alternatively, the Document Designer might choose to specify a set of default properties for the object-type, allowing end users to override certain of these properties (e.g., fonts) for individual objects in individual documents. The Designer's Workbench allows the Document Designer to specify the properties of various objects by choosing options on Property Sheets; similarly, the Quill editor allows the author of an individual document to control the properties of individual objects by choosing options on Property Sheets that contain those properties specified as overrideable by the Document Designer. A style specification might permit all properties to be overridden by users, thus enabling Quill to be used with all the flexibility of a WYSIWYG system. A style specification for a different type of document might rigorously specify all properties in order to enforce the style standards of an organization. Other style specifications might implement an intermediate approach, exposing some properties but not others, according to the policy of the Document Designer for specific types of documents or classes of users.

A prototype implementation of Quill is underway at Almaden Research Center, using IBM RT PC workstations and the experimental QuickSilver operating system and "Whim" window manager [Good85]. The principal characteristics of the Quill prototype are as follows:

- Quill is based on the document model of the Standard Generalized Markup Language [ISO86]: a document is a hierarchy of nested elements, and the semantics of an element may depend on its position in the hierarchy. Validity of document structure is enforced according to an external SGML Document Type Definition.
- Quill allows a user to edit a document by either logical or physical actions. An example of a physical action is a keystroke or other editing action applied directly to a WYSIWYG display. An example of a logical action is changing the markup of an element from "numbered list" to "bulleted list", which automatically reformats the list and affects the appearance of its items.
- Quill formats documents under the control of an external style definition that can specify complex processing, including remote effects such as resolving references and generating a table of contents. The style definition is created and edited by a facility called the Designer's Workbench.
- Quill allows a document to contain graphics and other materials as well as text, nested inside each other without restriction. Each type of material (e.g., graphics, mathematics, chemistry) can be manipulated by its own specialized editor, and the Quill system can be extended by the addition of new specialized editors. The representation of graphic objects using SGML, and the mechanisms used to support extensibility in Quill, have been described in other papers [Cham87b, Cham87c].

2. Elements, Attributes, and Properties

In the document model of the SGML Standard, a document consists of a hierarchical collection of *elements*. Each element is identified by a *tag*, which consists of a *generic identifier* (element name) and zero or more *attributes*, each of which has a name and a value. Each type of element has its own set of attributes, which are defined in a formal *Document Type Definition*. In addition to its tag, an element may have *content* which consists of character data and other elements.

The SGML Standard specifies no fixed set of elements and attributes, but allows them to be defined by the creator of the Document Type Definition (DTD). Quill will conform to the SGML Standard in that the Quill Document Designer can specify any desired set of elements and attributes. During an editing session, the Quill user can view and edit the attribute values of any element in the document. In addition, the Quill user can view and edit the *properties* of an element; these are presented in the form of a Property Sheet like the one shown in Figure 1. The Property Sheet contains values for properties such as fonts, alignment, etc., that control how Quill formats the given element. By examining the Property Sheet, the user can see the values of the properties, and, *where authorized by the Document Designer*, can modify these values. Those properties whose values are not user-modifiable for a given element appear shaded on the property sheet. The user can change an unshaded property by pointing to its value with the mouse and clicking the mouse button; this causes a menu of appropriate values to appear, from which the user can select the desired value by another click. Where appropriate, units (e.g., inches, picas, millimeters) also appear on the Property Sheet and can be changed by mouse clicks. At the bottom of the Property Sheet are three buttons that allow the user to confirm or cancel the revised set of properties, or to reset all properties to their default values.

The Quill Designer's Workbench allows the Document Designer to view and edit the Property Sheet for any type of element in a given Design. The property sheets seen by a Designer are much like those seen by an end user while editing a document. The Designer can specify property values in either absolute form (e.g., "14 points") or relative form (e.g., "4 points larger than the current size"). The Designer can change the value of any property, and, in addition, can control which properties are "locked" against user overrides (clicking on the name of a property cycles it between "locked" and "unlocked"; "locked" properties appear shaded on the property sheet). The property values specified by the Document Designer become the default property values for the given element, subject to user overrides if so authorized.

During an editing session, Quill maintains a data structure called the "Logical Tree" which contains a node for each element in the document.

Figure 1: A Property Sheet

Page	Break:	YES		
	Width: 8.5 INCH		Height:	11 INCH
Margins:	Top: 1 INCH	Page Number:	Value:	CONTINUE
	Bottom: 1 INCH		Style:	ARABIC
	Left: 1 INCH		Horiz. Pos.:	3.2 INCH
	Right: 1 INCH		Vert. Pos.:	0.6 INCH
Section	Break:	YES		
	Number of Cols.: 2		Column Width:	3 INCH
Column Shape	Break:	NO		
	Line Break Top:	YES		
	Line Break Bottom:	YES	Sticky at Bottom:	NO
	Alignment:	JUSTIFIED	Left Indent:	0 INCH
	Top Space:	1 LINE	Right Indent:	0 INCH
	Bottom Space:	1 LINE	Hanging Indent:	3 P.P
	Keep:	NO	Widow Prevention:	YES
	Tabs: 0.25 0.50 0.75 1.00 1.25 1.50 1.75 2.00 2.25 2.50 INCH			
Font	Type Family Name: TIMES ROMAN			
	Point Size:	10 Pts	Weight:	MEDIUM
	Italics:	OFF	Width:	NORMAL
	Baseline Offset:	0 INCH	Line Space:	12 P.P

[Confirm]   [Cancel]   [Reset]

Each node points to a set of default properties for its element-type, as defined by the Document Design. In addition, each node in the Logical Tree records those properties, if any, which have been given specific values for the individual element represented by the node. Thus, when some editing change is made to the element (e.g., a keystroke causes a character to be added to its content), the applicable properties are readily accessible for reformatting the element. It is a key characteristic of WYSIWYG systems that any element in the document may be reformatted at any time due to user actions, and therefore each element must be represented by a data structure that contains all the information necessary for its reformatting.

At the conclusion of a Quill session, when the document is to be saved in an SGML file, it is necessary to represent user overrides to individual properties using SGML syntax. The SGML Standard provides a feature called "Link Sets" for this purpose, which can be used to associate one or more "processing-oriented attributes" (properties) with an individual element of a document.

The purpose of property sheets is to permit end users, where so authorized, to exercise direct control over the appearance of elements in their documents. This control may be used for "fine tuning" of a document by introducing page breaks and similar small adjustments at places chosen by the user. Direct user control may also be used, with a relatively "permissive" document style, for creation of special effects in advertising copy and other types of documents whose appearance is not rigidly specified. By means of property sheets, Quill supports a spectrum of usage ranging from completely style-driven document types with no user-changeable properties to very flexible document types in which every property is controllable by the end user. These quite different usages, and many points in between, are supported with a common document syntax and user interface. The Designer's Workbench provides controls over the set of properties that are user-changeable, thus making user influence over document appearance a matter of policy rather than a hard-wired property of the formatting system.

Encoding property overrides in SGML Link Sets ensures that the property overrides are seen only by a specific process (the Quill formatter) and not by other applications which may be processing the document file.

It might be argued that direct user control over physical properties such as fonts and alignment is counter to the intent of SGML, which was designed for the description of "logical" documents. Of course, use of purely logical markup is very reasonable and useful, and the Quill Document Designer can force all markup to be purely logical simply by not authorizing any properties in the document to be overridden by users. Most generic-markup systems, however, provide some facilities for "final tuning" of the appearance of documents according to user discretion. It seems that automatic formatters have not yet reached such a state of perfection that users can resist "tinkering" with the final form of their pages. The mechanism provided by many markup-based systems for this "tuning" is insertion of low-level "control words" into the document by the user for such purposes as forcing line and page breaks or selecting a font. These low-level control words often use a syntax quite different from the logical markup; they do not conform to the hierarchical structure of the document; and they result in possibly conflicting instructions to the formatter (e.g., a user instruction may call for a page break in the middle of an element that is defined to be atomic). As a result, low-level controls imbedded in an SGML document often lead to unexpected behavior and unhelpful error messages. The association of formatting properties with SGML elements, as in Quill, provides the "fine tuning" controls that are frequently needed, but does so in a way that never conflicts with the SGML syntax or semantics, and is under the direct control of an authorization mechanism.

Exposing property sheets to end users does, however, involve an important tradeoff. It is possible, by direct user control over document appearance, to introduce device dependencies (e.g., by naming a specific font) or style dependencies (e.g., by placing page breaks in places that are appropriate only for a specific style). These kinds of dependencies are the price that must be paid for the flexibility of "user tuning". If a document is intended to be used with more than one style or printer, it is important that "tuning" properties be kept to a minimum and used with full knowledge of their potential harmful effects.

3. Specifying Semantic Algorithms

It is a major objective of Quill to provide a facility for document designers to create new types of SGML elements and to define their semantics. Such a facility must meet two important requirements: it must be easy to use for specifying relatively simple elements, yet it must be capable of specifying complex semantics when necessary.

As described in the previous section, the behavior of many simple elements can be completely specified by means of a property sheet. The property sheet exposes all the variables that directly control the Quill formatting engine. Property sheets are capable of specifying element formatting rules such as "print my content in italic type, four points larger than the surrounding text", or "keep my content together on the same page, and print it in a monospaced font". Since property sheets allow the document designer to specify tag semantics by simple menu interactions, they meet the first Quill objective of providing an easy-to-use facility for defining simple elements.

The second objective, of providing a means for specifying complex semantics, requires an additional mechanism. As an example of a complex element, consider an index that is automatically generated by an "index" tag. The index generation process involves collecting information from throughout the document, alphebetizing the index terms, eliminating duplicate page numbers, collapsing sequences of contiguous page numbers into ranges, etc. The index may be printed in one or more columns, with or without leader dots, and with various kinds of headings and subheadings. It is clearly infeasible to anticipate all possible kinds of index processing and list them as options on a property sheet—and an automatic index is only one example of an element with complex semantics.

The most powerful tool available for specifying semantic algorithms is a general-purpose programming language. For this reason, most existing systems that format documents based on an external style definition use some form of programming language in the style definition—for example, the ICEF2 system [Cham87a] uses a subset of Pascal for this purpose. However, semantic routines written in a programming language are usually based on a hidden assumption: that the document will be formatted from front to back, and that the semantic routines will be executed in order as the various elements are encountered in the document. This allows a semantic routine to share data with other routines, and with later activations of itself, by means of global variables. For example, a semantic routine for a "figure" element might increment the global variable containing the figure number by means of a statement such as `figno := figno + 1`. Hidden in this statement is the assumption that, when the routine is executed, the `figno` variable contains the correct value of the figure number for the current context in the document. In a WYSIWYG system such as Quill, however, any element in the document may be reformatted at any time due to user action. Thus a WYSIWYG system is a *reformatter* rather than a *formatter*, since its main job is to repair perturbations to a formatted document caused by the user. Figures anywhere in the document, for example, may be inserted, deleted, moved, or revised; therefore the semantic routine that defines the appearance and behavior of a figure must be executable at any time without any dependencies on the semantic routines of other elements.

We will define the term *WYSIWYG-able* in the following way: a semantic routine is *WYSIWYG-able* if it can be executed by itself at any time to reformat an individual element occurring anywhere in a document. To meet the objectives of Quill, it is necessary to define a semantic specification language that has the power and generality of a programming language, yet is WYSIWYG-able and also interfaces well with the property sheet approach to defining simple elements as discussed in the last section.

The language used for semantic specification in Quill is REXX [IBM84], a programming language implemented on several IBM machines. Each type of element in a document style is associated with both a property sheet and a semantic routine written in REXX. REXX provides the usual features of a high-level programming language such as looping, branching, and procedure calls. The key to the use of REXX as a specification language in Quill lies in the set of utility functions supported by Quill and made available to be called by the semantic routines of the various elements. These utility functions ensure that the semantic routines are WYSIWYG-able by recording all information needed for reformatting each element of the document in the "logical tree" data structure that is maintained during an editing session.

3.1. The OUTPUT Function

Perhaps the commonest utility function invoked by Quill semantic routines is the OUTPUT function, which places formatted text into the document. The OUTPUT function takes two arguments, as follows:

```
OUTPUT (properties, text)
```

If the `properties` argument is null (the usual case), the content of the `text` argument is formatted into the document according to the current element's property sheet (as overridden by the end user where permitted). The purpose of the `properties` argument is to allow the semantic routine to override one or more properties by specifying their names and values, such as `weight="bold"`. This type of override might be necessary if the element needs to print more than one piece of output having nonuniform properties; for example, an "abstract" element might print a heading in bold face, followed by the main part of the abstract in normal face. The semantic routine for such an element would consist of two OUTPUT functions, one with a property override to select bold face for the heading. An OUTPUT statement might also use a property override in order to set a property to some value that has been computed by program logic rather than simply selected in advance.[1]

---

[1] Note that a property on a property sheet can be overridden either by an end user or by an OUTPUT function. These two kinds of override serve different purposes, and it is considered unlikely that a style definer would permit end-user overrides of a property that is also overridden by the semantic routine. If such a conflict should occur, the property value specified by the OUTPUT function becomes effective.

The `text` argument of the OUTPUT function specifies the text to be placed into the document. This text string may contain certain symbols beginning with the escape character "\", representing special functions such as tabs. The commonest such symbol is "\[]", which represents "the content of this element". Therefore, the semantic routine for most simple elements consists simply of the function OUTPUT ('', '\[]');, meaning "print my contents, using my property sheet". This one-line semantic routine is provided as the default routine for all elements unless otherwise specified, so the definer of a simple tag can interact with the property sheet only and need not be aware of the semantic routine.

When a new element is inserted into a document, its semantic routine is executed. Each OUTPUT statement in the routine places text into the formatted document, and links the text to a "content" node in the logical tree that records the effective properties of the text. Insertion of the new element may cause surrounding text to be "fixed" by reflowing it according to the properties recorded in its own "content" node(s). When the content of an element changes (e.g., a character is inserted or deleted by a user keystroke), the line containing the change, and as many adjacent lines as necessary, are "fixed" by reflowing their text according to their recorded properties. It is not necessary to re-execute a semantic routine on each keystroke.

When an element is deleted from the document by user action, its content is removed from the logical tree, and nearby elements are "fixed" by reflowing their text according to their recorded properties. When an element must be completely reformatted (e.g., it is moved into a new context or its SGML attributes are changed by user action), this is handled as a deletion followed by an insertion of the element (all the logical children of the element must be reformatted at the same time).

3.2. Functions for Sharing Data

As noted above, the OUTPUT function is WYSIWYG-able because it records the information it needs for re-execution in the logical tree. A more subtle requirement for a WYSIWYG-able function arises when a semantic routine needs to share data with another routine or with another activation of itself. As noted previously, this sharing of data cannot be accomplished simply by updating a global variable, since the order of execution of the various semantic routines is unpredictable. We will illustrate the requirement for shared data, and the WYSIWYG-able functions provided by Quill for this purpose, by examining two example elements called <fig> and <figref>.

The <fig> element represents a figure that is to be printed together with its ordinal figure number (which must be generated automatically by the semantic routine). The <figref> element has an SGML attribute named "id"; its purpose is to generate a reference to the <fig> element with has a matching "id" attribute. For example, the SGML tag `<fig id="bicycle">` might print a figure with the generated caption "Figure 7"; the SGML tag `<figref id="bicycle">`, occurring either before or after the `<fig>` tag, would then generate the reference, "see Figure 7". As other figures are inserted, deleted, and moved, the number in the figure caption, and all references generated by `<figref>` tags, are automatically corrected.

The <fig> and <figref> elements illustrate two different kinds of shared data, which we will refer to by the names "local shared data" and "global shared data". Local shared data is represented by the propagation of the figure number from one <fig> element to the next. A local shared data item is characterized by a name (e.g. `figno`) and a value, but the value applies only to a local region of the document (e.g., between one <fig> element and the next). Global shared data is data that has validity throughout the document, such as the association of an ID with a particular figure number. A global shared data item is characterized by a qualified name that may include the ID attribute of an element (e.g., `figref.bicycle`) and a value. The value of a global shared data item may change over time, but at any given time it is valid throughout the document.

Quill provides two utility functions, LREAD and LWRITE, for handling local shared data, and two more functions, GREAD and GWRITE, for handling global shared data. Quill ensures that these data sharing functions are WYSIWYG-able by recording all shared data values in the logical tree, and by maintaining lists of all those elements in the document that read or write each shared data item.

When an element executes an LREAD for a given shared variable, Quill inserts the element into a linked list, called a "share list", consisting of all elements that read or write the given variable, maintained in their order of occurrence in the document. The LREAD function returns to the semantic routine the value recorded for the variable by the next-earlier LWRITE-type element in the share list. When an element executes an

LWRITE function for a given shared variable, it is linked into the share list in the appropriate position, and the value of the variable is recorded in the share list. If the value written by LWRITE is new or different from the value recorded by a previous execution of this element, it is necessary to re-execute other elements that depend on the value that has changed. The share list for the given data item is scanned in the forward direction, and all LREAD-type elements between the current LWRITE and the next LWRITE are marked for re-execution. Using spare cycles between user interactions, Quill will re-execute the semantic routines of the marked nodes, causing them to LREAD the new value of the shared data item. Thus, for example, when a new figure is added to the middle of a document, its semantic routine performs an LREAD to obtain the previous figure number, and also performs an LWRITE that causes the next figure element to be marked for re-execution. As each subsequent figure element is re-executed in turn using spare cycles, new figure numbers are propagated forward through the document.

Whenever an element is deleted whose logical tree node contains an LREAD or LWRITE notation, the deleted node is removed from any share lists in which it participates. In addition, if the deleted node had an LWRITE notation for some data item, all the following nodes on that share list are marked for re-execution, until the next LWRITE notation is encountered. Thus, for example, if a figure is deleted from a document, the following figures will be renumbered (one at a time).

The GREAD and GWRITE functions deal with global shared data, which propagates both forward and backward in the document. For each global shared data item, Quill records a value and an unordered list of elements that read the item. Whenever an element executes a GREAD function for a given shared variable, it is added to the share-list for that variable and the value of the variable is returned by GREAD. When an element executes a GWRITE for a given variable, the value of the variable is updated and all elements on the share-list for that variable are marked for re-execution. Using spare cycles between user interactions, Quill will re-execute the semantic routines of the marked nodes, causing them to GREAD the new value of the shared data item. Thus, for example, when the number of a figure changes, all references to that figure are marked for re-execution and updated using spare system cycles.

If an element that has performed a GWRITE is deleted from the document, the value of the corresponding variable becomes undefined, and all the elements on its share-list are marked for re-execution. Thus, when a figure is deleted, all references to that figure throughout the document will be re-executed (and will become unresolved references).

The key to the WYSIWYG-able property of the Quill data-sharing functions is (1) each function records all its dependencies directly in the logical tree; and (2) whenever a function causes a data item to change, it finds all the nodes in the logical tree that are dependent on the changed item and marks them for re-execution. This basic approach is applied in Quill not only to data-sharing functions but also to utility functions that return other information such as a count of the current element's siblings or ancestors of a given type. A function that returns a count of left-brothers of a given type, for example, records in the logical tree-node a dependency on this count, and any subsequent change in the number of left-brothers causes this node to be marked for re-execution.

4. The Quill Designer's Workbench

We have seen that Quill defines the semantics of a given type of element by means of a property sheet and a semantic routine written in REXX. The combination of a property sheet and a semantic routine is called a *look*. In addition to its look, the definition of an element-type consists of two additional parts, which are required by the SGML standard: the *content model* and the *attribute definition list*. The content model of a given element specifies, by means of a regular expression, the permissible content of the element, including character data and other required or optional elements and their orderings. The attribute definition list specifies the attributes of the given element type, with their permissible values and default values. The content models and attribute definition lists for a given set of element-types can be formally expressed as an SGML *Document Type Definition*, which describes the syntax for a particular type of document; the corresponding semantics are described by the set of *looks* for the given elements.

The Quill Designer's Workbench is a program that allows a Document Designer to create a Design file that consists of content models, attribute definition lists, and looks for all the elements in a given type of document. The user of the Designer's Workbench may be an individual responsible for creating and enforcing style standards for a whole organization, or he may be simply an end user creating or revising a document style for his own personal use.

The output of the Designer's Workbench is a Design file that specifies the syntax and semantics of a particular type of document. The Design file serves as input to the Quill editor as it formats a document of the given type. However, it is desirable that a given *type* of document (as defined by a set of elements) be formattable in several different *styles*. For example, a certain type of document, called a "Techdoc", might consist of elements called paragraphs, headings, examples, lists, footnotes, etc. A particular Techdoc, however, could be formatted according to several different *styles*, such as those used by *Communications of the ACM*, IEEE *Computer*, and *IBM Journal of Research and Development*. The content of the document, and the set of tags and attributes used in its SGML markup, would be identical in all three cases; but the appearance of the document would be quite different as it is formatted under the control of three different *styles* named, perhaps, "ACM", "IEEE", and "IBM".

Thus, a Design file produced by the Designer's Workbench encapsulates one document *type* (e.g., "TECHDOC"), and one or more named *styles* (e.g., ACM, IEEE, IBM) that can be used with the given type. Each type of element in the Design file has a single content model, a single attribute definition list, and a look (property sheet and semantic routine) for each style. The Designer's Workbench presents all these objects to the user by means of a Design Matrix, as shown in Figure 2. All the elements of a given document type are listed on the left side of the matrix, and all the styles available for the given type of document are listed across the top of the matrix. Commands are provided for adding new elements and styles to the matrix. A notation in each cell of the matrix indicates whether that object is currently defined. By pointing to a cell in the matrix and pressing the mouse button, the Document Designer can invoke a specialized environment for creating or editing the selected object: a content model, attribute definition list, or look (property sheet and semantic routine).

If a Design file contains several styles, it may be desirable for some elements to share a common look across multiple styles. For example, a <paragraph> element might have the same look in two different styles, whereas a <heading> element might have different looks. The Quill Designer's Workbench allows looks to be shared across styles, thus saving space and eliminating redundancy. When the Document Designer is editing a look, he is presented with a Look Usage Table that indicates

Figure 2: The Design Matrix for a Document Type

DESIGN MATRIX	CONTENT	ATTRIB	ACM	IEEE	IBM
Techdoc	*	*	*	*	*
Title	*		*	*	*
Body	*		*	*	*
Paragraph	*	*	*	*	*
List	*	*		*	*
Item	*			*	*
Example	*	*	*		
Figure	*	*	*	*	*

how looks are shared by the various styles for the given element. Commands are provided for creating new looks and for reassigning looks from one style to another.

5. Summary

The Quill project at IBM Research is exploring ways to combine the flexibility and ease of use of WYSIWYG systems with the formatting power and standard enforcement abilities of generic-markup systems. The resulting system will present a WYSIWYG user interface, but will format documents under the control of an external Design file that provides varying degrees of user control over appearance, according to the policy of the Document Designer. A tool called the Designer's Workbench is provided that enables the Document Designer to specify the syntax and semantics of each element in a given type of document, and to control those aspects of each element's appearance that can be overridden by end users. The appearance of each element is controlled by a "look" that consists of a property sheet and an (often defaulted) semantic routine. The semantic routines, needed only for complex tags, are written in the REXX language, using a set of functions that are specially designed for WYSIWYG processing. In order to be suitable for WYSIWYG processing, semantic routines must be executable at any time, in any order;

therefore they must record their dependencies in a shared data structure, and the semantic routine of each element must be automatically re-executed whenever a change occurs in one of its dependencies.

6. References

[Cham87a] Chamberlin, D.D. (1987). Document Convergence in an Interactive Formatting System, *IBM Journal of Research and Development*, 31, 1, pp. 58-72.

[Cham87b] Chamberlin, D.D., and Goldfarb, C.F. (1987). Graphic Applications of the Standard Generalized Markup Language (SGML), *Computers and Graphics*, 11, 4.

[Cham87c] Chamberlin, D.D., Hasselmeier, H.F., Luniewski, A.W., Paris, D.P., Wade, B.W., and Zolliker, M.L. (1987). Quill: An Extensible System for Editing Documents of Mixed Type. In *Proceedings of the 21st Hawaii International Conference on System Sciences*. Washington, DC: IEEE Computer Society Press.

[Good85] Goodfellow, M.J. (1985). Whim, the Window Handler and Input Manager. In *Proceedings of the First International Conference on Computer Workstations*, pp. 12-21. Washington, DC: IEEE Computer Society Press.

[IBM84] *Virtual Machine/System Product: Interpreter User's Guide*. IBM Publication No. SC24-5238.

[INT86] *Interleaf Workstation Publishing Software User's Guide*. Interleaf, Inc.

[ISO86] *International Standard ISO 8879: Information Processing - Text and Office Systems - Standard Generalized Markup Language (SGML)*. International Organization for Standardization.

[Reid80] Reid, B.K. *Scribe: A Document Specification Language and Its Compiler*. Ph.D. Dissertation and Technical Report CMU-CS-81-100, Carnegie-Mellon University, Pittsburgh, PA (1980). Scribe is a registered trademark of Unilogic Ltd., Pittsburgh, PA.

[Schn83] Schneiderman, B. Direct Manipulation: A Step Beyond Programming Languages, *Computer*, 16, 8, pp. 57-69.

IMAGE PROCESSING ASPECTS OF TYPE

ROBERT A. MORRIS

The University of Massachusetts at Boston and *Interleaf, Inc.*

ABSTRACT

Classical image processing models can be applied to individual letters and to text as a whole. By combining these models with contemporary models of human vision, some aspects of type design can be considered to reflect needs of the visual system.

1. Spectra

Type, both black-and-white and gray-scale, can be regarded as a function mapping points in the plane into intensities, which are numbers between 0 and 1. Since (western) type is made up largely of vertical strokes, we can sometimes conveniently represent it as a one-dimensional signal, with the intensity at horizontal position x, considered as the average intensity along the vertical line at x. In either the one- or two-dimensional case, it is possible to talk about the *spatial frequencies* present in the signal and about the amplitude of the image at each frequency. These spatial frequencies characterize the image and can reflect features of the type, detailed below. In addition, the human visual system has different responses to different spatial frequencies, and this affects the way we see type (see Section 2.).

1.1. *Generalities*

In the one-dimensional black-and-white case, spatial frequency can be conveniently thought of as the rate of alternation of the strokes between black and white, per unit distance. This distance is most appropriately measured not in a fixed linear measure, but rather in the amount of visual angle subtended by the image under study. Intuitively, this is reasonable: 100-point type viewed at 400 cm. will subtend the same visual angle as 10-point type at the normal 40 cm. reading distance. If we had no visual cues about the viewing distances, we would judge these to be the same size type (ignoring for now the important typographic principle that type should not be linearly scaled). For example, 10-point type at 40 cm. alternates between black and white at the rate of about 7–8 cycles per degree (*cpd*) of visual angle. (This can be confirmed with a ruler and simple trigonometry on the reader's favorite 10-point type.) This spatial subtense measure is also appropriate for the two-dimensional case, which we discuss later.

Even when we are viewing essentially analog type, such as might be produced by ink which flows on the page (as opposed to the discrete marking produced by laser printers or digital photo-typesetters on their original film), the visual system is *sampling* the image we see. This is because the image is perceived early in the process by discrete photoreceptors on the retina. The distance between these receptors is a limiting factor in the resolution with which we can perceive an image. It is known to be about 1 minute of visual angle, corresponding to a maximum perceivable frequency of 60 cpd. Some of the implications for digital typography of these limits were observed in [Bigelow83]. Omitting considerations of half-toning, in which multiple one bit pixels make one gray cell, this limit implies that pixels about 1/600-th inch apart can not be distinguished even at the minimum distances at which one can focus. Thus, a resolution of 1200 dots per inch (dpi) permits the finest distinguishable alternation of white with black, and, indeed, digital typesetters traditionally are manufactured at about this resolution.

Sampling continuous signals, either in the marking process or in the vision system, creates several well-known problems for whatever system is reconstructing the image. In the computer graphics literature, all of these are coloquially known as *aliasing*, but the major one is simply the roundoff error inherent in making a discrete choice from a continuous signal. This is most evident in the familiar "jaggies," or staircase effect, seen in curves and some diagonal lines. Aliasing results when two signals become indistinguishable due to undersampling. Both artifacts can be dealt with by increasing the sample rate, i.e., the resolution, but, in theory, never completely (see Ch. 12 of [Castleman79] for a treatment of the tradeoffs in dealing with sampled signals). Any signal with sharp edges is guaranteed to have components of arbitrarily high spatial frequency.

A famous theorem of signal processing theory, the Shannon–Nyquist sampling theorem, asserts that aliasing is not possible *for a band-limited signal* (one with an upper bound on frequencies present) when the signal is sampled at a rate at least twice that of the highest frequency. Unfortunately, any signal with sharp edges is never band limited. Increasing the sample rate of any signal can move the aliasing artifacts to frequencies not perceivable, but the "anti–aliased" gray-scale fonts in some use are smoothing the jaggies principally by reducing the roundoff error in the image's representation. In addition, some recent vision research ([Yellott84]) cpd has shown that the visual system is in fact not subject to as much aliasing as

Figure 1: *Pattern with multiple spatial frequencies*

might be expected from the 60 cpd limit on its sampling rate. This apparently is due to the fact that the sampling is not uniform, a "technique" also applied in sampling oscilloscopes, whereby periodic signals of higher frequency than the instrument's sample rate can be reconstructed by sampling at different points in successive cycles. We will not touch much on aliasing issues in type, nor directly on gray-scale fonts, which only recently have been modeled with sufficient rigor to advance beyond elementary stages ([Naiman88]).

It is easy to understand that the visual system has differing responses to different spatial frequencies by consideration of an image such as in Figure 1, due to Kirkham ([Sekuler85], p. 169). There are actually patterns at two spatial frequencies present, but the lower one, three extra clusters of dark dots, will become visible to most viewers only if they squint, which has the effect of filtering out the higher spatial frequency, making visible the pattern at the low frequency.

It is important to note that no enhancement of the low frequency has taken place, but rather only an attenuation of the higher one. An even more dramatic illustration of these issues can be had by viewing the figure from a distance of several feet instead of at arms length. This has the effect of raising both spatial frequencies, to the point where the response to the higher one is negligible compared to the response to the lower. The higher frequency pattern will then be a uniform gray and the lower one will be visible.

A signal can be decomposed into a weighted sum of all the spatial frequencies it contains by means of Fourier analysis. These frequencies can be computed by Fourier Transforms in one or two dimensions. The resulting collection of complex numbers is called the *spectrum* of the signal

Since our interest is in sampled signals, namely the digital representation on a discrete grid of black-and-white characters we can study the *Discrete Fourier Transform* (DFT) whose k–th sample frequency $F(k)$ is given in one-dimension by $F(k) = \Sigma f(n) \exp(2\pi i k n/N)$, where $f(n)$ is the signal at the n–th sample point, N is the number of samples, and the sum is taken over all N samples. In the corresponding two-dimensional case we would consider a signal which is given a value at integer points (u,v). In both cases we assume that f is 0 outside some interval (rectangle, in the two-dimensional case). For black-and-white characters, f will always be 0 or 1, namely the pixel value at coordinate (u,v).

The DFT has several advantages. The main one is that it enables us to use bit-mapped fonts as the samples from which to compute the transform with no further sampling required. In addition, it is efficiently computable by well-known Fast Fourier Transforms. Also, there is a discrete inverse transform analogous to the inverse Fourier Transform from which one can perfectly reconstruct the original discrete signal given its DFT. Finally, under suitable conditions it gives a good approximation to the complete spectrum. We do not dwell here on the conditions which make this true, nor on techniques for improving this approximation when it fails, but we turn next to some specific spectra which we have computed with FFT's, so that some of these points can be illustrated.

1.2. *Average amplitude spectra for lines of text*

In general the spectrum is a complex valued function. The magnitude of the spectrum is the *amplitude spectrum* and its square is called the *power spectrum*, for adequate physical reasons in simple cases (cf. Sec. 4.3 [Oppenheim83]). It is thus a measure of how much signal is present at each frequency. Earlier we suggested that the spatial frequency due to the strokes of letters, which we call the *letterform frequency,* is an obvious component of a line of text, and we shall see next that it is a major one. A second component is the *wordform frequency* due to alternation between black and white of the words of text in a line such as might be perceived from a distance too great to distinguish letters (i.e., at which the spatial frequencies presented by the strokes are too high to be perceived). Without more detail, suffice it to say that we might expect to see fequencies in the spectrum corresponding at least to

Figure 2: *Idealized text signals.*

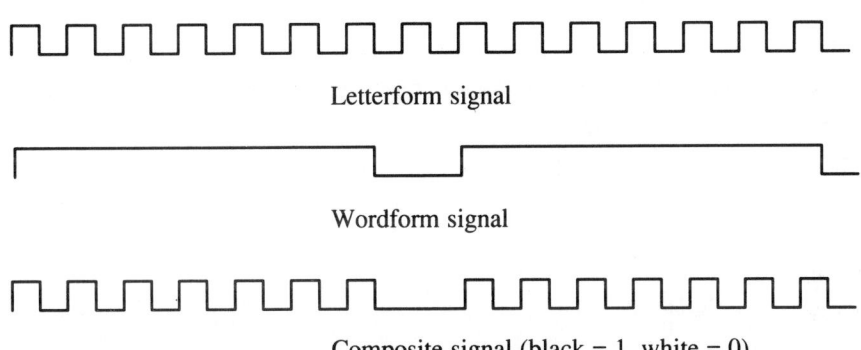

these two rates of alternation. Idealized text is roughly a product of the stroke pattern and the wordform pattern (Figure 2). A more accurate model multiplies the wordform signal by the duty cycle (the fraction ''on'' of the letterform signal), reflecting the overall grayness of the font. The spectrum of such a composite signal will contain each of the fundamental frequencies, all of their harmonics (with decreasing amplitude), and all the sums and differences of all of these frequencies.

We can test this expectation against a trivial text string which conforms quite closely to this model, namely repetitions of pair of ''words'' consisting of upper case l's in a sans-serif font (llll llll). We use the Computer Modern (cm) family in our studies because MetaFont provides a powerful tool for making manipulations of the image as well as for varying sample rate (i.e., resolution). We have also begun studies with Lucida fonts [Bigelow86], which were kindly provided us by Bigelow and Holmes. Several spectra are shown in Figure 3. Computer Modern bitmaps in the TeX pxl format were used. These are named *<fontname>.Npxl*, where N/500 is the resolution in dots per inch at which the fonts were made. Except for the Chinese characters, all examples in this paper are at 300 dpi.

These spectra are computed by finding the amplitude spectrum on each scanline and averaging over all the scanlines in the text. All of the spectra shown are normalized to the amplitude at frequency 0 (often called the *dc* component after the electrical applications), which represents the average intensity of the signal, i.e., the ratio of ''on'' to total duration of the signal. It is also interesting to average over an entire page, as is done by Rubinstein and Ulichney [Rubinstein87]. However, since we want to relate this to human vision and reading fixates one line at a time, we do not do this. Averaging over a page will have the effect of raising the average signal (the dc) due to having more white space. With the normalization described, this will reduce the variation shown among frequencies in the text itself. An alternative in this case might be to normalize to the maximum non-dc amplitude, which will gen-

Figure 3: *One-dimensional spectra*

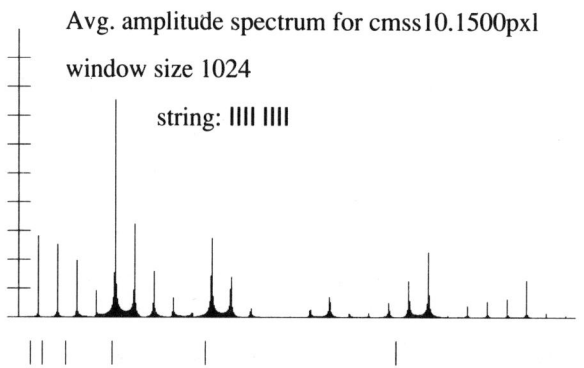

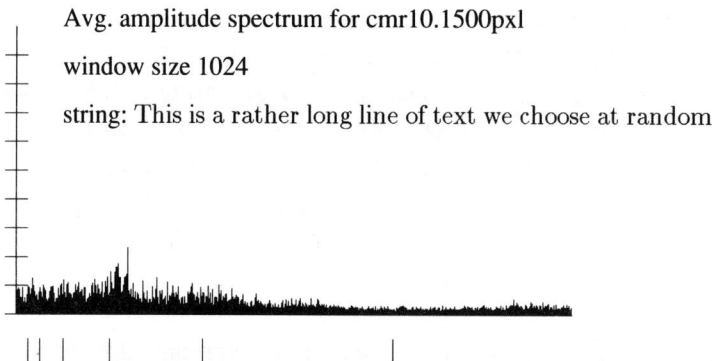

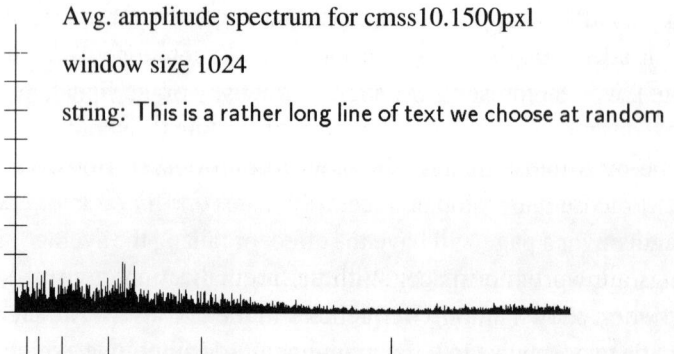

erally be the letterform frequency. The dc gives a measure of the overall grayness of the font.

The spectra are computed through a truncation window as shown. For strings containing fewer samples than this window, the signal is considered to be replicated throughout the window. The legends show the string as produced from the actual pixels in the bitmap representation of the font. If d is the viewing distance in pixel width's, then the viewing angle is $\text{Arctan}(1/d)$. For example, if we regard the bitmap as displayed on a 300 dpi device viewed at 18 inches (5400 pixel widths), the angle subtended by one pixel is $\text{Arctan}(1/5400) = .0106$ degrees, or about 38 seconds of arc. The total frequency span on each axis would be 1/.0106, or about 94 cpd, but amplitude spectra are symmetric about 1/2 the maximum frequency, and these graphs are plotted only to that frequency, i.e., about 47 cpd with the viewing hypotheses above. Below each graph are tick marks at one octave intervals, beginning at 1 cpd. In the trivial string, the principal component is close to 8 cpd, and this could have also been deduced by trigonometry from the bitmap. (The upper case I in cmss10 is 4 pixels wide with 11 pixels of setwidth, i.e., 7 white pixels between characters. The space between the "words" is 13 pixels.) Real spectra are, of course, more complex, as shown in the spectra for cmr10 and its san-serif cousin cmss10. The serif face generally has thinner strokes, which puts relatively more energy in the principal frequency; both faces have peaks a little above 8 cpd. The over-boldness of the sans-serif face corresponds to raising the value of the wordform signal (which, recall, is multiplied by the duty cycle of the letterform signal); this is what leads to more energy in the lower frequencies. This is visible in the spectra, with cmss having slightly more energy around 2 cpd.

It is not necessary to compute FFT's to ascertain the principal frequencies present in these average amplitude spectra. It suffices to count strokes in a line, calling each one cycle, and to divide by the visual subtense of the measured line. This gives the letterform frequency. Similarly, counting words produces the wordform frequency. This method produces results that are quite accurate for Computer Modern and the heavily tuned bitmapped Interleaf Classic font, as well as for Bigelow and Holmes' Lucida fonts, and there is no reason it should not be for others. In Table 1 we show some of the computed frequencies obtained by this kind of measure applied to a large text (one hundred lines of Bronte's *Wuthering Heights*). All letters were assumed to have two strokes, except i, j, l, and t (one each) and m, and w (three each). Visual subtense was computed from the font metrics assuming an 18-inch viewing distance.

A few things are worth noting. First, these frequencies are generally in agreement with those given by the DFT methods, although of course this counting scheme does not reveal amplitude. Second, apparent from these measurements is

Table 1: *Predominant Spatial Frequencies of Several Fonts*

Font	fl	fw	Font	fl	fw
cmr7	10.39	1.31			
cmr8	9.85	1.25	cmss8	10.29	1.31
cmr10	8.20	1.04	cmss10	8.33	1.12
cmr12	6.79	.89	cmss12	7.46	.95
cmr17	5.20	.66	cmss17	5.37	.69
cl06	10.57	1.27			
cl08	9.16	1.10	cmr = Computer Modern Roman		
cl10	7.83	.93	cmss = Computer Modern Sans-Serif		
cl12	6.71	.80	cl = Interleaf Classic		
cl14	5.80	.70	Type size in points is indicated in font name.		
cl 18	4.53	.55	fl is letterform , fw is wordform frequency.		

that the designers of all of these fonts have not scaled the fonts linearly down to small sizes. If they had, cmr7 would have a letterform frequency of 10/7, that of cmr10, i.e., 11.7 cpd. One study of human vision [Legge87], described below, suggests that readability drops off rapidly at high spatial frequencies, and this would seem to argue in favor of these expanded fonts.

1.3. *Two-dimensional spectra*

Two-dimensional amplitude spectra reveal features of individual letters which are not discernible by the scanline averaging described above, and also suggest ways to quantify certain differences among typefaces (serif vs. san-serif faces, for example). Figure 4 shows the spectra of several letters in various faces. The spectra are centered at the origin, with a distance of about 47 cpd on each axis. In each of these discrete amplitude spectra, the frequency samples represented are at about 94/128 = .74 cpd because these spectra were computed through a window of 128 samples. Note also that the characters are horizontally centered in a white space, which adds a horizontal low frequency artifact to the spectra.

Some features in the spatial domain can be deduced from these two-dimensional spectra. For example, in the spectrum of the cmr10 upper case X, one can see that there is more low frequency energy in the spectral feature at 45 degrees than in that at –45 degrees. Since the amplitude spectra represent *variation* in intensity, these directions will generally be at 90 degrees to the letter features. Thus the spectrum reflects that one stroke is thicker than the other, namely the one at angle –45 degrees in the character.

Figure 4: *Two–dimensional spectra of characters*

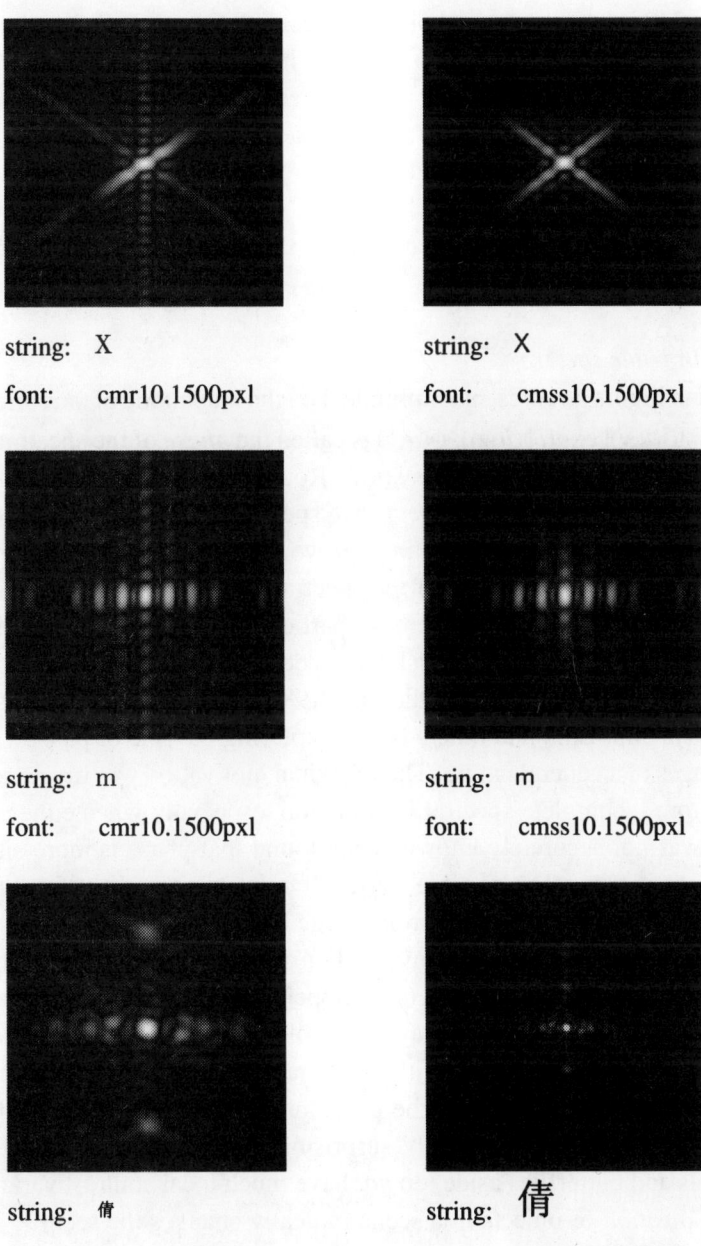

Of particular interest is the difference between serif and sans-serif characters. In the Computer Modern fonts the serifs are largely horizontal, which means they represent variation in the *vertical* direction. For example, the serif upper case X shows a repeating vertical pattern near the center line which is not manifest in the sans-serif spectrum. The pattern repeats about 14 times in the upper half, which means its base frequency is about 47/14 = 3.36 cpd. Put another way, the serif presents a pattern repeating at a distance of 1/3.36 = .30 degrees of visual angle. A similar difference can be seen between the serif and sans-serif lower case m. A character the same except for a thinner serif would generally have similar low frequency amplitude, but more, or higher intensity, highs. We suggest below that this additional energy is at visually relevant frequencies, and this may lend weight to arguments that serifs add to legibility.

1.4. *Phase in letter spectra*

The spectra in Figure 4 represent amplitude, i.e., the magnitude of the complex values $F(u,v) = |F(u,v)| \exp(i\phi(u,v))$. $\phi(u,v)$ is called the *phase* of the spectral value at the two-dimensional spatial frequency (u,v). Roughly speaking, phase is a measure of the position of patterns in an image. If two spectra differed only in phase, and by a constant amount, then the original images would be translations of one another. On the other hand, the amplitude of the spectral values is a measure of the local contrast variation of the image. If there is a particularly high spectral amplitude at a given frequency, then the image has a lot of repetition of a pattern at this frequency.

In a series of papers beginning in the early 1980's ([Hayes80], [Oppenheim81)), Hayes, Oppenheim, Lim, and others began exploring the role of phase vs. amplitude for images of a general nature. Their original motivation was the reproduction of signals from incomplete spectral information, especially when either phase or magnitude was not accurately known. They found that phase is more significant than amplitude in several reasonable senses. If one takes the phase from the spectrum of image A and the amplitude from image B, combining them to make a synthetic spectrum, and then takes the inverse Fourier Transform, the resulting image is generally recognizable as image A (see [Oppenheim83] Figure 4.35 for an example). This suggests that amplitude plays little role, and, in fact, the aforementioned series of papers give iterative algorithms for reproducing an image using essentially constant amplitude and only the phase of the spectrum under study. Upon reflection, this might not be entirely surprising, given that most images in the world, zebras and butterflies aside, do *not* have much local contrast variation, but varying the *position* of objects in a scene radically changes the scene.

Figure 5: *Reconstruction from phase only (left), one bit of phase (right)*

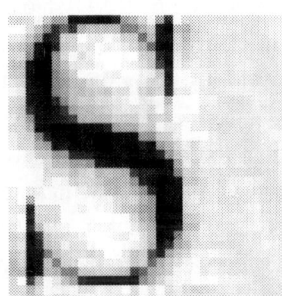
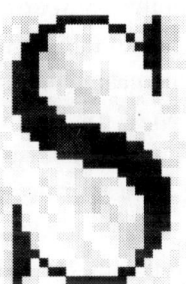

In work with my colleague Guozhen Duan (Duan88), we wondered whether these generalities applied to letter shapes as well. Indeed, when we examined amplitude spectra of entire lines of text, as opposed to individual letters, we found that, just as in the case of the one-dimensional scanline averaging spectra, only a few predominant frequencies were distinguishable, the rest being present over a not very wide range of amplitudes. This may have important implications for human vision. The visual system has radically different responses to different spatial frequencies, with an overall peak at about 4 cpd. The example of Figure 1 shows that very low, as well as very high, frequencies may need substantially more amplitude to be distinguishable when among intermediate frequencies. Although we have not done so, we suggest that a more meaningful way to normalize spectra of images is to weight the spatial frequencies by the human visual system's response. The human vision literature is sufficiently consistent about the gross structure of this response, if not about the details, that such a project seems reasonable. For type, this is likely to reveal, as suggested in Section 2. below, that font artists have been designing type along lines consistent with contemporary models of high visual response (which, of course, would be a reaffirmation of the vision models, not the designs! Undoubtedly skilled font artists already have the "correct" notion of what is easy to see, no matter whether the vision scientists do or not.)

Duan proposed, for technical reasons, that we consider the amplitude spectra of each character to have the same features as that of a square black box of about the same size. The iterative algorithms of [Hayes80] amount to this: Take a discrete spectrum with at least twice as many samples as there are points in the support of the image (that is, if the character vanishes outside an NxN rectangle, take an MxM DFT with Mx2N). In this enlarged spectrum, replace the amplitude with the "virtual" amplitude of Duan, or perhaps some similar amplitude spectrum which is independent of the character (for example, [Hayes80] uses constant amplitude for this initial estimate). Take the inverse DFT to obtain a new image. Next construct a restricted image which coincides with the new one on the NxN rectangle, but is 0 outside it. Finally, compute a new spectrum by taking the MxM DFT of this image and replacing its phase with the phase of the initial MxM DFT.

Roughly speaking, increasing the frequency sampling corresponds to increasing the frequency resolution of the spectrum, i.e., a finer division of the spectrum is computed. The algorithm sketched above is known to converge only under conditions on the so-called z-transform of the samples – conditions which seem not to hold for general binary sample sequences such as describe black-and-white characters. However, it is always the case that the error between the true image and the iterated approximation is non-decreasing and, in real cases, the image seems always to be quite recoverable. Garcia and Calero ([Garcia84]) suggest that initial amplitude estimates should depend somewhat on the image content, and this is the direction we are exploring. Note that the inverse transform may not return to an image with only two levels in it, nor even necessarily look like the original character. But after only a few iterations of this procedure, the original character is easily recognized, especially if some threshold is selected and all gray values below that are set to black and all above it set to white. We can take this as an indication that the amplitude of the spectrum is relatively unimportant in distinguishing characters from one another. This is illustrated in Figure 5, which represents a reconstructed upper case S from Computer Modern Roman digitized at 300dpi, after 30 iterations of the Hayes algorithm as implemented by Duan. In related investigations, we found that using all the amplitude information and only one bit of phase information also recovered the character quickly with similar iterative algorithms. [Curtis84] gives some abstract conditions for an image to be reconstructed from 1 bit of phase data, and shows that as the image size gets larger, the probability approaches 1 that a randomly chosen image meets these conditions.

1.5. *Chinese*

We have begun studies with the the Song font of Chinese characters produced with MetaFont by Hobby and Gu [Hobby83]. Chinese characters have substantially more horizontal strokes than do western fonts. This is visible in the amplitude spectra as 90 degree rotational symmetries not common in western spectra. The character represented in Figure 4 also shows the presence of a strong diagonal stroke at right angles to the corresponding spectral feature. This character is shown at two resolutions, with more high frequency visible in the high resolution spectrum. The low resolution picture can be regarded as an enlargement of the center of the high resolution one (but note that they are not entirely comparable because each character is in a 128x128 window with white side bearings extending to the window edge.

Since the higher resolution character fills this window more, it does not show as much of the low frequency energy which represents the artificial replication through the window.)

At this writing we have not begun reconstruction studies with Chinese characters of the sort described above. The complexity of Chinese characters would lead to the conjecture that stroke position, hence phase in the spectrum, is even more critical for them than for western characters.

2. Vision

2.1. *Visual models and type models*

In recent years, a substantial amount has been learned about spatial vision (Sekuler85, pp. 145–178). In particular, it has been known since 1968 that monochromatic vision can be modeled by independent spatial frequency tuned channels, in much the same way that color vision can be modeled by three channels tuned with peaks at the frequencies of red, green, and blue light. The fundamental evidence for this consists of measuring a subject's response to two different spatial frequencies, then adapting the subject to one of these frequencies, causing the visual system to reduce its response to that pattern. If the frequencies are sufficiently widely separated, the response will not be reduced at the non-adapted frequency.

There is much literature on the details of these channels. Recently, work of Wilson [Wilson84] suggests that there may be as few as six channels, each with a response which is given by the difference of two Gaussian functions, and having peaks approximately at .8, 1.7, 2.8, 4, 8, and 16 cpd. Generally, these channels overlap in pairs, but not otherwise. In essence, the channels behave as filters, each responding to signals within its passband. The information of all of them is summed in a way that makes the entire pattern present an image to the visual system. This kind of model is confirmed by psychophysical experiments with humans, as well as by probes inserted into *single cells* of the visual cortex of cats and monkeys. Cells can be isolated that respond to patterns of some frequency and orientation but not to others. There is intuitive appeal to multi-channel models, in that they can easily distinguish signals from (uniformly distributed) noise. (The noise is that which has equal output in all channels. All else is signal. In fact, this observation has been used to reduce noise in medical images [Baker80].)

We will speculate in this section how some of the spectral properties of type, which we have described above, fit in with these models of human vision. Roughly, we want to argue that type designers have implicitly designed with parameters which cause the type to evoke high response from the human visual system. It is difficult to separate our cognitive processes, in particular the recognition of words, from the reading process. Type designers attempt to do this with their initial design color studies, in which conventional collections of letters are studied. In the final analysis, though, type is about words, and the design of a typeface is not complete without the study of the appearance of real text.

Very few psychophysical studies have been made about reading with attention to spatial frequency models of vision. The most careful of those few is a series of works by Legge et al., culminating in [Legge87]. That work relates reading rate to text contrast and character width. It makes an experimental conclusion which is consistent with a well-known typographic phenomenon, for which we describe a somewhat theoretical foundation below. Legge's conclusion is that at the high contrast typical of reading, the reading rate is highest for characters subtending about .25 degrees. Given that most characters have approximately two strokes, this means that the spatial frequency presented by the strokes is about 8 cpd. As our table of measurements above shows, this is about the frequency of most 10-point type, and it is well known that type gets *harder*, not easier to read as its size increases well above 12-point. Most reading authorities speculate that this decreased legibility comes from the requirement to make longer saccadic eye motions, the motions between fixations which we make when reading, with the attendant reduced information content per line. We will suggest below that the multi-channel models imply that bigger type actually presents information at frequencies less discernible to the early part of the visual system.

The Legge study mentioned above also relates reading rate to psychophysical contrast, but this is not the same thing as the contrast which type designers manipulate when they vary stem weights. (Note that Legge's experiments were done on CRT's, not paper, possibly a consequential difference.) In type design, what is changed is the duty cycle (the fraction "on") of the letterform signal idealized in Figure 2. Indeed, even that example is unreal in that the white space between strokes is typically several times the stroke width. The duty cycle of the wordform signal, however, is an artifact of the mean word width, which is, of course, a function not only of the type but of the language as well. For example, German text is often printed in 9-point type, which then tends to have wordform frequencies similar to larger English type, even though higher letterform frequencies (however, the response curves for human visual response are broader at their peaks than on their shoulders, which means that we might expect more tolerance in the letterform than the wordform frequencies). In addition, a more accurate form of this idealized model multiplies the wordform signal by the duty cycle of the letterform signal to account for the overall average grayness of text without regard to the details of letters. That notion of contrast – sometimes called the color of the text – then becomes built into the compound signal model and can have filters, such as proposed in [Wilson84] applied to the signal.

It is beyond the scope of this paper to detail the application of multi-channel filtering models to type models, but the central feature is this: The overall peak of visual response is not near 8 cpd, but rather near 4 cpd. If the visual system were responding only to the strokes in letters, we would expect best response not from 10-point type but rather from something about twice as large. What is known is that recognition of individual words or even letters *does* increase as size increases above 12-point, although reading rate for text decreases. The overall response to a compound signal, such as presented by text (namely, the major frequencies presented by strokes and by words), can indeed be shown to decrease as the stroke frequency decreases below 8 cpd (i.e., the type size increases above 10-point). Thus, we can speculate that 10-point type is actually easier for the early visual system to process than much bigger type, and we need not resort to eye motion explanations.

2.2. Two–dimensional vision

The one-dimensional model of Wilson can be extended to two-dimensions (Wilson83), but we have not attempted much to combine it with type models, as our two-dimensional work has largely consisted of the reconstruction studies described in Section 1.4. There is some evidence in the vision literature that monochromatic vision is more sensitive to phase than to spectral amplitude changes and this would be expected if natural images have most of their information in their phase. Since this seems to be the case for letters also, once again it would suggest that type designers have implicitly chosen "optimal" variables to manipulate. Roughly speaking, radical changes in spectral amplitude throughout a font could be accomplished by radical changes in stroke width. It is probably difficult for the unskilled eye to detect these changes as much as mis-positioning of strokes, which are phase changes. For example, a lower case m with its third stroke too close to the second might be more easily mistaken for an n than would one whose strokes were uniformly a little too thick. Indeed, the amplitude spectra of an m and an n are nearly identical because repeated m's and repeated n's present little difference from one another in their rate of alternation of black and white.

On the other hand, serifs, especially horizontal ones (as would be the case in most western letters), do present additional information both in phase and amplitude, and our preliminary indication is that they are at visually relevant frequencies, i.e., their presence enhances the signal in the Wilson model.

Acknowledgments. The FFT's were coded by Richard Ratta, YuBing Chen and Guozhen Duan and converted to generate PostScript by the author. Most of the two-dimensional data described were taken by Duan, who also implemented the reconstruction algorithms. The manuscript was prepared with the Interleaf Technical Publishing system in Times-Roman type producing PostScript output. The spectra and reconstruction images were made from encapsulated PostScript embedded in the document. Thanks to Bigelow and Holmes and to Interleaf, Inc. for the use of their font data. PostScript is a trademark of Adobe Systems. Lucida is a trademark of Bigelow and Holmes. The research was supported by NSF Grant DCR–85–03154 at UMASS/Boston.

References

[1] K. D. Baker, and F. D. Sullivan (1980), "Multiple Band Pass Filters in Image Processing," *IEEE Proc.* **127(E)**, No. 5, Sept. 1980, pp. 173–184.

[2] C. Bigelow and D. Day (1983), "Digital Typography," *Scientific American,* **249**, No. 2, pp. 106–119.

[3] C. Bigelow and K. Holmes (1986), "The design of Lucida: an integrated family of types for electronic literacy," *Text Processing and Document Manipulations,* J.C. vanVliet, editor, Cambridge University Press, Cambridge. (This is the proceedings of the Nottingham Conference, EP86.)

[4] S. R. Curtis, J. S. Lim, and A. V. Oppenheim (1984), "Signal Reconstruction from One Bit of Fourier Transform Phase," *IEEE Conference on Acoustics, Speech, and Signal Processing,* pp. 12A.5.1–12A–5.4.

[5] G. Duan and R. A. Morris (1988), "Phase information in characters," work in progress, Dept. of Math. and C.S., Univ. of Massachusetts at Boston, MA.

[6] K. R. Castleman (1979), *Digital Image Processing,* Prentice–Hall, Englewood Cliffs, N.J.

[7] N. Garcia and A. Calero (1984), "Faster Phase Only Image Reconstruction," *IEEE Conference on Acoustics, Speech, and Signal Processing,* pp. 12A.3.1–12A–3.4.

[8] M. H. Hayes, J. S. Lim, and A. V. Oppenheim (1980), "Signal Reconstruction from Phase or Magnitude," *IEEE Transactions on Acoustics, Speech, and Signal Processing,* **ASSP–28**, No. 6., pp. 672–680.

[9] J. Hobby and G. Gu (1983), "A Chinese Meta-Font," Stanford Technical Report, Stan–CS–83–974, Stanford Department of Computer Science, Stanford, CA.

[10] A. Naiman (1988) *The Use of Grayscale for Improved Character Presentation,* Ph.D. dissertation, in progress, Department of Computer Science, University of Toronto.

[11] A. V. Oppenheim and J. S. Lim (1981), "The importance of phase in signals," *Proc. IEEE,* **69**, pp. 528–541.

[12] A. V. Oppenheim and A. S. Willsky with I. T. Young (1983), *Signals and Systems*, Prentice Hall, Englewood Cliffs, N.J.

[13] G. C. Phillips and H. R. Wilson (1984), "Orientation bandwidths of spatial mechanisms measured by masking," *J. Opt. Soc. Am. Series A,* **1,** pp. 226–232.

[14] R. Rubinstein (1988), *Digital Typography*, Addison–Wesley, Reading, MA, to be published.

[15] R. Rubinstein and R. Ulichney (1987), personal communication. See also, [Rubinstein88].

[16] R. Sekuler and R. Blake (1985), *Perception,* Alfred A. Knopf, New York, N.Y.

[17] H. R. Wilson and D. J. Gelb (1984), "Modified line-element theory for spatial frequency discrimination," *J. Opt. Soc. Am. Series A,* **1(1)**, pp. 124–131.

[18] J. I. Yellott, Jr., B. A. Wandell, and T. N. Cornsweet (1984), "The beginnings of visual perception: the retinal image and its initial encoding," Chapter 7 in *Handbook of Physiology – The Nervous System III*. The American Physiological Society, Bethesda, MD.

OPTIMAL LINE BREAKING IN MUSIC

WAEL A. HEGAZY*
JOHN S. GOURLAY**

*Ohio State University, Columbus, Ohio
**ArborText, Inc., Ann Arbor, Michigan

ABSTRACT
For a variety of reasons music line breaking, or "casting off" as it is called by musicians, is not susceptible to simple treatment in automatic music formatting software. The powerful line breaking method used by Knuth in the text formatting program TEX can almost do the job for music, but it falls short in being unable to handle the complex motions of notes when lines of music are stretched or shrunk. This paper describes a generalization of the line-breaking model used in TEX in which *springs* (analogous to TEX's glue) penetrate boxes and connect to interior points. A line-breaking algorithm based on this model is described, and implementation details that make it computationally feasible are discussed.

1. Introduction to the Problem

Among the many "exotic" document formatting problems currently receiving attention, music formatting is one of the most challenging. For some time, the MusiCopy project at The Ohio State University has been searching for algorithms to automate many of the kinds of formatting decisions made routinely by human music copyists in preparing high-quality musical scores [Gourlay87]. One of the recent investigations has been into the problem of line breaking, or "casting off" as it is called by musicians.

A fairly evident feature of printed music is that the last line of a piece or movement is always full. Unlike a paragraph of text, a piece of music conventionally cannot end with a short line, and music copyists must be willing to revise early line-breaking decisions in the likely case that their initial choice of breaks does not lead to a full last line. Automated line breaking for music must exhibit the same flexibility in looking ahead or backtracking, or it will be forced to stretch or shrink the last line by intolerable amounts. It is also considered desireable that long works of music fill the whole last page, causing copyists sometimes to set an entire piece slightly tighter or looser than they would otherwise to force the piece to fit in a number of lines that is a multiple of the number of lines per page.

A related issue in music is that certain page breaks and sometimes line breaks can be very troublesome for performers, who must be able to deliver a smooth performance from music they have not rehearsed thoroughly. We cannot expect automated systems to detect these breaks, but it must be possible for users of music printing software to be able to encourage or discourage certain line and page breaks while the software maintains uniform spacing throughout the piece.

Another complexity of music is that certain bits of text, for example clefs and key signatures, are repeated at the beginning of every line. It is possible for these features of the music to change from time to time during a piece, not only in appearance but in size, and so they must be introduced and accounted for by a line-breaking algorithm rather than treated as a constant background on which the rest of the music is printed.

A last and very important feature of music relevant to line breaking is the complex motion of notes with respect to one another as the line they are in is stretched or shrunk. In text we desire uniform spaces between words, regardless of the widths of the words themselves. In music, on the other hand, the important distances, which depend on the durations of the notes, are measured from the left edge of one note to the left edge of the next, leaving variable amounts of white space depending on the actual widths of the notes. Notes must not be allowed to overlap, even in tight spacings where the edge-to-edge distances could otherwise become very small, and so the position of a note in a line is not usually a simple linear function of the amount by which the line is stretched or shrunk.

The difficulties of casting off music have not been overlooked by others, but there appears to be no published algorithm that attempts to deal with them. Gomberg [75] and Byrd [84], both of whom have described algorithms for automatic music formatting, discuss the problems but simply defer any useful line-breaking decisions to the users of their software. Byrd's software will do "first-fit" line breaking (in which each line is filled as full as possible and never reconsidered), but he suggests that his users will usually want to choose their own breaks. Ross [70], as well as others writing for musicians and copyists, offers little guidance other than to avoid certain musically bad breaks, and to keep spacing as uniform as possible.

The goal of this paper is to describe an approach to music line breaking that can successfully deal with all of the above problems. The algorithm is a generalization of the line-breaking algorithm devised by Knuth [81] for the text formatter TEX, with which we assume the reader is familiar. Section 2 of this paper introduces the necessary generalizations to Knuth's model and Section 3 describes a simple but slow version of the algorithm. Section 4 then presents some modifications that make the computations practial.

2. A Music Line-Breaking Model

Knuth's line-breaking model can handle all of the problematical features of music except the last. Specifically, if there is no glue at the end of a paragraph, his algorithm will automatically find an optimal setting with a full last line. If there is a particular word space at which an author would like to discourage a line break, he or she need only specify an appropriate penalty value at that point. TeX can also force a paragraph into a specific number of lines, satisfying the need to fill a last page of music, or alternatively the whole algorithm can be applied a second time to find optimal page breaks as was done by Plass [81]. Finally, with the simple and powerful hyphenation feature called the *discretionary break*, a line break can be designed to modify or insert things like clefs at the end of the previous line and the beginning of the new one.

This leaves only the problem of the relative motions of notes during stretching and shrinking. As we have already said, these do not obey the simple linear rule followed by text. In Figure 1 we see three versions of the same measure, the first one severely shrunk, the second at its natural width, and the third severely stretched. If we look first at the pair of eighth notes, we see that their spacing changes smoothly with the line length. If notes never had large printed widths, this is what should happen in all cases. If we look at the last pair of notes, however, we see that the space between these notes is the same in both the shrunk and natural versions of the measure. If we imagine an animation of the measure shrinking from its maximum to its minimum size, the space between these notes shrinks smoothly until about the time the measure reaches its natural width. At this point the pair of flats in front of the last note abruptly stops any further shrinkage of the space. An extreme case of this occurs between the first two notes, whose spacing never changes at any line length. The flats belonging to the second note are so wide that they always require more space than would be appropriate for this pair of notes in the absence of the flats. (The ideal spacings of notes depend on their durations in a logarithmic fashion described elsewhere [Gourlay88], so we will not concern ourselves here with how the numbers are arrived at.)

A good physical analogy for this behavior is to think of notes and any associated accidentals (flats or sharps) as occupying boxes, just as words do

Figure 1: *A measure shrunk, spaced normally, and stretched.*

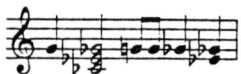

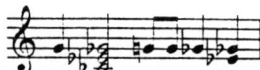

in Knuth's model, but instead of being separated by glue, they are connected with *springs* that penetrate the boxes and connect to common points at the left edges of the noteheads. While springs can penetrate boxes, boxes cannot penetrate each other, and when they come into contact they prevent the springs from shrinking as far as they might otherwise.

Note that the the vertical spacing of lines in a column of text, maintaining uniformly spaced baselines, is a special case of this problem.

Like glue, every spring has values for ideal width, stretchability, and shrinkablility, and for a given amount of strech or shrink, there is a corresponding *fitting force* (analogous to Knuth's "adjustment ratio") that can be used exactly as Knuth does to compute badness and demerits and to find the optimum series of line breaks. The computation of the fitting force is complex, however, because as the line gets shorter, fewer and fewer springs are available to absorb additional reductions in width. With attention to detail, however, it can be done efficiently.

3. Overview of the Algorithm

Under this model, the input to the line-breaking algorithm consists of a sequence of *items* describing the behavior of the springs connecting the notes. Each item has four parts, called w, y, z, and b, where w is the ideal width of the spring, y is its stretchability, z is its shrinkability, and b is the width at which the two boxes it connects collide, what we call the *blocking width* of the spring. If $b > w$ we say that the spring is *prestretched*. Interspersed among these items are penalties, indicating the locations of *legal break points*, and which in practice will occur just prior to barlines.

As in text, however, most of the possible sequences of breakpoints are absurd, in the sense that they would result in lines that either are packed with so many measures that they can never fit into the desired line width, or have very few measures that they are ridiculously loose. Therefore, the number of sequences of breakpoints that the line-breaking algorithm need to consider can be brought down significantly by defining an acceptable range of forces permitted in fitting sequences of measures into a desired line width (Knuth's "tolerance"). We will denote such a range by $[f_{min}, f_{max}]$, where f_{min} has a negative value and f_{max} has a positive value, following the convention that a stretching force is positive and a shrinking force is negative. As Knuth pointed out with text, dynamic programming can be used to further reduce the number of sequences of breakpoints by discarding all but the best subsequence leading up to a given breakpoint.

These ideas are sufficient to bring the optimum line-breaking algorithm to practical efficiency for text, but it is still not sufficient in the case of breaking musical scores into lines. We introduce the algorithm in this form, nevertheless, and concern ourselves with the final efficiencies in Section 4.

3.1. The Main Idea

Overlooking the computation of the fitting force for the moment, the algorithm is very much like TEX's. As the measures of a piece of music are read, an *active list* is kept of breakpoints that can be the beginnings of lines whose ends are yet to be read. Only if the fitting force of these lines is within the tolerable range are the breakpoints kept on the list. These are the *feasible breakpoints*. As they are dropped from the list, they are assembled into a network that shows the optimum series of feasible breakpoints up to that point. At the end of the piece the optimum sequence of breakpoints can be read from the graph.

Figure 2 shows a piece of music with small numbers labelling the legal breakpoints, while Figure 3 shows the graph representing the optimum-breakpoint computation. The numbered circles represent the feasible breakpoints, and the lines connecting them are labelled with the demerits for the line. Following the headed arrows up from the last breakpoint produces the series of breaks with the minimum total demerits. It is worth mentioning here that the line breaks chosen by the algorithm for this piece are identical to the line breaks chosen by a professional musician for the same piece. It took a few hours to cast off the piece manually, whereas an implementation of the algorithm on a personal computer did the job in a few seconds.

In outline, this is the algorithm:

⋮

⟨ **for** every legal breakpoint b ⟩ **do**

```
begin
  ⟨ Initialize the feasible breakpoints at b to the empty set ⟩
  ⟨ for every active breakpoint a ⟩ do
    begin
      ⟨ Compute the fitting force f for the potential line from a to b ⟩
      if f < f_min then ⟨ remove a from the active list ⟩
      elseif f > f_max then ⟨ exit inner loop ⟩
      else ⟨ record a feasible break from a to b ⟩
    end
  ⟨ if there is a feasible break at b ⟩ then
    ⟨ append the best such break to the active list ⟩
end
⟨ Use the last feasible break in the active list to
      trace back the optimum breakpoint sequence ⟩
  ⋮
```

Since legal breakpoints occur only between measures, and since the size of the active list is bounded by the maximum number of measures per line, the number of times the body of the inner loop of the algorithm is executed is bounded by $mpp \times mpl_{max}$, where mpp is the number of measures in the piece and mpl_{max} is the maximum number of measures per line. The main operation inside the inner loop is that of computing the fitting force for the measures between a feasible breakpoint a and a legal breakpoint b. This operation should be made as efficient as possible since the efficiency of the whole algorithm depends, mainly, on the efficiency of this operation. The rest of this section summarizes the characterization of the fitting force needed to fit a given group of measures (or items) into a desired length.

3.2. Finding The Fitting Force

The problem of finding the fitting force can be formulated as follows: given a sequence of items, I, and an amount of stretch or shrinkage, s (to fit the potential line into the desired line width), what is the necessary fitting force, f, that is needed to stretch or shrink the whole group of items I by s? We will adopt the convention that both s and f are positive for stretch and are negative for shrinkage. Since f does not depend on the order of items in I, we will refer to I as a set rather than a sequence. Each item in I is represented as a 4-tuple for the w, y, z, and b values of the item.

The idea behind finding the fitting force can probably be understood best in terms of a function that maps an amount of stretch or shrinkage,

Figure 2: *A piece with optimal line breaks.*

for a set I of items, into the required fitting force. Such a function will be denoted by $\phi_I(s)$. The function $\phi_I(s)$ is a piece-wise linear function whose line segments depend on I. For the purpose of defining $\phi_I(s)$ for an arbitrary set of items I, the set I is partitioned into three disjoint sets, I_{PR}, I_{SNP} and I_{NSNP} as follows:

I_{PR}: Contains the prestretched items in I; i.e., those items for which $y > 0$ and $b > w$. The elements of I_{PR} are denoted by (w_1, y_1, z_1, b_1), ..., (w_m, y_m, z_m, b_m). Without loss of generality, it can be assumed that:

$$\frac{b_1 - w_1}{y_1} \leq \frac{b_2 - w_2}{y_2} \leq \cdots \leq \frac{b_m - w_m}{y_m}$$

I_{SNP}: Contains those non-prestretched items in I that can shrink; i.e., those items for which $b < w$ and $z > 0$. The elements of I_{SNP} are denoted

Figure 3: *The computation for the piece of Figure 2.*

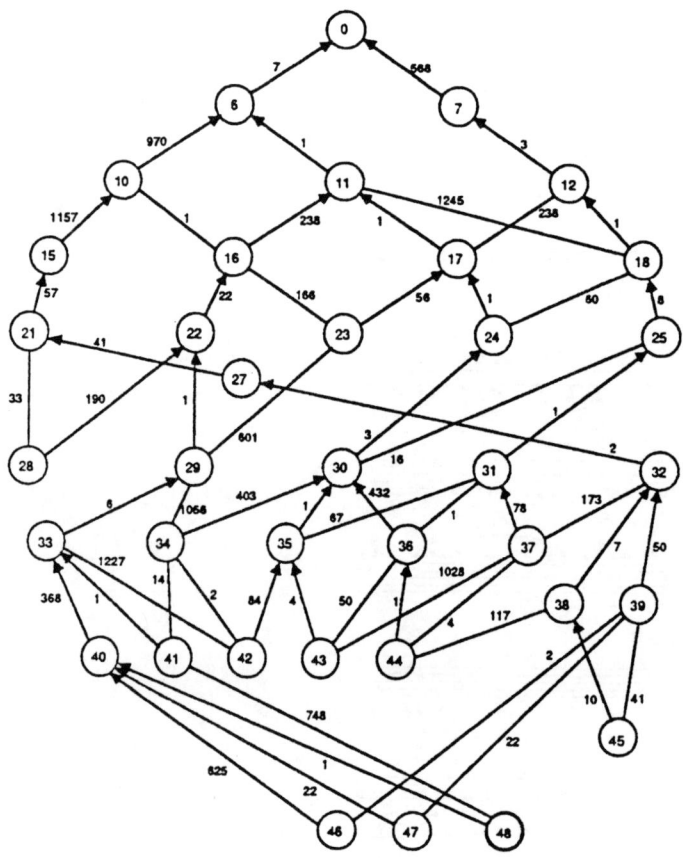

by $(w'_1, y'_1, z'_1, b'_1), \ldots, (w'_n, y'_n, z'_n, b'_n)$. Without loss of generality, it can be assumed that:

$$\frac{w'_1 - b'_1}{z'_1} \leq \frac{w'_2 - b'_2}{z'_2} \leq \cdots \leq \frac{w'_n - b'_n}{z'_n}$$

I_{NSNP}: Contains those non-prestretched items in I that cannot shrink; i.e., those items for which $b = w$, or $b < w$ and $z = 0$. The elements of I_{NSNP} are denoted by $(w''_1, y''_1, z''_1, b''_1), \ldots, (w''_p, y''_p, z''_p, b''_p)$.

Using the above notation, the function $\phi_I(s)$, for an arbitrary I, is represented graphically in Figure 4. The function $\phi_I(s)$ will be called the characteristic function of I, or the characteristic function of the potential line whose items make up the set I. The expressions next to the arrows pointing at the boundaries between line segments represent the values of

Figure 4: *Fitting force as a function of stretch or shrink.*

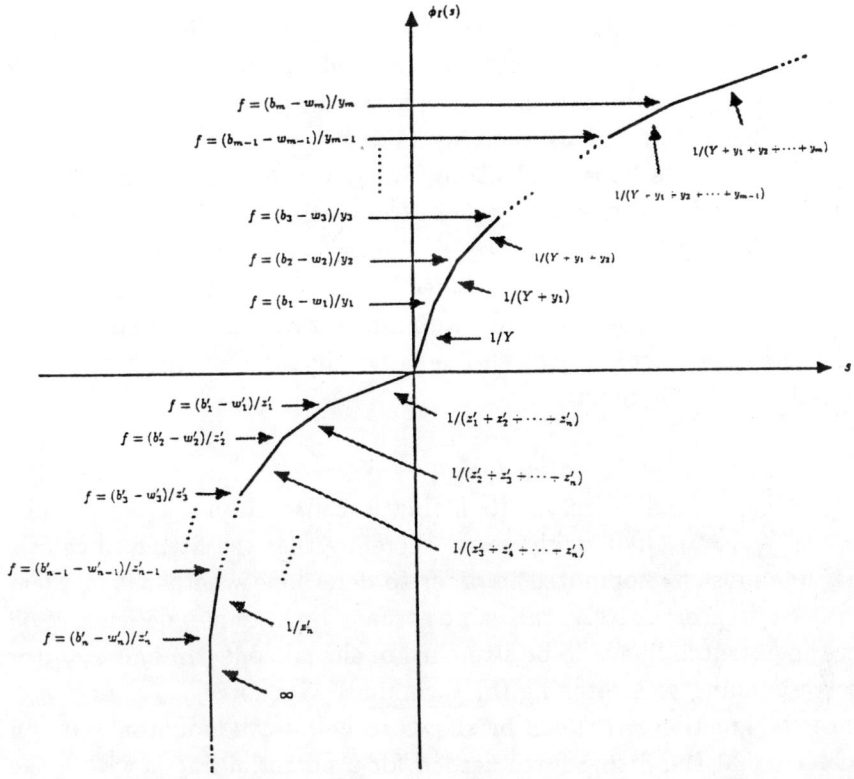

the force at these points. The expressions next to the arrows pointing to the line segments themselves represent the slopes of the segments, with $Y = \sum_{i=1}^{n} y'_i + \sum_{i=1}^{p} y''_i$.

According to the specifications of $\phi_I(s)$, as shown in Figure 4, it is apparent that finding the fitting force for some I and s inevitably involves two main steps. In the first step, the elements of the set I are scanned so that I can be partitioned into I_{PR}, I_{SNP} and I_{NSNP}. The sums $\sum y + \sum y''$ or $\sum z'$ might be computed while the elements of I are being scanned. The second step involves constructing as many line segments, among those which represent $\phi_I(s)$, as necessary to reach the segment that corresponds to the given value of s.

4. Improving the Algorithm's Efficiency

According to the outline of the algorithm given in the preceding section, the fitting force is computed for every potential line. This would take too much time unnecessarily. In the first place, a large portion of the potential lines are not feasible lines (i.e., they need fitting forces outside any "reasonable" permissible range), and the time needed to compute the fitting forces for these lines can be saved if an efficient way is used to filter out the infeasible lines. Furthermore, computing the fitting forces for the feasible lines can be made more efficient, on the average, by taking advantage of the fact that many of these feasible lines need fitting forces within the first positive or the first negative line segment of $\phi_I(s)$. Computing the fitting force that is within the first line segment of $\phi_I(s)$ can be made much more efficient if it is known, beforehand, that it is indeed within the first segment. More efficiency, therefore, can be obtained if a simple test can be used to determine whether the fitting force for a given line is within the first line segment of the line's characteristic function.

4.1. Filtering Infeasible Potential Lines

A potential line is feasible only if its fitting force is within a given permissible range, $[f_{min}, f_{max}]$. It might seem, therefore that the fitting force of a potential line must be computed in order to determine whether it is a feasible line or not. Fortunately, this is not true. For example, depending on whether the potential line is to be stretched or shrunk, one can find s_{max} (or s_{min}) corresponding to stretching (or shrinking) with force f_{max} (or f_{min}). And since the function $\phi_I(s)$ can be shown to be always monotonic, it can be concluded that the fitting force needed for a potential line is within the permissible range if and only if $s_{min} \leq s \leq s_{max}$, where s is the amount of stretch (or shrinkage) needed to fit the potential line into the desired line length.

This way of filtering out the infeasible potential lines, however, does not seem to be efficient enough. The purpose of such filtering is to save the time of computing the fitting force in the cases where its exact amount is not going to be used. It, therefore, makes no sense to do this filtering in a way that might take more time than the time needed for computing the exact fiting force. This can be the case here due to the fact that many of the infeasible potential lines need fitting forces that are within the first line segment of their characteristic functions, in which case the fitting force can be computed most efficiently. Therefore, a more efficient way for filtering out the infeasible potential lines is sought.

A better approach towards filtering out the infeasible potential lines would be to approximate $\phi_I(s)$ in such a way that makes computing the "approximate" fitting force efficient enough for the filtering purpose. Let $\phi_I^A(s)$ be such an approximation of $\phi_I(s)$. The approximation must be such

Figure 5: *A fitting-force function and an efficiently computed approximation to it.*

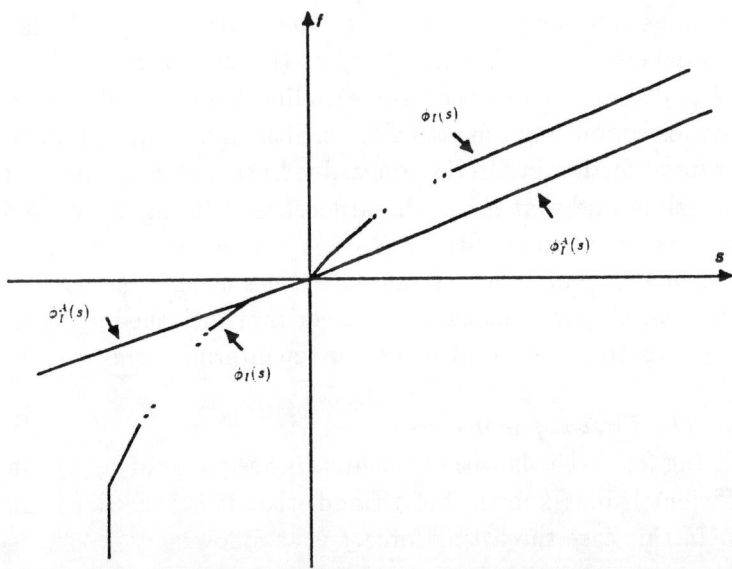

that no potential line that is actually feasible would ever be considered infeasible by the approximation. In other words, for every given value of s, it must be true that $|\phi_I^A(s)| \leq |\phi_I(s)|$. An appropriate function $\phi_I^A(s)$ would approximate $\phi_I(s)$ by two line segments as follows:

$$\phi_I^A(s) = \begin{cases} s/(\sum_{i=1}^n y_i' + \sum_{i=1}^m y_i + \sum_{i=1}^p y_i''), & \text{if } s \geq 0; \\ s/\sum_{i=1}^n z_i', & \text{otherwise.} \end{cases}$$

As shown in Figure 5, $\phi_I^A(s)$ satisfies the condition that $|\phi_I^A(s)| \leq |\phi_I(s)|$ for any given value of s. In the case of stretch ($s > 0$), $\phi_I^A(s)$ is a straight line that passes through the origin, and whose slope is equal to the slope of the last line segment of $\phi_I(s)$. In the case of shrinkage ($s < 0$), $\phi_I^A(s)$ is a straight line that passes through the origin, and whose slope is equal to the slope of the first line segment of $\phi_I(s)$. Using $\phi_I^A(s)$, the magnitude of the force corresponding to a given value of s is never overestimated. Besides, $\phi_I^A(s)$ is such a simple function that filtering out infeasible potential lines using it is quite efficient and independent of the number of items in the line, unlike the case when $\phi_I(s)$ is used. Note that the sums $\sum y'$, $\sum y''$, $\sum y$, and $\sum z'$ need not be computed, over and over, for each potential line. Instead, the sums are computed from the beginning of the piece to the current place, and two such sums are subtracted to obtain the sum for what lies between them.

Filtering infeasible potential lines using $\phi_I^A(s)$ is an imperfect filtering, in the sense that some infeasible lines are not filtered out. In particular, for any value of s where $\phi_I^A(s) < f_{\max} \leq \phi_I(s)$ (in case of stretch), or $|\phi_I^A(s)| < |f_{\min}| \leq |\phi_I(s)|$— (in case of shrinkage), a line is considered feasible when $\phi_I^A(s)$ is used for computing the fitting force, although the line, in fact, is infeasible. This imperfection in filtering infeasible lines does not represent a problem; an infeasible line that is not discarded sooner using $\phi_I^A(s)$ will be discarded later, after its exact fitting force is computed using $\phi_I(s)$. Nevertheless, the probability of detecting infeasible lines using $\phi_I^A(s)$ is high enough to make the overall performance of the algorithm with the imperfect filtering, using $\phi_I^A(s)$, better than it with the perfect filtering, using $\phi_I(s)$.

4.2. Checking For The First-segment Cases

Computing the fitting force that is within the first line segment of $\phi_I(s)$ can be made most efficient if it is known, beforehand, that it is indeed within the first segment. In this case the fitting force f is as follows:

$$f = \begin{cases} 0, & \text{if } s = 0; \\ s/\sum_{i=1}^n y_i', & \text{if } s > 0; \\ s/\sum_{i=1}^n z_i', & \text{otherwise.} \end{cases}$$

And since $\sum_{i=1}^n y_i'$ and $\sum_{i=1}^n z_i'$ are computed anyway for each potential line, for the purpose of filtering out the infeasible potential lines, computing the fitting force that is known to be within the first segment of the line's characteristic function boils down to a single division operation.

Referring to Figure 4, the fitting force f is within the first segment if and only if $f \leq \min_{1 \leq i \leq m}(b_i - w_i)/y_i$, in case of stretch, or $|f| \leq \min_{1 \leq i \leq n}(w_i - b_i)/z_i$, in case of shrinkage. Given an amount s of stretch (or shrinkage), it can be determined whether the required fitting force f is within the first segment or not as follows:

f is within the first segment

$$\iff \begin{cases} s/\sum_{i=1}^n y_i' \leq \min_{1 \leq i \leq m}(b_i - w_i)/y_i, & \text{if } s \geq 0; \\ s/\sum_{i=1}^n z_i' \leq \min_{1 \leq i \leq n}(w_i' - b_i')/z_i', & \text{otherwise.} \end{cases}$$

The minima $\min_{1 \leq i \leq m}(b_i - w_i)/y_i$ and $\min_{1 \leq i \leq n}(w_i' - b_i')/z_i'$ could be computed, for every feasible potential line, by scanning through all the items in the line. However, experience has shown that it is more efficient to precompute these minima for each measure in the piece and then find the minima for each potential line by scanning through the measures of that potential line.

Checking every feasible potential line to see whether or not its fitting force is within the first segment of the line's characteristic function would save time only if the fitting force turns out to be within the first segment. Therefore, the overall saving in computation time depends on the probability that the needed fitting force is within the first segment. Such probability tends to get smaller as f_{max} and $|f_{min}|$ increase. For high values of f_{max} and $|f_{min}|$, it is possible that checking for the first-segment cases can have a negative effect in terms of computation time. However, a limited experience with using the music line-breaking algorithm has shown that for $f_{min} \geq -1$ and $f_{max} \leq 1$, the algorithm's performance is improved by checking for the first-segment cases.

Acknowledgements

We would like to thank Dean K. Roush for his permission to use his composition "Lacrimosa" as an example in this paper, and for the contribution of his expertise in music notation. This work was partially supported by the National Science Foundation under grant number IST-8514308.

References

[1] Byrd, Donald A. (1984). *Music Notation by Computer*, Ph. D. Thesis, Indiana University.

[2] Gomberg, David A. (1975). *A Computer-Oriented System for Music Printing*, Ph. D. Thesis, Washington University.

[3] Gourlay, John S. (1987). "Computer Formatting of Music," In *PROTEXT III Proceedings of the Third International Conference on Text Processing Systems*, ed. J. J. H. Miller. Dublin, Ireland: Boole Press.

[4] Gourlay, John S. (1988). "Spacing a Line of Music," In *PROTEXT IV Proceedings of the Fourth International Conference on Text Processing Systems*, ed. J. J. H. Miller. Dublin, Ireland: Boole Press.

[5] Knuth, Donald E. and Plass, Michael F. (1981). "Breaking Paragraphs into Lines," *Software—Practice and Experience*, **11**, 1119–1184.

[6] Plass, Michael F. (1981). *Optimal Pagination Techniques for Automatic Typesetting Systems*, Ph. D. Thesis, Stanford University.

[7] Ross, T. (1970). *The Art of Music Engraving and Processing*. Miami: Hansen Books.

DRAG: A GRAPH DRAWING SYSTEM

HOWARD TRICKEY

AT&T Bell Laboratories

ABSTRACT

Drag is a system which produces a picture of a combinatorial graph, given only connectivity information. It differs from other such programs in that the user has fine control over what nodes look like and where the edges touch the nodes. Also, planarity is used to help find an aesthetically pleasing drawing.

1. Introduction

Preparing the diagrams for a document can take up a significant portion of the total preparation time, so any tool that aids in drawing diagrams is a useful adjunct to a document preparation system. Many diagrams can be regarded as graphs—nodes with interconnecting edges. For example, Aho, Sethi, and Ullman [Aho79] contains over 200 graph diagrams, constituting more than 75% of the pictures in the book. This paper describes *Drag*, a program that could have drawn many of those pictures given a specification of the graph connectivity and the node drawing method. The goal is to produce layouts of sufficient quality that they can be published as is, or after only minor editing.

Other people have written graph drawing programs, but the goal has usually been to have a tool for quickly inspecting a graph, often on a screen [Robins87, Rowe87]. Thus, the emphasis is on getting acceptable results in a reasonable amount of time on graphs that may have hundreds or even thousands of nodes. Mostly, the graphs drawn by these programs aren't pretty enough to go into a high quality document as is, and the user can't get better results by expending a little more effort in making up the specification. Also, for many graphs the user must be able to specify exactly how to draw the nodes and where each edge should be attached on each node. Furthermore, graphs are often *hierarchical* in the sense that the nodes have *ranks*: Several researchers have pointed out that it is important to make the ranking evident

Figure 1: (a) Minimum specification output; (b) Detailed specification output

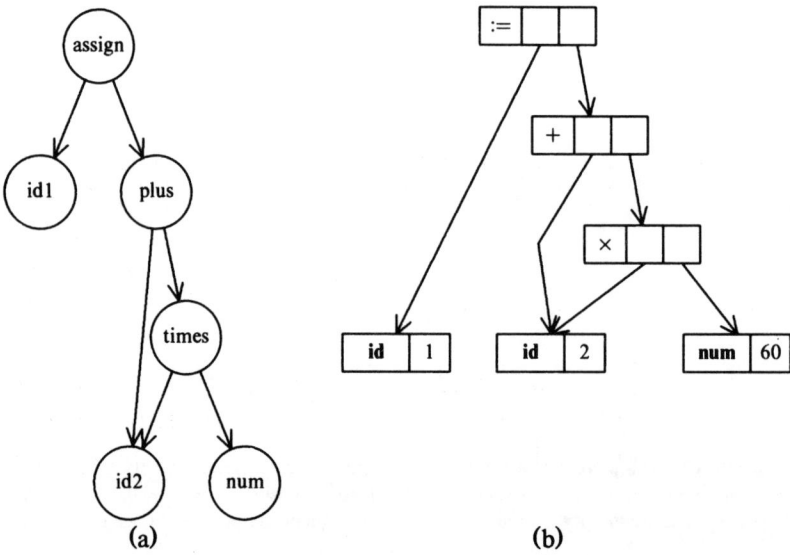

by a strategy such as lining up all nodes of a given rank in a row, and placing the rows in rank order, top-to-bottom on the page [Carpano80, Rowe87]. Directed Acyclic Graphs (DAGs) are easy to comprehend when displayed this way, with ranks assigned as "shortest (or longest) distance from a source (or to a sink)".

2. Drag Descriptions

The principle that guided the Drag user interface was: allow anything in the spectrum between a *minimum specification* (connectivity only) and a *full specification* (connectivity, how to draw each node and edge, places on nodes where edges attach, node ranks and subranks). A minimum specification is a set of *edge* statements, such as:

```
assign -> id1, plus;
plus -> id2, times;
times -> id2, num;
```

Drag's output is shown in Figure 1(a); Figure 1(b) results from adding other Drag statements, to be discussed below. Labels and other attributes can be added to an edge statement, as in `x->"lab" dashed y`. To specify a particular attachment point (a *port* in Drag terminology), a node can be followed by a set of port choices: `x.e|w` means attach to either port e or port w on node x, but not to any other port that x might have.

The default way of drawing a node is to use a circle, with the node name centered inside it. A *node* statement like

```
node id1 pair "id" "1" rank 4;
```

tells Drag that node `id1` is of type `pair` (with a user-defined drawing method), has labels "`id`" and "`1`", and should appear on the fourth rank. Users can define drawing methods for nodes using *nodetype* statements. The idea is to give a fragment of IDEAL[1] code that draws a node of the given type. Drag has hooks to let the node sizes be determined by the dimensions of the node labels.

Other Drag statements let one include another file, give IDEAL code that is to appear outside the individual nodetype boxes, give TeX or troff code to appear before the diagram, and give an alternate direction of rank progression (left-to-right, say, instead of the default top-to-bottom).

Most people should just use edge and node statements, relying on the built-in nodetypes or nodetypes available in a library. But if one expects to do a large number of graphs of a certain type, it might be worth the effort to design some custom nodetypes. For example, I wrote a silicon compiler which could dump its internal graphs in Drag format, so it was very easy to produce diagrams like Figure 2 for debugging purposes. The shapes of the nodes reflect their functions (register, operator, etc.), and their ranks show which microcode cycle the operation is scheduled for. Two label arguments give an internal reference number and a variable name or other information.

3. Graph Drawing Methods

Graph drawing can be divided into two phases: (1) getting the approximate layout plan—where nodes go in relation to each other (as in "x left of y") and how the edges snake between the nodes; and (2) the assignment of final positions to things. The latter phase is guided by neatness and stylistic aesthetics. The first phase seems to be harder for computer programs. Looking at the graph drawing literature [Batini84a, Carpano80, Reingold81, Wetherell79], and at books containing a lot of graphs, one finds or deduces rules such as: minimize edge crossings; place connected nodes close to each other to avoid

---

[1] See Van Wyk [Van Wyk82] for a description of IDEAL. Very briefly, it has variables whose values are complex numbers, and you give a system of simultaneous equations sufficient to fix all the numbers. Then `conn` and `at` statements draw lines and place labels.

Figure 2: Graph of a compiler data structure

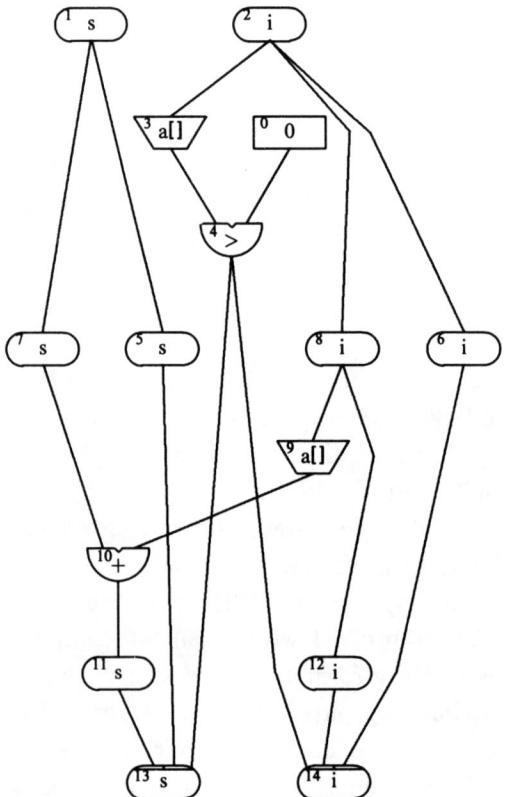

long edges; don't route edges so that they make long detours around other nodes; emphasize patterns in the connections; put certain nodes in "preferred positions" to emphasize their function (e.g., put nodes connected to the outside world on the boundary of the diagram; put "important" nodes in the center); maintain a consistent relation between edge direction and direction on the page (e.g., place nodes to make edges go top-to-bottom).

These rules conflict with each other, so one has to prioritize them. It is important to consider the type of graph to be drawn when deciding on the relative rule priorities. For graphs where the edges represent a precedence relation or the flow of some commodity, the consistent-edge-direction rule seems to be very important. For graphs where the edges are undirected, indicating a symmetrical relationship, it is often most useful to emphasize patterns in the graph. Graphs with big nodes need to be drawn in a way that saves space.

The most common graph drawing method emphasizes consistent edge directions (call this the *Barycentric DAG* method) [Carpano80, Gansner87, Majewski86, Robins87, Rowe87, Sugiyama81]:

1. Assign ranks to the nodes. A typical method: make a directed acyclic graph (DAG) out of the input graph by ignoring edges that lead back to places already seen during a search through the graph; then let the rank of a node be the greatest number of edges in a path from a source to that node. Then most edges go from a lower-rank node to a higher-rank one. Nodes will be put in horizontal rows, each row corresponding to a particular rank number, and the rows will be arranged top-to-bottom in increasing rank order.

2. Make all the edges go between two adjacent levels by adding *dummy* nodes to serve as intermediaries on edges that used to jump levels.

3. Assign subranks: order the nodes from left-to-right within each row, trying to make the estimated horizontal position near to that of nodes in rows above and below it. One way to do this is to sort based on the average position (*barycenter*) of nodes above and/or below. Several iterations of this give better results. The hope is that this ordering will cut down on the number of edge crossings in the final diagram.

4. Assign physical positions to nodes (the previous step just established the order); try to make dummy nodes line up so that long edges are straight.

This works reasonably well, but a person can often look at the results and say "why didn't it put this part of the graph over here, to avoid those crossings?", and the answer is that the algorithm doesn't know about the topology of the graph.

Woods [Woods82] designed a graph drawing algorithm that does know about the topology of the graph. It starts by finding a *planar embedding*—a way of drawing the graph on the plane so that edges don't cross. He assumes the graph is planar, so that this can be done. A planar embedding can be represented by listing the order of edges around each node, the edges bounding the *faces*, and identifying one face as the unbounded *outer face*. Woods uses a graph-theoretic concept known as (s, t)-numbering to assign nodes to levels. The key property of the assignment is that all nodes except those on the top and bottom levels are connected both to nodes above and nodes below them. This leads to an easy level-by-level algorithm for assigning subranks such that there are no edge crossings. A problem with Woods' method is that the graph tends to get spread out over many levels, violating the rule that says to keep connected nodes close to each other. He proposed some expensive postprocessing to make local improvements. Another problem is that edge directions can't be made consistently upwards or downwards.

Batini, Tamassia, Nardelli, and Talamo [Batini84a, Batini84b] also start by finding a planar embedding. They then find an *orthogonal graph*: a representation where all edges are sequences of horizontal and vertical segments. (Nodes have to be represented by more than one grid point to handle the case of more than four edges incident on a node.) A network flow problem is solved to find the angles within each face, minimizing the number of bends in edges, and then the edge's lengths are found by decomposing the faces into rectangles. Minimizing the number of bends in the edges does tend to keep connected nodes close to each other, so the results are better than those found by Woods' method. But again, edge directions are haphazard.

None of the references mentioned address two of the problems pertinent to illustration-quality graphs: users need to be able to specify ranks and subranks on occasion, and nodes can have different dimensions and have edges attached to particular points. It isn't too hard to extend the barycentric DAG method to allow for these things—it mainly involves recognizing that edges might go between nodes on the same level, and they might have to route around a node to its other side. A predecessor to Drag used that method, but the lack of topology knowledge appeared to be a stumbling block. As for the other methods, it seems impossible to add user-specified ranks to any them; furthermore, they all do poorly at drawing DAGs or almost-DAGs, where the consistent-edge-direction rule is very important.

Drag offers a choice of layout methods: a new *ranked planar* method, or a version of the Batini et al. *orthogonal minimum bend* method. The latter can only be used if there are no user-assigned ranks.

4. Drag Processing

Drag follows the procedure shown in Figure 3. After reading the input, Drag calls a text formatter (LaTeX or troff) to get exact measurements for all the labels. Then it calls IDEAL to get the dimensions and port positions of all the nodes. Next, one of two methods is applied to get a *layout*: an assignment of nodes to rows, the order of nodes within each row (including dummy nodes used to route edges that cross several levels), and the edge routing topology. Both methods make a planar embedding of the graph, a process that may end up discarding certain "crossing" edges; crossing edges are added after the main layout procedure. Finally, the nodes are given absolute positions, the

Figure 3: Drag processing steps

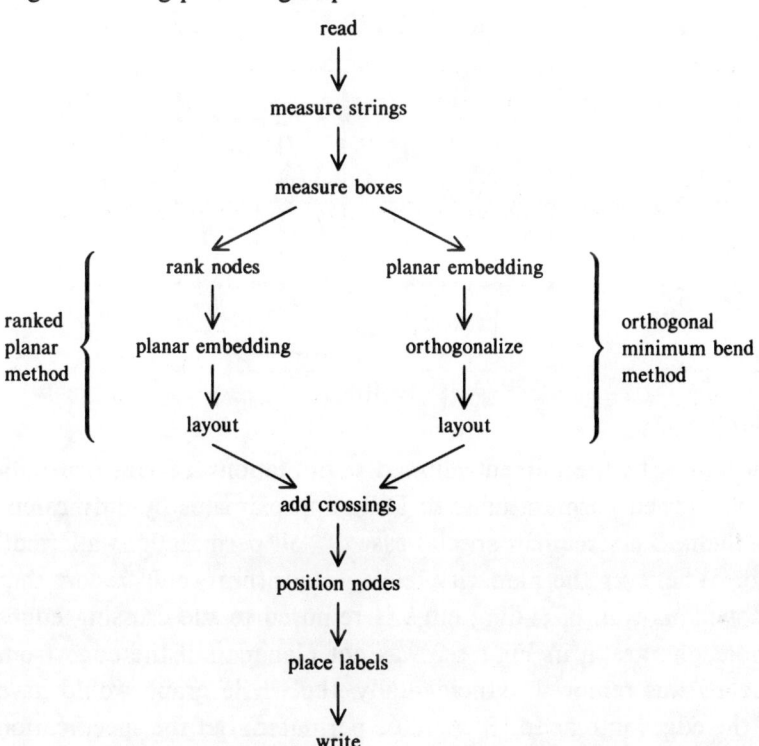

edge labels are placed, and the graph is written as an IDEAL program.

4.1. *Ranked Planar Layout Method*
If the user hasn't assigned ranks, Drag uses the scheme described in the barycentric DAG method: the rank is the longest path from a source to the node in an acyclic subgraph of the input graph. When the input edges aren't directed (the specification says `x--y` instead of `x->y`), it is often better to use the shortest path from a source, so that alternative is available.

The next step is to find a planar embedding for the graph. Drag uses a variant of an easy-to-implement planarity tester of Demoucron, Malgrange, and Pertuiset [Demoucron64]. Faster planarity testers are known, but this isn't the bottleneck in Drag. A complication is that we also want to avoid crossings near nodes due to the final routing to an attachment port. It is especially complicated since the user can give a choice of ports. Drag calculates a set of *allowed permutations* of edges around a node, and the planarity testing algorithm only says that a given edge can be attached within a given face

Figure 4: Two layouts with the same node ranks and subranks

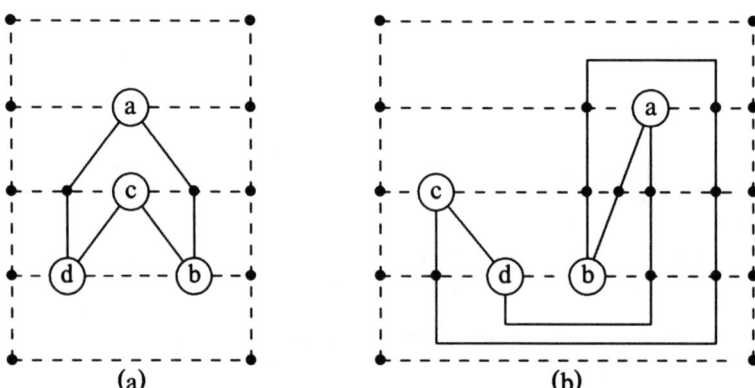

(a)　　　　　　　　　　　(b)

if that is consistent with the current allowed permutations. There can be a large number of allowed permutations, so Drag approximates by only calculating some of them. The frequent special case of "all permutations allowed" is handled also. Whenever the planarity testing algorithm would report that the graph is not planar, an offending edge is removed to the crossing edges set. For example, the graph in Figure 2 was not planar until the edge from node 9 to node 10 was removed. (Incidentally, the whole graph would have been planar if the edges into node 13 could be permuted, but the specification said no.)

The quality of the final layout varies greatly with the embedding chosen. Currently, the main heuristic used is: if there is a choice, make newly created faces as small as possible. This tends to avoid long edges that are stretched to fit around large pieces of graph inside a small face.

Given a planar embedding and a rank assignment, one might think that the rest of the layout process is easy; certainly, it should be easy if subranks are user-assigned, too—then we only need figure out the details of edge routing. But consider Figure 4, which gives two layouts for the same planar embedding of a graph with user-assigned ranks and subranks. Figure 4(a) is what Drag produces; Figure 4(b) was done by hand, but one wrong choice in the layout process could force that layout.

Drag regards a layout as a planar embedding of an extension of the original graph. The extended graph includes the dummy nodes (•'s) and dummy edges (dashed) of Figure 4, so that there is an *outer frame* which defines the ranks. Edges of the original graph get expanded into a sequence of edges, going through intermediate dummy nodes, so that the layout embedding has edges only between nodes on the same or adjacent ranks. Thus, this layout embedding has enough information to finish the drawing—all that remains is to fix the spacing between nodes of a given rank.

Layout starts with an empty frame, and then edges of the original graph of laid out, one by one. Nodes are *installed* by splitting a horizontal frame edge, and the first thing done is to install one node from each connected component of the original graph. Thereafter, an edge is either *connected* between two installed nodes, or *attached* to an installed node, causing the installation of the node at the other end.

Connecting is the easier case: the face of the original graph in which the connection is to be made corresponds to a group of faces in the layout embedding. Drag finds the shortest path through those faces, and routes the edge along that path, installing dummy nodes as it goes. For an attachment, a decision has to be made about where to install the new node along the rank where it is supposed to go, if the user hasn't already assigned subranks. Drag finds shortest paths to all suitable places, and uses the shortest of those. If there is a tie, Drag sometimes knows about an already-installed node that will eventually be connected to the new node, and the distance to that eventual destination can be used to break the tie. Attachments are easier if the edges are processed in a particular order: first Drag lays out a spanning tree, so that all the nodes get installed in the outer face. Then the rest of the edges follow the simpler connection case.

The orthogonal minimum bend layout method won't be discussed here, but it also results in a layout embedding.

Crossing edges are added to the layout embedding as follows: for each rank between the two end nodes, see if the there are two adjacent faces touching the rank, where the faces can be reached from the end nodes by crossing only dummy edges. The best of these pairs is chosen (based on the estimated horizontal position of the adjacent faces), and connections are made to new dummy nodes touching the faces. Finally, Drag remembers the new pair of dummy nodes so that it can connect them directly later on. A more complicated routing occurs if there are no suitable adjacent faces.

4.2. *Node Positioning*

Drag currently spends a large portion of its time deciding how much vertical space to put between rows, and how much horizontal space to put between nodes within rows. It makes sure that certain minimum distance requirements are met: node to node, node to edge (except where they touch), and edge to edge (except where they touch a common node port). After that, it may insert extra horizontal space to satisfy these criteria:

centering Nodes should be centered around a common connected node in the next or previous row (it's not clear whether dummy nodes should be included in this).

straightness Long edges (going through dummy nodes) should be straight rather than bending at every dummy node.

width The width of the graph shouldn't be too large.

It is often impossible to satisfy all of these simultaneously; Drag minimizes a weighted sum of deviations from the ideal. It does this by solving a linear program.

Unfortunately, the linear program can grow quite large. Drag cuts it down by forcing long edges to be straight, except at the dummy nodes adjacent to the two ends. Even so, performance was unacceptable for 50 node graphs until sparse matrix methods were employed.

Another aspect of node positioning involves the detailed routing of edges to the ports. If an edge approaches a node from the top, and it needs to attach to a port on the bottom, Drag allocates routing channels around the node. And edges between nodes in the same row are routed in horizontal channels between the rows. (The channels are allocated paying attention to an "endpoints-between" relation, to avoid or minimize crossings.) These node and row channels are taken into account when the minimum spacing rules are obeyed.

Edge labels can be positioned after nodes are placed. Drag keeps track of where labels have been placed already, so that it can avoid overlapping labels.

5. Implementation

Drag is a ten thousand line C++ program. It produced the graph parts of all the diagrams in this paper; Figures 5 and 6 are more examples. It runs in acceptable time for the kinds of graphs that fit on one page. For example, Figure 2 takes 11 seconds on a Sun 3. Fifty node graphs can take several minutes; Drag could use a less costly node placement algorithm for graphs above a certain size threshold.

Drag is still being improved. Among the planned enhancements: partitioning of large graphs into page-sized pieces, with cross references; an option to replace edges with short cross referencing arrows; an option to use splines instead of bent long edges; better final routing to ports.

Figure 5: A finite state machine example

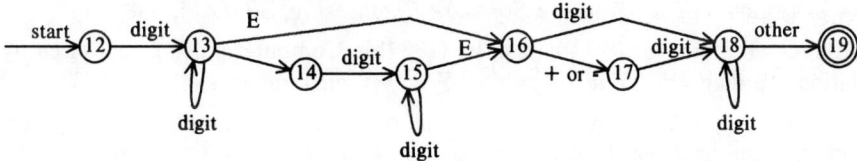

Figure 6: An example done by orthogonal minimum bend method

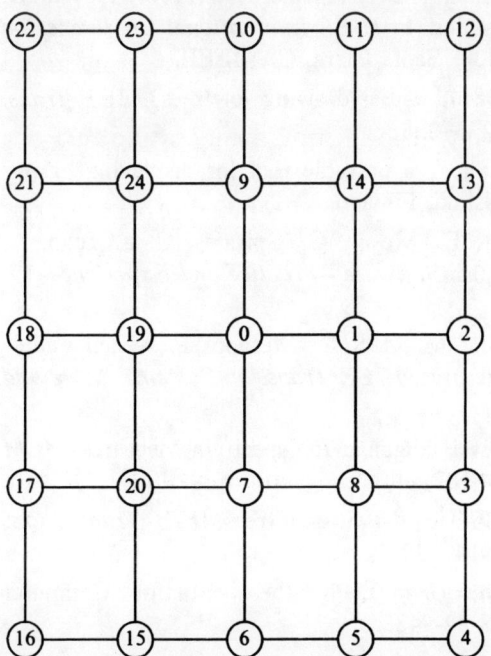

References

[1] Aho, A.V., Sethi, R. & Ullman, J.D. (1985). *Compilers: Principles, Techniques, and Tools*, Reading, MA: Addison-Wesley.

[2] Batini, C., Nardelli, E. & Tamassia, R. (1984a). A layout algorithm for data flow diagrams, *IEEE Trans. on Software Engineering*, **SE-12**, 4, 538–546.

[3] Batini, C., Talamo, M. & Tamassia, R. (1984b). Computer aided layout of entity relationship diagrams, *The Journal of Systems and Software*, **4**, 163–173.

[4] Carpano, M.-J. (1980). Automatic display of hierarchical graphs for computer-aided decision analysis, *IEEE Trans. on Systems, Man, and Cybernetics*, **SMC-10**, 11, 705–715.

[5] Demoucron, G., Malgrange, Y. & Pertuiset, R. (1964). Graphes planaires: reconnaissance et construction de représentations planaires topologiques, *Rev. Francaise Recherche Opérationnelle*, **8**, 33–47.

[6] Gansner, E.R., North, S.C. & Vo, K.P. (1987). DAG—A program that draws directed graphs. AT&T Bell Laboratories Technical Memorandum.

[7] Lamport, L. (1986). LaTeX: *A Document Preparation System*, Reading, MA: Addison-Wesley.

[8] Majewski, M.A., Krull, F.N., Fuhrman, T.E. & Ainslie, P.J. (1986). Autodraft: automatic synthesis of circuit schematics. In *IEEE International Conference on Computer-Aided Design*, pp. 435–438. Santa Clara, CA: IEEE.

[9] Reingold, E.M. & Tilford, J.S. (1981). Tidier drawings of trees, *IEEE Trans. on Software Engineering*, **SE-7**, 2, 223–228.

[10] Robins, G. (1987). The ISI Grapher: a portable tool for displaying graphs pictorially. In *Symboliikka '87*. Helsinki, Finland.

[11] Rowe, L.A., Davis, M., Messinger, E., Meyer, C., Spirakis, C. & Tuan, A. (1987). A browser for directed graphs, *Software—Practice and Experience*, **17**, 1, 61–76.

[12] Sugiyama, K., Tagawa, W. & Toda, M. (1981). Methods for visual understanding of hierarchical system structures, *IEEE Trans. on Systems, Man, and Cybernetics*, **SMC-11**, 109–125.

[13] Van Wyk, C.J. (1982). A high-level language for specifying pictures, *ACM Transactions on Graphics*, **1**, 2, 163–182.

[14] Wetherell, C. & Shannon, A. (1979). Tidy drawings of trees, *IEEE Transactions on Software Engineering*, **SE-5**, 5, 514–520.

[15] Woods, D.R. (1982). *Drawing Planar Graphs*, PhD thesis. Stanford Computer Science Technical Report STAN-CS-82-943.

HYPERTEXT: THE WAY FORWARD

P. J. BROWN

Computing Laboratory, University of Kent at Canterbury

ABSTRACT
Hypertext is currently a popular area of endeavour, but only a relatively small number of application domains have been successfully pioneered. This paper outlines the areas where further research and development are vital if hypertext is to realize its full potential.

1. Introduction

Hypertext has the potential to revolutionise the way we present information to on-line users. Although the ideas behind it are relatively old [Bush45], only recently has the necessary hardware and software been sufficiently accessible to allow hypertext to be used widely.

Over the past year there has been an explosion in the number of people using hypertext, and a corresponding explosion in the number of experts pontificating about it. Nevertheless the subject is still in its infancy, and is arguably in the same state as programming languages in the fifties — an analogy that will be frequently used in this paper. The potential is there, but we still do not know how much of that potential will be realised. In this paper I discuss nine areas where research and development need to be done. The success or otherwise of this work will, I believe, determine whether hypertext becomes, on the one hand, an all-pervasive discipline or, on the other, a moderately interesting backwater.

2. The 'Hypertext 87' workshop

In November 1987 the first international gathering of hypertext practitioners took place, at the *Hypertext 87* workshop at Chapel Hill, N.C.. Being the first such event, it attracted great enthusiasm, and almost all the important figures in the field were there.

The proceedings of the workshop represent, to a first approximation, the current state-of-the-art in hypertext, and I have used the material heavily in this paper. In particular I have made a lot of use of ideas that came out of van Dam's keynote address (which is not included in the printed proceedings given out at the workshop, and therefore cannot be directly cited), and the seven issues proposed in Halasz's paper.

3. Integration

One of the shortest yet most powerful contributions to Hypertext 87 came from Meyrowitz [Meyrowitz87]. His views are well explained by an imaginary scenario.

Assume that in, say, the Macintosh environment there is no cut-and-paste paradigm. Instead there is a special tool, MacMove say, which is devoted to this function. To use MacMove, users have to convert their files to a special MacMove format. MacMove can then be employed to do the necessary cutting and pasting. Having done this work, the user saves the output from MacMove and then converts this back to its original format, so it can be used by the original tool again.

If this scenario represented the real Macintosh approach to cut-and-paste, then all the blood would have been drained out of the facility.

Unfortunately the scenario exactly corresponds to what we are doing with hypertext systems. They are typically closed worlds, with special techniques for importing and exporting files. Once imported, material is often emaciated, e.g. you might be able to import a picture created by tool X but, once imported, you cannot then call tool X on the fly to change the picture.

Not only are users unable to interact dynamically between hypertext systems and the rest of the computing environment, but, once they have created a hypertext corpus (I use the word *corpus* to mean a set of interlinked hypertext documents), they can frequently only use it with the system that created it. They cannot feed the information to another hypertext system, nor can they apply other tools — for example a style checker/corrector, a language translator, or an 'expert system' information filter — which would add value to the corpus.

Perhaps even more challenging than integrating with other systems is integrating with other paradigms. A good example of this is the Find command. Most computer users are familiar with using the Find command to search through linear text, and thus they expect a similar facility in a hypertext system. It is, indeed, easy to implement a Find command within a hypertext system — badly. To do it well, so that the user knows *what* he is searching and understands *how* he is moving round the hypertext corpus, is a real challenge [Halasz87], [Brown88].

Such problems are, of course, germane to any new discipline, and, at the technical level, one can argue endlessly about whether standards are necessary or premature. Nevertheless it is high time for a change of approach from those of us who design hypertext systems: instead of expecting the world to change to meet our needs, we must adapt to meet the needs of the world.

4. Quality of authorship

The second area is concerned with training people. Consider the evolution of computer software manuals prepared using traditional means and printed on paper. For the first twenty years the standard of these was truly appalling. Only in the last ten years have authors learned how to produce these manuals well, and the standard is now quite high (though appalling manuals have not been eliminated). The art of writing these manuals is not greatly different from the art of writing other manuals, yet it took us twenty years to master it.

Hypertext documents are hugely different from paper documents, and it is totally unrealistic to expect authors immediately to master the art of hypertext writing. We know from the field of electronic publishing that providing the tools is not enough; it just allows amateurs to do really ghastly things. Fortunately, in electronic publishing, there already exist professional designers, and their layout skills carry over to the new technology. There is thus a counterweight to the over-enthusiastic amateurs, and a goal for which these amateurs can strive.

In hypertext we just have the tools, but no professional designers. Current hypertext documents are nearly all the works of enthusiastic amateurs. Many of them are indeed truly ghastly. Unfortunately, although one glance at the work of an amateur let loose on an electronic publishing system will give an impression of its quality, this is not true of a hypertext document. One needs to waste a good deal of time trying to use a document before the quality of authorship becomes obvious.

Although this can be regarded as a problem that will take years to solve, it can be turned around and regarded as an asset: even the poorly written hypertext documents that we are producing now have found some success; just think of the success awaiting well-written hypertext documents.

5. Finding higher-level abstractions

Following on from the previous area, it is not even true that we provide authors with the best tools. What current hypertext systems do is to provide a means of connecting material together with goto's. It is the equivalent of a programmer being provided only with assembly language. We need to look at higher-level abstractions. Engelbart has proposed that hypertext documents should have a *hypergrammar* to define their structure. This is akin to the grammar of a natural language, which restricts the form of sentences and thus helps readers, once they are familiar with the grammar, to understand the material.

It is possible that the search for good higher-level abstractions will fail. There is a feeling that the nature of information itself is such that it is full of spaghetti-like links; hence if hypertext represents such information the spaghetti will be inherent. Nevertheless, as Brooks [Brooks87] has pointed out, a talent of a good author is that he can simplify material by cutting links so that the information appears more coherent; thus higher-level abstractions should at least help to present the simplified view, even if the complete view needs to descend to the spaghetti level.

6. Catering for change

In the life-cycle of a program, the cost of maintenance dwarfs all other costs. The same doubtless applies to hypertext documents. Indeed in the current state of development the maintenance costs will be even higher because of two of the problems cited earlier:
- we are using low-level abstractions ('writing in assembly-language').
- we are inexperienced, and thus our efforts will require a lot of change over the years.

Cost of maintenance depends critically on two issues. Firstly it depends on how well the maintenance staff can understand the authors' original intentions — both at the 'grand-design' level and at the detailed level. We know next to nothing about documenting the design of a hypertext corpus, and will need to start with informal methods, using words and diagrams. To produce documentation at the detailed level, authors should be able to annotate *links*, as distinct from the material that the links connect. Thoth-II [Collier87] is a system that is specially good in this respect; its underlying philosophy is: 'Every link has a reason, and that reason should be recorded by the author in a commentary that is attached to the link'.

The second issue arises when the maintenance staff have understood the original material and have formulated the changes they need to make. If these changes are merely in the text this is easy, and it is relatively easy for other media (like most authors, I use the word 'hypertext' to encompass hypermedia). It becomes difficult, though, when changes in the hypertext structure are needed — as they usually will be. Direct manipulation of the structure is probably easiest to understand, but few current systems support this. Indeed many of them give authors no feel for what they are doing, and drastically wrong changes are all too easy to make.

Maintenance also brings with it a third issue: version control. Currently many hypertext systems provide no facilities for this, relying instead on the availability of general-purpose version control tools. These general-purpose tools may not cater for such topics as different versions of links, and thus hypertext systems may need to include their own version control mechanisms. A leader in this is the HAM abstract machine for the Neptune system [Campbell87].

7. Testing and validation

All too often, when reading a hypertext document, you try to follow a link and get an error message because the author has forgotten to define the destination of the link. Alternatively the link may lead to a 'stub' where the author has written 'I will fill this in later', but has forgotten to do so.

The most common reason why such errors creep in is that the author has no tools for testing and validation of a hypertext document. There is also a lack of searching tools, even for simple searches such as 'Find everything that links to this point'. Such tools are specially valuable when the author changes a document, and for general maintenance. Indeed tools for testing and validation are probably even more necessary for 'maintenance releases' of a document than for the original.

8. Big systems

To take a further analogy with programming, it took us a long time to learn that programming in the large is different from programming in the small. The corresponding lessons for hypertext are still to be learned, since every current hypertext corpus is at best of a medium size. (Document Examiner [Walker87], Augment [Engelbart84], and the applications of Guide in the motor industry are examples of some of the bigger ones now available.)

Many people, including Nelson [Nelson80], the great hypertext pioneer, dream of linking all the world's knowledge in one massive hypertext corpus. There are immense problems to be solved before this is achievable.

9. Collaborative authorship

A popular application of hypertext is in areas where documents have multiple authors, who may be working simultaneously. This will obviously arise in large projects but can also arise in small ones.

An example of the latter would be a policy document which is circulated (in hypertext form) to a group of people to add their own annotation, supporting or criticising the original — or even refuting someone else's annotation. There are problems here with integrity of the hypertext corpus, but these problems have been tackled in other areas and may be quite tractable. More serious, perhaps, are the problems of presenting a mass of arguments and counter-arguments to the reader in a coherent way.

10. Navigation

Perhaps the most common complaint made by people using current hypertext systems is that they 'get lost'. This applies both to readers, who are simply seeking some information, and to authors, who need to be aware of the underlying structures.

The term 'getting lost' is a catch-all for several sub-problems. It can mean:
(a) the reader does not understand the travelling facilities of the hypertext tool.
(b) the reader does not understand the way the author has modelled the information (e.g. how he has defined the hierarchy — if there is one — and how this is augmented by additional links). Either the reader has a different model or no perception at all of what the model is. (Similarly,

this can apply even to an author that is looking at his own material, written a few months previously.)
(c) getting lost in the same way as one gets lost in a road system, e.g. taking a wrong turning, then taking several subsequent turnings, and, when one finally realises something is wrong, not knowing where to go back to.

These are undoubtedly real problems, but their importance can be exaggerated. When we try to master a new body of knowledge by reading books we often get lost too — though lost in different ways to those described above. It is unrealistic to expect a novice to move easily round a new body of knowledge, even if presented by a talented author using the optimum medium.

Indeed hypertext systems offer many advantages over books, for example:
- easy backtracking to each previous decision point — most systems allow you to leave a trail of orange peel.
- showing a map of where you are (e.g. as in Thoth-II or IDG [Feiner81]).

The current problems with hypertext users getting lost are probably more to do with the inexperience of authors than with inherent difficulties. Though the problems of navigation are a challenge, they are not, I think, the most important ones facing us, and that is why I have delayed their discussion until towards the end of this paper.

11. Real costed projects

I will end with an area that is of undoubted concern to us all: the question of economics. There is a dearth of real applications of hypertext that have been properly costed so that their value can be judged. Given this lack, the cynics continue to mock the 'hype' in hypertext. (This is, perhaps, an unfortunate property of the word 'hypertext'; if expert systems had been termed 'hyperexpertise' or 'con ...', then the jibes would be easy there too.)

Costs of authorship are a serious issue. In the field of CAI, for instance, many promising projects have been killed by the empirical law that it takes 100 hours of an author's time to produce one hour of material. There are few, if any, published analyses of the authorship cost of hypertext documents, but it is likely that the 100 to 1 factor still applies, at least in 'browsing' applications where the task of the author is to present information in a good form for readers to peruse. Indeed if a project entails preparing and integrating material in diverse media then the ratio may be 1000 to 1. Moreover the costs of maintenance come on top of the original authorship costs, and will eventually dwarf them.

To justify the costs we need to measure the benefits. Here we have some evidence that users prefer hypertext documents to paper ones, at least for complex tasks. Shneiderman [Shneiderman87] is a great pioneer and evangelist for such experiments. Walker supplements this with empirical evidence: when users had their computer documentation available in an on-line hypertext form, the corresponding paper documentation was often left in its packing-case.

Such positive evidence is doubly encouraging (even though there is doubtless much negative evidence to match it), given the current rudimentary state of authorship, but we have little idea of the economies of scale that will be needed to justify production costs. What will be the cost of 'stackware' aimed at a small market of, say, 1000 potential buyers, and will buyers be willing to pay?

12. Summary and conclusions

The nine areas outlined have been: integration, quality of authorship, higher-level abstractions, catering for change, testing and validation, big systems, collaborative authorship, navigation, and real costed projects. All provide opportunities for challenging research projects, and anyone with ability in software or in communicating information can contribute. Few if any of the areas lend themselves to dramatic 'solutions'. Instead we must hope for steady progress, each step extending the viability of hypertext by a small amount. It is much better to see such steady advance than to have hypertext as a fashionable research area where huge numbers of researchers suddenly rush in and then, equally suddenly, rush out again, leaving nothing behind but their extravagant claims.

13. Acknowledgements

I have cited several individual papers that have contributed to plotting the likely future of hypertext. I am also grateful to numerous individuals who, mainly by questions and discussion at the Hypertext 87 workshop, have helped refine my knowledge and appreciation.

14. References

[1] Brooks, F.P., Jr. (1987). After-dinner speech, *Hypertext 87*.

[2] Brown, P.J. (1988). Linking and searching within hypertext, *Electronic Publishing — Origination, Dissemination and Design*, **1**, *1*.

[3] Bush, V. (1945). As we may think. Atlantic Monthly, **176** 1, pp.101-108.

[4] Campbell, B. & Goodman, J.M. (1987). HAM: a general purpose hypertext abstract machine, *Hypertext 87*, pp.21-32.

[5] Collier, G.H. (1987). Thoth-II: hypertext with explicit semantics, *Hypertext 87*, pp.269-290.

[6] Engelbart, D.C. (1984). Authorship provisions in Augment, *IEEE 1984 COMPCON Proceedings*, pp.465-471.

[7] Feiner, S., Nagy, S. & van Dam, A. (1981). An integrated system for creating and presenting complex computer-based documents, *Computer Graphics*, **15**, 3, pp.181-189.

[8] Halasz, F.G. (1987). Reflections on NoteCards: seven issues for the next generation of hypertext systems, *Hypertext 87*, pp.345-366.

[9] Meyrowitz, N. (1987). The missing link: why we're all doing hypertext wrong, position paper, *Hypertext 87*.

[10]Nelson, T.H. (1980). Replacing the printed word: a complete literary system, in *Information Processing 80*, pp.1013-1023.

[11]Shneiderman, B. (1987). *Designing the User Interface*, Reading, Mass.: Addison-Wesley.

[12]Walker, J.H. (1987). Document Examiner: delivery system for hypertext documents, *Hypertext 87*, pp.307-324.

ABSTRACTION AND INTEGRATION IN IDE, AN EDITING AND FORMATTING ENVIRONMENT

MATTHEW KAPLAN

Department of Computer Science, Brown University

ABSTRACT

Recent interactive document preparation systems can be divided into two groups. One of these supports complex structured documents that combine text and graphics. These systems emphasize *abstraction* in the user interface and support only partial formatting during editing. The other group concentrates on displaying accurate facsimiles of page images during editing. These systems have placed restrictions either on complexity of the document's logical structure, or on graphical complexity. Thus, they emphasize *integration*, at some expense of generality. This paper describes IDE, an editor/formatter that displays a printable facsimile at all times, yet also supports a high degree of structural complexity and the ability to mix text and graphics. This paper discusses how IDE mediates the conflicting demands of abstraction and integration in its user interface.

1. Introduction

In recent years, automated assistance for document preparation has diversified. We now have batch formatters that can turn document content, including text, tables, equations, line drawings, and charts and graphs into correspondingly complex page formats. There are also structured document editors that can properly represent the structures of text and other content, which can simplify editing and formatting [Furuta86] WYSIWYG editor/formatters such as Interleaf [Interleaf87] simplify creation of documents containing graphics, which are most effectively produced when the user sees an exact representation of the formatted document during editing.

However, we lack comprehensive systems that combine the advantages of all these systems and thus allow interactive composition, examination, and display of documents containing several kinds of text and graphics. This paper presents an overview of IDE (Interactive Document Environment), a prototype interactive editor/formatter that allows structured text and graphics to be created and combined within formatted pages. In IDE content is edited abstractly, though users have accurate graphical feedback at all times.

The next section defines abstraction and integration, two important properties that characterize our system. Section 3 describes IDE's capabilities with respect to previous systems. Section 4 explains how editing structured multimedia content is simplified by incorporating abstraction into our user interface. Section 5 summarizes IDE's capabilities, and section 6 discusses the system's organization, and explains how programmers can extend IDE to edit and format use new kinds of content.

2. Abstraction and Integration

As we use it in this paper, *abstraction* is the temporary removal of irrelevant information from an object, for the purpose of focusing attention on more relevant aspects. The temporary nature of abstraction implies an inverse: *integration*. Integration is the combination of different pieces of information to produce a coordinated whole. In different phases of editing, context takes on differing importance. Thus, abstraction should be applied when context is distracting, while integration is necessary at other times. IDE's user interface supplies two kinds of paired abstraction-integration facilities: style separation and zooming.

(a) *Style separation / automatic reformatting.* Users edit abstract content, i.e. content that has not yet been formatted. The concrete content is derived from abstract, editable content by automatically formatting after each edit. Thus, users are temporarily shielded from graphical details during editing, but these details are available for inspection whenever desired.

(b) *Zoom in / zoom out.* To minimize clutter on the screen, content editors display only one level of detail by substituting placeholders for detailed content. For example, the table editor displays table entries as labeled gray rectangles, abstracting their contents. The user can zoom in on abstracted content by clicking on its placeholder in an editor, or by clicking on its formatted version. In either case, an editor is activated for the abstracted content, which can then be examined and changed. This ability to expand hidden content, moving between abstract editors for different kinds of content, is a form of integration.

Let's see how these techniques apply in figure 1, a typical IDE screen. On the right is an abstract table editor; the left shows a page containing the formatted table. (a) Removing or adding an entry to the abstract table immediately causes the formatted table to be updated to show the current table contents. (b) Clicking on the entry labeled **Margin Note** replaces the table editor by an editor for that diagram. The same effect is achieved by clicking over the formatted table entry on the left.

3. Relation to Previous Systems

Recent multimedia editor/formatters have limited ability to represent and display non-standard layout and content. Interleaf, for example, concentrates on conventional technical and office reports. More general page layout was made available in Janus [Chamberlin82], but with limited success; text is restricted to full- or half-page width in that system, and laid-out pages are displayed inaccurately during editing. Also, Janus is text-oriented: graphics must be produced outside the system and pasted into holes left in a Janus layout.

Editor/formatters that use a batch text formatter as a back-end formatting engine, e.g. [Furuta86], don't integrate the editing and formatting phases, an important capability when graphics and text are to be used together. Interactive systems without page layout, such as Tioga [Teitelman85] and Grif [Quint86] suffer from this problem to a lesser degree: line breaking and typographic style are well integrated with editing, but pagination is a batch process.

In IDE, users can edit different kinds of content (text, tables, diagrams) without leaving the system. We provide easy-to-use page layout tools that don't restrict text width. Furthermore, we display an accurate rendition of the formatted document during editing.

4. Abstract Editing and Concrete Viewing

IDE's uses a two-pane screen format, with different parts of the display dedicated to editing and to viewing. In this section we explain why we chose this approach over the more intuitive WYSIWYG paradigm of directly editing the formatted representation of the document.

In structured documents supported by IDE the information displayed in a concrete text and the information contained in an abstract one are not equivalent. For example, formatting replaces the logical structure of text by the formatted structure of graphically nested pages, blocks, lines, etc. Style-dependent format information is present in the formatted content but absent from the abstract content. In some kinds of graphics, as well, concrete and abstract content differ. For example, in an editor for parametrized surfaces (not implemented in our prototype) users would edit by changing the abstract parametrized equations, although shaded images would be displayed. Internally, IDE represents the substantially

Figure 1: *formatted table and table editor*

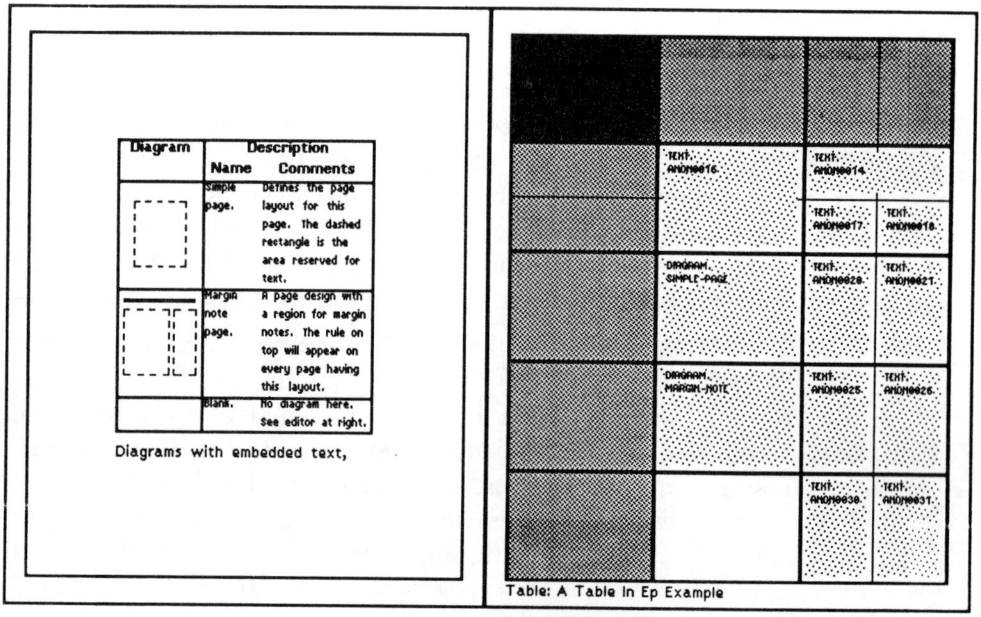

different abstract and concrete forms of document content separately.

To avoid losing content by overwriting it during reformatting, all document content present in or derivable from the abstract representation. Thus abstract editing is simplest for the system. It is often more convenient for the user too, since formatting constraints tailored to printed matter can be inappropriate on interactive displays. For example, structured text editors often allow users to hide the text of irrelevant sections when editing so that screen space is used most effectively. A concrete editing paradigm in which the editor displays content in printable form prohibits this.

An abstract editing paradigm without a concrete (i.e. exact-representation) display, as is used in tnt, is appropriate as long as the displayed content is immediately recognizable. But when abstract and formatted representations differ substantially, combining abstract editing with concrete viewing is much more effective; in the example above, users would want to see the rendered parametrized surface, in addition to the equations.

Even with text, concrete editing could mislead the user by suggesting that all concrete aspects of the document can be edited. For example, a user would rightly expect a concrete editor to provide functions such as "loosen the leading between these two lines." When style and content are separated, this request is ambiguous since leading, capitalization, and various other appearance properties are determined by combining of abstract content (e.g. letters in words), abstract structure (e.g. location of sentence or paragraph breaks) and formatting style. Which, or what combination, of these three should the system change to loosen the leading? Abstract editing eliminates this ambiguity by allowing users to edit structured content or style but not the formatted document.

5. Prototype Summary

This section overviews our abstract content editors. Section 5.1 makes some general remarks about our representation. Section 5.2 summarizes style and logical-structuring facilities. Sections 5.3 through 5.5 briefly describe our editors for text, tables, and diagrams.

We first define the scope of our implementation. IDE is a substantial prototype, written in object-oriented Lisp on a Symbolics Lisp Machine. Our goals were the ability to edit an open-ended class of text and graphics, with accurate interactive feedback from the system. IDE was constructed to help evaluate representations and formatting techniques needed to achieve these goals, thus we stressed generality and assigned secondary importance to ease-of-use. Our current prototype does not produce hard-copy; incompatibility of available screen and laser-printer fonts precluded a simple solution to this important problem. Although this limits the usability of our prototype, we preferred to await the availability of printer-compatible screen bitmaps than to devise ad hoc solutions. Similarly, the content editors described in this section are underdeveloped. Concentrating on generality in our content representations and user-interface paradigms, we have placed less emphasis on details such as command set and display format in abstract content editors. As we discuss in section 6, IDE's design supports programmer extension, so further development of our editors will be straightforward.

5.1. Mixing and Nesting Abstract Content

We consider all kinds of content to be equally important, and allow different kinds of content to be composed in similar ways. Our prototype supports three kinds of content: structured *text*, *tables* and *diagrams*, (line drawings). We generally allow different kinds of content to be used interchangeably. For example, our text editor can insert not only words, but also diagrams and tables (both inline and page-width). Similarly, a table entry can be a text, a table or a diagram, text, tables and diagrams can be placed anywhere within a diagram. Internally, we do this using an abstract representation similar to tnt's.

Like tables and diagrams, which can have several independent formatted texts in them, IDE documents can contain multiple independent streams of text and graphics. For example, bilingual or magazine formats, where several different texts are printed on one page, can be created in our prototype. Users define page layout by creating page designs (sketches of laid-out pages) with IDE's diagram editor, and declaring each text stream to appear in a certain text region defined in the page design. Multiple streams can also be dependent, i.e. derived from and positioned with respect to a larger text. Footnotes and margin notes are implemented as dependent multiple streams.

We also support shared content. For example, a single (abstract) table or diagram can be incorporated into several texts or used several places in a single text. Similarly, parts of a text may be excerpted and used elsewhere, in summaries, indices, or other texts.

5.2. Style and Structure

There are three ways to change the document: by creating or editing abstract *content*, by changing the *logical structure* of abstract content, or by changing the formatting *style*. Changes to content, structure, and style can all be performed interactively without leaving the system. Before surveying content editing, we discuss style and logical structure.

Style

Our style mechanism is similar to that of other recent formatters. Associated with units of abstract content are *tags*, which are used to select *style rules* when formatting. Style rules tell the formatter what graphical conventions to use when deriving a concrete formatted object from a unit of abstract content. Among the properties controlled by style rules are font and page layout for text, and column-widths for tables.[1]

Some tags are assigned explicitly by the user. For example, names in a text could be marked with a proper name tag that would set off a

---

[1] Format specifications for diagrams have described in [Beach83]. Though incorporating diagram style into IDE presents no unusual design or implementation difficulties, we have neglected this feature to trim the implementation effort.

style rule indicating capitalization. Other tags are automatically derived from text structure. For example, the first word in a sentence is automatically given a `start of sentence` tag, which sets off a different style rule to cause capitalization. Tags are inherited (through the logical hierarchy in text, from rows and columns in tables) and applicable style rules are selected by arbitrary predicates on presence and absence of tags at nodes. Thus, style rules take the form

tag predicate → *format parameter assignments* .

For example, the first word of each chapter would be set in uppercase through the action of the following:

`start of chapter` ∧ `start of sentence` → `CAPITALIZATION=UPPERCASE` .

This says that words inheriting the two tags on the left-hand side should be formatted in uppercase. These two automatically-generated tags are inherited only by the first word of the first sentence in each chapter. CAPITALIZATION is one of a fixed set of *formatting parameters* used by the text formatter, and UPPERCASE is one of a fixed set of values that CAPITALIZATION can take. The set of format parameters varies with content type. For example, tables do not use CAPITALIZATION, but do use a RULE WEIGHT parameter not applicable to text. The list of applicable formatting parameters, and the possible values, are defined as part of the formatter for a particular kind of content. Thus, while users can change the values assigned to formatting parameters by editing style rules with a menu-based interface, the set of available parameters can only be changed by modifying the formatting method (see section 6).

Structure

The logical structure of text is defined by a context-free grammar that users can edit with a menu-based interface. By combining user-defined text structure with corresponding style rules, non-standard formats, e.g. for program code or recipes, can be produced. As described in section 5.4, table structure, (i.e. number of rows and columns, etc.) can also be defined by users. Diagrams in our prototype are hierarchically structured, but may have any number of elements, of any type. A more complete abstract diagram representation would allow structure to be defined. For example, cartoons in newspapers might have a fixed four-frame horizontal structure.

5.3. Text Editing

IDE's text editor lets the user create texts conforming to the hierarchical text structure. The usual structure editor operations are allowed. An internal node with unfilled fields can be *expanded*. For example, a `recipe` node might expand into two other internal nodes: `ingredients list` and `instruction list`. Nodes can be *inserted* before or after some other node, or *deleted, split* or adjacent nodes *joined* if this does not cause logical structure to be violated. Users can also delete a contiguous region of text, or insert a list of words. The focus can be moved between levels in the hierarchy. For example, node operations can apply to words, paragraphs, or chapters. As discussed above, there is also an operation to explicitly associate a *tag* with a text node.

There are a few less typical operations. Regions in a text can be *excerpted*. Excerpted text can be inserted into a table, diagram or text like an independently defined text. Nodes can also be *annotated* with another text. In the abstract display, annotated nodes are marked by an asterisk. Users zoom in on the abstracted annotations to inspect or change them. Depending on the tags attached to an annotation, it will be formatted as a footnote or a margin note.

5.4. Table Editing

A single hierarchical structure for tables is insufficient, since entries are organized both vertically within a row, and horizontally within a column. It is important to capture the row-column structure of tables, so that operations such as exchanging rows or transposing rows and columns don't require complex transformations of the table data structures. However, tables can't be structured as a simple two-dimensional array of table entries because of complications arising from spanning headers and entries. Beach [Beach86] discusses table formatting in greater detail.

We use a pair of two-level hierarchies to represent the row and column structures in abstract, unformatted tables. One of these hierarchies divides the table's height between its rows; each row is subdivided into sections. The second hierarchy structures columns analogously: for brevity, when we use "row" in the following, the corresponding statement on columns is implied.

Table contents are represented as a set of *entries*. An entry specifies where a unit of abstract content (a text, a table, or a diagram) is to be placed in the table, i.e. which row and which subdivisions of the row the entry occupies. No entry can cross a row or column division.

However, entries can freely span subdivisions of rows or columns.

Table structure defines the kinds of rows in the table and the number of subdivisions in each kind of row. For example, the table shown in figure 1 has two kinds of rows: a single `header` row followed by some number of `content` rows. The `header` is subdivided into two parts: the main heading contains the word, **Description**, with subheadings, **Name** and **Comments**. The **Diagram** label spans the two subdivisions. Unlike the `header` rows, `content` rows aren't vertically subdivided. The column structure has a single `diagram` column on the left, and a single `description` column on the right. The `diagram` column is not subdivided, while the `description` is divided in two. Table style determines the relative widths of columns, and the position and weight of vertical and horizontal rules.

In the abstract table editor at the right of figure 1, the thick lines separate rows and columns while thin lines separate their subdivisions. The labeled light gray rectangles represent table entries and the white rectangle represents unused table space. The dark gray areas at the top and left are used to select rows and columns with the mouse. Users can *delete* entries selected with the mouse, or *insert* new entries into the table, using the mouse to select the regions these entries will occupy. New *rows* of a given kind can be *inserted* or *deleted*. Other operations, e.g. for exchanging rows and transposing rows and columns, were left out of our prototype, but could be added without great difficulty.

5.5. Diagram Editing

Diagrams are rectangular regions that can contain entries: either primitive diagram elements such as circles or rectangles, or other diagrams, texts and tables. The diagram formatter positions entries by aligning their sides to arbitrarily spaced horizontal or vertical *gridlines* organized into *grids*. Thus, grids define position and dimensions of diagram entries. Operations are available to define grid-aligned *regions* of a diagram and to select units of abstract content to *fill* these regions. A diagram editor window is shown in figure 2. The dashed rectangles represent unfilled regions, the labeled gray rectangles are entries (i.e. filled regions). Grid lines are normally invisible, as in figure 2, but are displayed while defining regions and editing gridline spacing.

6. Representation, Adaptation and Extension

In this section we briefly discuss the mechanisms that permit interactive response and extensibility. Details omitted from this brief overview are

Figure 2: *the diagram editor*

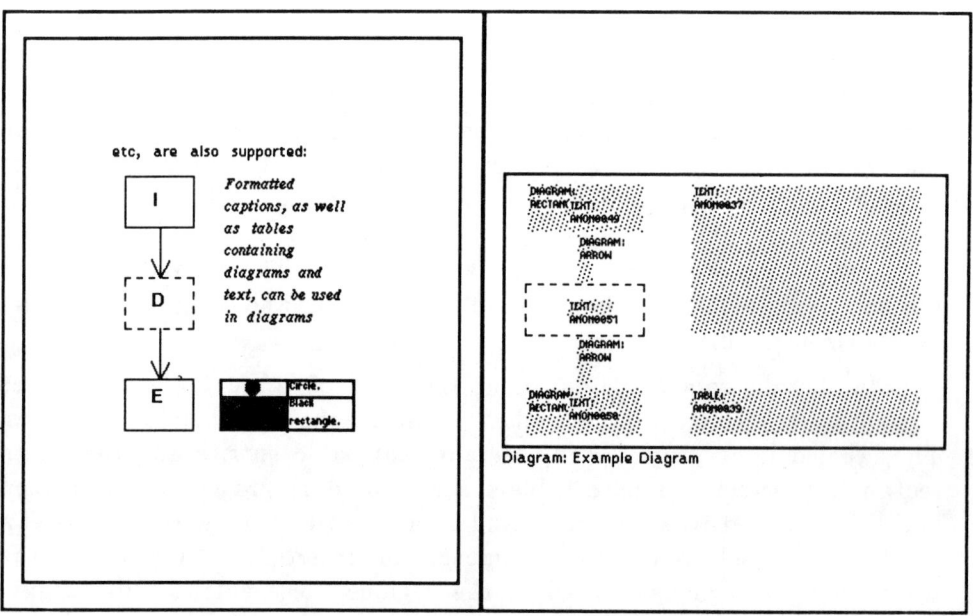

given in [Kaplan88] We use an object-oriented model for document content. For each kind of content (e.g. text, table, and diagram) two object classes are defined, to represent the abstract and concrete contents. The abstract class must implement the editor operations and a formatting method, which yields the corresponding concrete object.

The document remains properly formatted through the action of our *consistency-maintenance* control paradigm. Each object has a *consistency condition* and a *local adaptation* method. Consistency conditions are predicates that evaluate whether an object is well-formed; for example, a table's consistency condition requires that the entry heights match the row height. If an object is ill-formed, applying local adaptation will correct the situation locally, though this may disrupt consistency of another object; e.g. if the table grows to accommodate a taller entry, page layout could be affected. Thus, changes propagate from object to object. The objects to which propagation can occur are identified by explicit dependency links attached to each object. Most dependencies either point from a part to a whole concrete object (e.g. from table entry to table) or from an unformatted object to the corresponding formatted object. The first kind control reformatting when an object in a composed layout changes size, while the second kind insure that the concrete view accurately represents the abstract content.

Two properties of this representation and adaptation model support *extensibility* of IDE by system programmers. First, objects can have arbitrary internal representation and formatting behavior. Secondly, consistency conditions and adaptation make use of only local state and externally-visible properties of objects they depend on, so adding a new kind of content does not require changing existing object classes. Thus, a new kind of content can be added to the system by defining abstract and concrete representations, and supplying code for the editing and formatting methods.

Consistency maintenance causes adaptation only in those objects that require it, and is thus incremental. However reformatting can still be slow if local adaptation methods are expensive. Since text changes are usually small, even when the text itself is long, we save much time by using an incremental reformatting algorithm to adapt to changes in abstract text. This algorithm reconstructs only damaged parts of the formatted text, leaving the rest intact. Together, incremental text reformatting and (incremental) consistency maintenance make it feasible to present an accurate formatted view at all times.

7. Summary

We have described IDE, an integrated editor/formatter for multimedia documents. IDE supports graphical content and layout as well as text, and accurately displays the formatted document as it is edited.

Abstraction and integration play dual roles in IDE's user interface. Users view the document concretely, but edit it abstractly. Abstraction limits the amount of irrelevant context and detail presented to the user. Though directly editing the concrete formatted content is natural in simple domains, abstract editing is more valuable where many kinds of content can be combined. The danger that abstraction will hinder ease of use by obscuring the relationship between content and formatted appearance is countered by IDE's high level of integration: switching between different abstract editing contexts and examining the concrete effects of abstract edits is fully supported.

We briefly described our prototype editors for text, tables and diagrams, and the underlying representational and adaptive framework used to implement these editors. This framework supports incremental formatting and extension of the system to new kinds of content.

Acknowledgements

I am indebted to Rick Furuta for his careful readings of earlier drafts. His efforts have greatly improved the form of this paper.

References

Beach, R.J. & Stone, M. (1983). Graphical style: Towards high quality illustrations, *Computer Graphics*, **17**, 3.

Beach, R.J. (1986). Tabular typography. In *Text processing and document manipulation*, ed. J.C. van Vliet, Cambridge, England: Cambridge.

Chamberlin, D.C., et. al. (1982). Janus: an interactive document formatter based on declarative tags, *IBM Syst. J.* **21**, 3.

Furuta, R.K. (1986). An Integrated, but not Exact-Representation, Editor/Formatter. In *Text processing and document manipulation*, ed. J.C. van Vliet, Cambridge, England: Cambridge.

Interleaf. (1987). *Technical Publishing Software Reference Manual*. Cambridge, Mass.

Kaplan, M. (1988) *An environment for maintaining formatted documents*. Ph.D. Dissertation. Brown University, Providence, RI

Quint, V. & Vatton, I. (1986) Grif: An interactive system for structured document manipulation. In *Text processing and document manipulation*, ed. J.C. van Vliet, Cambridge, England: Cambridge.

Teitelman, W. (1985) A tour through Cedar. *IEEE Trans. Soft. Eng.*, **11**, 3.

INTENT-BASED PAGE MODELLING USING BLOCKS IN THE QUILL DOCUMENT EDITOR

ALLEN W. LUNIEWSKI

IBM Almaden Research Center

ABSTRACT
This paper describes Blocks, the mechanism for controlling page layout in the Quill document editor. The Blocks mechanism consists of a small number of primitives that can be combined to model many interesting pages. By providing a set of general-purpose tools, the blocks mechanism supports a variety of typographic features including multiple columns, footnotes and floating figures. Blocks also provide the basis for one form of extensibility in Quill - supporting multiple editors for flowing text. The Blocks mechanism simplifies the implementation of the formatting part of editors since the formatter need only be concerned with formatting an input stream into a rectangular box.

1. Introduction

This paper describes Blocks, the mechanism used to implement the layout of pages, and the placing of document contents on those pages, in the Quill document editor. The paper first presents a brief overview of Quill and describes the Blocks mechanism. The sections that follow introduce various features of Blocks, beginning with a very simple page model and working toward more complex pages, and concluding with a discussion of how Blocks contribute to the extensibility of the Quill design.

Quill is a research project in document editing and formatting whose purpose is to combine the advantages of two approaches to document formatting: (1) the "generic markup" approach, exemplified by the ISO Standard Generalized Markup Language (SGML) [ISO86]; and (2) the "direct manipulation" or "WYSIWYG" (What You See Is What You Get) approach, exemplified by Interleaf [Int86] and Xerox's Ventura [Xer87] products. The principal goals of Quill are as follows:

- Provide a WYSIWYG editor that explicitly represents, and allows manipulation of, both the physical and logical views of a document.
- Achieve a "seamless" merging of various media, especially text, image and graphics, in an unrestricted hierarchy.
- Produce an extensible framework so that new editors can be easily "plugged in" to Quill.

Quill is organized into a system shell and a collection of interacting editors. Each editor is responsible for editing and formatting a specific type of material, such as text, graphics, mathematics, or chemistry; each editor has its own set of commands and specialized knowledge about its own type of material. The interface between the system shell and the editors is carefully defined and is the basis for extensibility (see [Cham87]).

The shell is the heart of the system. It insulates the rest of Quill from the underlying operating system by providing needed services to other parts of Quill. The shell is also the basic "traffic cop" controlling what happens next in a Quill session.

The editors are responsible for the editing and display of the document. Editors use shell services to interact with the user to create and edit documents. The editors translate editing requests into modifications of internal data structures and use those data structures to display the document in the Quill window. Editors are also responsible for translating those data structures into output files such as printer files and SGML files.

2. Page Modelling in Quill

A major aspect of a formatter is the collection of page models that it supports. A page model specifies how pages are organized into areas containing various materials such as columns of text, footnotes, and running titles. A simple page model might consist of a single column of text per page, while a very complicated page model would support all of the features required by a production publishing house.

Since complex page layout is not a primary goal of the Quill project, the initial Quill prototype will support a relatively simple page model with the following characteristics:

- A document consists of one or more pages.
- A page consists of one or more sections.
- A section consists of one or more columns of equal width.

- Pages may also have: running titles, footnotes, and floating figures.

The number and width of columns can vary from section to section. The number of sections on a page can vary from page to page. The user can force text to begin a new page, section or column.

Page layout in Quill could be implemented by a collection of special-purpose mechanisms to support various features such as footnotes and floating figures. Instead, however, Quill will use a general mechanism called Blocks which is able to support the same set of features with greater simplicity, maintainability, and extensibility.

3. Introduction to Blocks

The blocks model is an intent-based page layout mechanism, in the sense that editors specify the intended appearance of formatted pages rather than detailed procedures for realizing that appearance. The Quill Blocks Manager works cooperatively with the editors to achieve the desired page formats. Blocks insulate the editors from most of the details of page layout, thus making the implementation of new editors simpler.

The blocks model has three basic notions: blocks, input streams and editors. A block is a rectangular part of a document. Blocks are nested inside each other, forming a hierarchy in which the root block is the document itself. An input stream is an ordered sequence of tokens that comprise (part of) a document. There may be multiple input streams within a single document (*e.g.*, one for text and a second for floating figures). An editor is a program responsible for managing the editing and display of a subsequence of an input stream in a given block.

An input stream is an ordered sequence of atomic units, called *tokens*. Tokens are either regular or special. Regular tokens represent the content of the document itself, and are not interpreted by the Blocks Manager. Special tokens are used by editors to communicate their formatting intent to the Blocks Manager.

An *editor* is responsible for editing the contents of an input stream and for presenting that stream in formatted form on an output device. Editing of a stream, usually through insertion and deletion of tokens, is done at the request of the user. The editor interprets the tokens, in any manner it chooses, to produce the displayed or printed document. Thus a text stream might have tokens representing words and punctuation while a music stream would have tokens representing notes, rest marks, etc. The editors and the Blocks Manager interact through procedure calls to partition the input stream among the various blocks in such a way that each block is filled with the appropriate amount of material.

A *block* is a rectangular region of arbitrary size. Blocks may be properly nested within one another to an arbitrary depth. A document is represented as a single block (typically with many descendant blocks). A block with no children is called a *simple block*. A simple block is the rectangular area of a document in which an editor performs its editing activities. A block that has one or more children is called a *compound block*. Compound blocks are used to organize the contents of a document and are manipulated solely by the Blocks Manager. Thus a document represented in blocks can be thought of as a tree of blocks with the document block at the root and simple blocks, which are associated with input streams and editors, at the leaves of the tree. This view of a document is represented in Figure 1, which shows a three page document.

The basic properties of a block are geometric: its size (current, minimum and maximum, in both directions), and its x and y location relative to its parent. Any of these may be fixed. The Blocks Manager determines all of the variable geometric attributes of blocks. A variable location and size for a block is useful if it contains variable sized material such as flowing text. Blocks of fixed size and location are useful for such things as running titles.

A *block template* is a singly rooted tree of blocks with a name called its *block kind*. Block templates are the "model" by which blocks are created during the processing of a document. The collection of block templates associated with a document comes from two sources: the design file and the editors.

The *design file* describes how a generic class of documents, a document type, should be formatted given its SGML representation. Part of a design file is a collection of block templates. These templates represent the parts of the document whose properties are known at the time that the document type is defined.

During the editing process, editors may need to create new block templates in response to editing requests. For instance, suppose that the user can choose the number of columns in a section. Since the number and spacing of columns is arbitrary, it is impractical to have a template block for every possible multi-column section in the design file. Thus,

Figure 1: Block Model for a Document

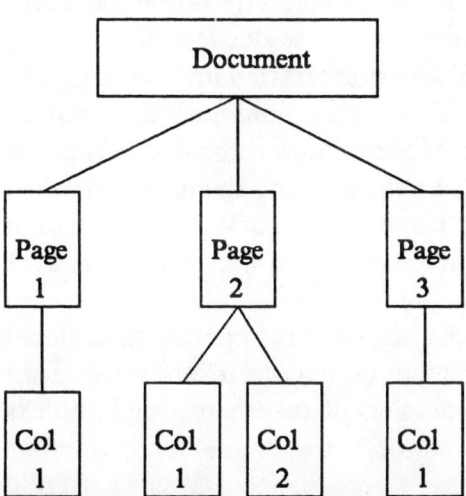

at the time of the user request, the editor creates a new block template with the appropriate number of columns.

Every block may have a previous sibling and a next sibling. Each block may also specify a *template successor*. A template successor, specified by naming a block kind, specifies how a next sibling can be created if needed (e.g., if a page block becomes too full, requiring a new page to be created to hold the excess material). Once created, the new sibling is called the *instantiated successor* of the original block.

A simple block may have a single subsequence of an input stream associated with it.[1] A compound block never has an input stream associated with it. A block that has an input stream associated with it is said to "consume" that input stream. The ordered sequence of simple blocks that consume an input stream "covers" the input stream from beginning to end and no two blocks consume the same input token. Consider two adjacent blocks in that sequence. The earlier block is called the *flow predecessor* of the following block and the following one is called the *flow successor* of the preceeding block. The Blocks Manager distributes the tokens of the various input streams among the various simple blocks of the document to ensure this covering property.

---

[1] However, it is not necessary to have an input stream associated with a simple block. If there is no input stream then the editor must use a mechanism outside of the block model to determine the block's appearance. For instance, the block might have a constant appearance (*e.g.*, a logo).

The blocks approach places clearly defined sets of responsibilities on the editors and the Blocks Manager to ensure correctly formatted documents and to provide WYSIWYG editing of those documents.

An editor has two basic responsibilities: interact with the user and interact with the Blocks Manager. User interactions include receiving input and updating the display. The editor is responsible for taking the tokens associated with a simple block and presenting them, in formatted form, to the user. The editor must also respond to requests for information and action from the Blocks Manager and must describe certain conditions to the Blocks Manager when they happen.

The basic responsibility of the Blocks Manager is to ensure that global formatting is correct - that is, to ensure that each input token is consumed by the correct simple block. The allocation of tokens to simple blocks is done to meet certain constraints:

- make the current size of a block be the same as the space the editor reports is required for formatting the tokens consumed by that block.
- ensure that all intents specified by special tokens are met.
- minimize the amount of white space, space not allocated to any child block, in a compound block.

These constraints require the Blocks Manager to maintain geometric constraints on the blocks that comprise a document and adjust the tokens consumed by each simple block. In addition, the Blocks Manager must respond to requests for information and reports of exceptional conditions from the editors.

This separation of responsibility results in a system with centralized global knowledge and algorithms (the Blocks Manager) coupled with localized, and distributed, knowledge for interaction with the user (the editors). Blocks are a tool used by the editors to achieve WYSIWYG document formatting and editing.

4. Simple Text Processing

Consider a very simple document in which each page is a single column of text. If the last page of the document overflows, a new page is created to hold the overflow. This document is easily modeled using blocks. The block model for this document consists of a document block of infinite size inside of which is a single block template, call it pageTemplate.

pageTemplate contains a single, fixed size, child block called columnBlock; the size and location of columnBlock are chosen to leave appropriate margins on each page. columnBlock consumes tokens from the input stream textStream and the text editor is its editor. columnBlock has no template successor since it is the only column on a page. pageTemplate has pageTemplate as its template successor; that is, pageTemplate reproduces itself as needed. An empty document consists of a single instantiation of pageTemplate within the infinite document block.

Suppose that an instance of this simple document consists of a single page that is full. This means that the block representation of this document consists of a single instantiation of pageTemplate. Thus, the instance of columnBlock within the instantiated pageTemplate has neither a flow successor nor a flow predecessor.

Now suppose that the user edits the last line of the document, say by adding a new word, making the line too large to fit on the page. The text editor reports to the Blocks Manager that page one's column block is "broken" with a reason of *too full*. The Blocks Manager notes that the block is broken, queues the work to fix that block for a later time and returns to the editor (work is queued for subsequent processing when CPU cycles are available in order to increase responsiveness). Eventually, when Quill is otherwise idle, the shell calls the Blocks Manager asking it to perform any pending work. At that time, the Blocks Manager will fix the broken block. It first tries to grow the broken block. This fails since columnBlock is of fixed size. The Blocks Manager next tries to find a flow successor for column block. This is done by first trying to instantiate the template successor for columnBlock. This fails since columnBlock has no template successor. Next an attempt is made to instantiate a template successor for the parent of columnBlock. This succeeds, resulting in a second instance of a pageTemplate (and thus, also, of its child, a columnBlock). As a side effect of this, the Blocks Manager notes that the columnBlock in the first pageTemplate now has a flow successor, the columnBlock in the second pageTemplate since both accept the same stream and are "adjacent" in the document.[2] The Blocks Manager now

---

[2] The flow successor for a block is the next simple block in the document that accepts the same stream as the original block. In this case, "next" is defined in terms of the leaf order of the simple blocks. As a side effect of instantiating blocks, the Blocks Manager adjusts the flow successor and flow predecessor for effected blocks.

asks the text editor for the tokens that are excess in the first columnBlock (*i.e.*, the excess word). The Blocks Manager informs the text editor that the first columnBlock no longer consumes those tokens and that the second columnBlock does. In this way, the excess word from the first page "flows" to the second page. The text editor will, when Quill is idle, perform the needed reformatting of the two columnBlocks and display the properly formatted document to the user.

Now suppose that the user decides that the word just added was not correct and deletes it. This results in the Blocks Manager and the text editor moving the word from the second page back to the first in an operation that is roughly the inverse of what just transpired. In detail, the user deletes the word from the first page. The text editor notes that the first column is no longer full enough so it reports, to the Blocks Manager, that the columnBlock is broken with a reason of *not full enough*. When Quill is otherwise idle, the Blocks Manager will fix that block. At that time, it will ask the text editor how much is needed to fill the first columnBlock and then ask the text editor if it can supply that much material from the second columnBlock. In this case, the request to the second block will succeed and the Blocks Manager will inform the text editor that the specified tokens are no longer consumed by the second columnBlock but, rather, by the first columnBlock. At this point the Blocks Manager notes that the second pageTemplate is the last block in the document and consumes no input tokens so it destroys the block, leaving a one page document. The text editor will reformat the first columnBlock and display the results to the user.

This example has illustrated a number of points about the blocks model. First, editors detect that blocks are broken for various reasons and report them to the Blocks Manager, which is responsible for fixing them. Second, the Blocks Manager fixes broken blocks by querying the editors as to the size of various things and then moving tokens from one block to another, informing editors of the move. Third, the Blocks Manager finds a flow successor for a block that is too full, instantiating template successors for that block if needed. Finally, the Blocks Manager detects when blocks are no longer needed and destroys them.

5. Breaks: Starting New Blocks

At times a document writer wants to place some text at the beginning of some physical unit (*e.g.*, top of a page or top of a column). These effects are achieved in the blocks model using *break tokens*. A break token is a special token inserted into an input stream by an editor to specify the desired effect. To specify that effect precisely, the notion of a *block class* must be introduced.

A *block class* is a set of block kinds and is another part of the block model for a document. For instance the block class *Pages* might consist of block kinds for pages that are left pages, right pages and also first pages of chapters. A given block kind may be in zero or more block classes; thus block classes may intersect.

A break token specifies a block class. The editor's intent by including the break token is:

Let b be the simple block that consumes the break token, t, in the formatted document. t must precede all regular tokens in b. If b is not in the block class specified in t, start at b and look at each of its ancestors until a block is found, call it c, that is of the block class specified in t. b must be the first block contained within c that consumes the stream that contains t.

The Blocks Manager moves tokens from block to block, possibly creating new blocks in the process, to ensure that this condition is satisfied. This condition is simply, and quickly, checked for validity by first verifying the location of the token within the subsequence consumed by its block and then verifying that that block is the first block of some appropriate ancestor block to consume that stream. Thus only a few nearby tokens within a stream need be examined and only a few blocks examined in the chain of ancestor blocks to validate that the intent is met.

To illustrate the use of break tokens, let us return to the example of the single page document. Suppose that the editor supports user defined page breaks. To implement page breaks using blocks, the document designer must ensure that a block class, call it Pages, exists, and that pageTemplate is a member of that class. If the user specifies that a page break should occur at some point in the document, the editor inserts a break token at that point with Pages as the named block class and informs the Blocks Manager that a special token has been inserted into the input stream. The Blocks Manager will immediately check to see if the break token assertion is true. If it is not, the break token, and all following tokens consumed by the block consuming the break token, are flowed to successive flow successors until the break token assertion is satisfied. As further editing occurs, it is the Blocks Manager's responsibility to ensure that the break token assertion remains true. If an editing action were to make it false, the break token, and all following tokens, are flowed towards the end of the document until the assertion is satisfied.

6. Synchronizing the Formatting of Input Streams

Many typographic effects involve controlling the location of one document element relative to another. For instance, a footnote should appear on the same page as its callout if possible and, in any event, on a page no earlier than its callout. Similarly, a floating figure should appear on a page no earlier than its point of definition. In order to achieve these effects, two new special tokens, called anchor tokens and anchored item tokens, must be introduced.

An anchor token names the anchored item token that it is related to. It denotes a callout point (*e.g.*, the place at which a footnote is referenced). An anchored item token represents the "called out entity" (*e.g.*, the footnote itself). It has two components: a block class and a list of the anchor tokens associated with it. The list of anchor tokens is used to verify the anchor/anchored item constraint as one or the other moves about in the document. The block class is the heart of the constraint:

> *Given an anchor token a and its associated anchored item token ai. Let b_a be the nearest ancestor of the block that consumes a that is of the block class named in ai. Let b_{ai} be the nearest ancestor of the block that consumes ai that is of the block class named in ai. Then a and ai satisfy the anchored item constraint if and only if b_a appears no later in the document than b_{ai}.*

Verifying that this assertion is true is relatively easy. All that need be done is walk from the given anchor token towards the root until an ancestor of the appropriate block class is found. Similarly, walk from the anchored item token towards the root until an appropriate ancestor is found. At this point, verifying the assertion simply involves determining which node is earlier in the tree - a simple exercise involving walking to the root of the tree from each node. For most documents, it is anticipated that the tree depth will be relatively small making these walks very fast.

Ensuring that this assertion is satisfied as editing occurs is also simple. If an anchor token moves to a block that is later in the document, then the corresponding anchored item token must be moved towards the end of the document until the assertion is satisfied. An attempt to move an anchored item token to an earlier block in the document will be vetoed if it would violate the assertion. If an anchor token moves within a block in a manner that would allow the block to shrink (*e.g.*, a footnote callout moves to an earlier line), then the possibility that this shrinkage would allow the anchored item token to flow toward the front of the document must be examined. If an anchor token moves toward the front of the document, the assertion will remain satisfied.[3] If an anchored item token flows towards the end of the document, no checking is required since such a movement can *never* cause the constraint to become false. Thus proper formatting is ensured by a local checking of validity and by moving anchored item tokens within the document as needed.

Now consider a simple example. Imagine that the simple one column document previously used has room for footnotes at the bottom of each page. There will be a footnote stream that runs through these footnote areas.[4] To insert a footnote in the document, the text editor places an anchor token in the text stream at the point of reference and a related anchored item token in the footnote stream, naming *Pages* as its block class. The text editor does not need to be concerned with the relationship between the footnote and the callout; the Blocks Manager will ensure that the assertion is true. The only chore that the text editor has taken upon itself is the need to notify the Blocks Manager whenever the callout moves to a previous line on the page. The Blocks Manager will guarantee that the footnote is on a page not earlier than the callout, and on the same page as the callout if possible.

Imagine that the above document is properly formatted with a callout near the bottom of page one and the one line footnote on that same page. Suppose that the user adds text before the footnote callout, pushing the callout far enough towards the bottom of the page that there is no

---

[3] However, it might be possible to move the anchored item token towards the front of the document to keep it as close as possible to its anchor token. This possibility must also be examined.

[4] Ordinarily, footnotes do not flow from one page to another. However, such a flow can occur if the callout of the footnote is so near the bottom of a page that only part of the footnote can appear on that page.

longer enough room for the footnote. The text editor notes that the text area is too full and calls the Blocks Manager informing it that block is broken with a reason of *too full*. At this point, the blocks manager has two choices: move the extra line to the next page or shrink the footnote area by one line (and thus move the footnote to the next page). With the information at hand, the choice is an arbitrary one from the point of view of the Blocks Manager. To make this predictable, the notion of *block priorities* is introduced. Within a compound block, the children blocks are each assigned a priority. A block of higher priority has first chance at white space within a block. Thus, in the case at hand, assume that the footnote area is of higher priority than the text area (the proper choice, it turns out, to get the expected appearance of documents with a footnote ending up near its callout). After noting that the text area is of lower priority than the footnote area, the Blocks Manager will begin moving lines to the next page, one at a time. Eventually, it will think about moving the line containing the callout to the next page. It does so but notes that this violates the constraint on anchor tokens so it also moves the anchored item token, the footnote, to the next page. At this point, the text block on page one has shrunk enough so that it is not too full. However, the pageTemplate that is page one now has excess white space (since the footnote area is now empty). Thus the Blocks Manager marks the pageTemplate block as broken with a reason of *not enough*. This causes the Blocks Manager to begin filling blocks on that page from highest priority to lowest. The highest priority block is the footnote block and so it is tried first. The first thing on page two is a footnote that is called out on page two so it cannot be moved to page one. So, the next lower priority block is tried - the column block. The first line to be moved back contains the footnote callout. Moving it to page one is permitted since the callout will still precede the footnote itself so the line is moved. At this point, page one is full; the callout is on page one and the footnote is on page two. The anchor/anchored item constraint is satisfied. Since there is no room for the footnote on page one, it is as close to its callout as is possible. Thus the document is properly formatted.

If the user now deletes text before the anchor point on page one, the text editor must inform the Blocks Manager as the anchor token "floats" upward on the page. Eventually, enough room will appear at the bottom and the footnote will be moved to page one (and lines below the callout moved to page two).

In moving tokens around to satisfy constraints such as this, the danger of oscillation is present. The Blocks Manager would oscillate if it continuously moved the formatted document between two states with no intervening user action. The Blocks Manager avoids the problem of oscillation by careful algorithmic design and by means of block priorities that clearly define which block has first priority to occupy white space when it becomes available.

7. Dynamically Changing the Layout of the Document

The last special token is the *change template successor* token. This token is used to dynamically change the layout of a document, due to the properties of some element in the document or to a user editing action. A change template successor token names a block class and a block kind. The token changes the template successor for the block that consumes it (or for the nearest ancestor block that is in the named block class) to be the block kind named in the token. As with other special tokens, the effect of this token is specified as a constraint. The constraint concerns the definition of the template successor for a block:

> *The template successor for a block is the block kind named in the last change template successor token consumed by that block, or one of its descendants, which names it as a block to have its template successor changed. If a block, or one of its descendants, does not consume a change template successor, then its template successor is the same as when the block was first instantiated (i.e., the same as in the block template that it was instantiated from).*

Thus change template successor tokens impose a constraint on the formatted document by specifying the template successor for the block that consumes them.

This constraint imposes a restriction on change template successor tokens: if a block is to have its template successor changed then only *one* of the subsequences of the streams consumed by it (or its children) may have *any* change template successor tokens within it. In practice, this means that only a single stream in a document will have change template successor tokens within it. This restriction was introduced to achieve predictability in the formatting process. Without it, the template successor for a block might be a function of the order in which the tokens within the various streams within that block got there.

A simple example will illustrate the use of change template successor tokens. Let us return to the initial one column document. In this case, we make the block model a little more complicated. Within the pageTemplate block place a section block and within that block place the column block. In this case, both the section and column blocks are given a maximum size that fits within the page (and its margins) but are initially empty. In the case of a document that remains a single column, the processing is much as in the initial example of this paper with the exception that the column block needs to grow as text is added to it. This will happen by first growing its parent, the section block, and then growing the column block.

Suppose that the user wants to switch to two column formatting. The text editor constructs a new block template, call it section2, that has two children - each a (narrower) column block. Neither the section2 block nor its children blocks has a template successor. The left column takes its input from the text stream. The right column also consumes the text stream but is connected, in the section2 template, as the flow successor of the left column. Thus any text that falls out of the left column will fall into the right column. Next, the text editor creates a new page template, call it pageTemplate2, that has as its only child a section2 block. The template successor for a pageTemplate2 is another pageTemplate2. The Editor now asks the Blocks Manager to add both section2 and pageTemplate2 to the block model.

Finally, the text editor introduces three special tokens into the text input stream. The first is a change template successor token that names a class that includes a section block as its block class and a section2 as the new template successor. The second is a change template successor token that names a class that includes a pageTemplate block as its block class and a pageTemplate2 as the new template successor. The third token is a break token that specifies the block class containing section.

If some text follows the break token, the break token will not be at the right place so a flow successor will be found. This will create a successor for section, the newly specified section2. This will cause the break token, and the following text, to move to the left column of the section2 block. Thus, the one column formatting will end and two column formatting will begin. If the user types even more text, eventually the page will fill requiring the creation of a new page. In this case the newly instantiated page will be a pageTemplate2, as specified in the change template successor token provided by the text editor. The effect is that the document has changed from one column formatting to two column formatting.

8. Extensibility through Blocks

Blocks are one means for providing extensibility in Quill. This extensibility comes in two forms: new flowing editors for flowing document content and support for various typographic effects in the context of a single general purpose mechanism.

Blocks provide the page layout facility within Quill. Although blocks support non-flowing document content (*e.g.*, a running title on a page), blocks are primarily designed to support document content that flows (*e.g.*, text). Flowing content is characterized by its ability to move from one page to another, filling arbitrary sized regions. Quill initially supports only English text in fixed-width blocks. The blocks mechanism supports arbitrary flowing document content and blocks that grow in both width and height. Thus, having a music editor that supports writing large amounts of musical score that flows from one sheet to another does not involve any new page layout mechanism - blocks will support it. Similarly, adding support for non-Western languages, including those that flow from right to left on a page (*e.g.*, Arabic), or from top to bottom on a page (*e.g.*, Chinese), does not affect the page layout parts of Quill. The editor for such new text need only be concerned with interacting with the user and with laying out document contents in a single rectangular region - a block.

The special tokens provided by the Blocks Manager permit a wide variety of typographic effects with no change to the basic mechanism. Floating figures and footnotes will be in an early version of Quill and are fairly well understood. The same mechanisms can support other effects. A parallel translation dictionary can be constructed using break tokens and suitable page templates. Documents with different layouts of even and odd pages are handled by changing the basic document block to be a block with two page blocks within it - one for the even page and the other for the odd page. End notes are handled by having a footnote area on each page of a chapter but making the footnote area the *lowest* priority item on the page; this will cause all footnotes to flow to the end of the chapter. As these examples illustrate, the range of effects possible with the blocks model is large. It is believed that blocks provide a sound basis upon which to explore such effects in a WYSIWYG environment.

9. Conclusions

This paper has described the blocks model for page layouts as used in the Quill document editor. The blocks model is a single generalized mechanism that supports a very wide variety of page layout needs. The blocks model is based on the following ideas:

- Document formatting is divided in a well specified manner between the Blocks Manager and the editors.
- Special tokens are used by editors to communicate document formatting intent to the Blocks Manager.
- The intentions expressed by editors can be "WYSIWYG" edited. That is, they can quickly and easily be checked using knowledge that is locally available to the Blocks Manager.

The blocks model has a number of important advantages over approaches that integrate document layout with editors:

- Editors are simpler since they need only be concerned with formatting into a (rectangular) block. The Blocks Manager handles more global formatting requirements.
- It is easy to add new editors since they need only satisfy the interface requirements of the Blocks Manager and of the system shell. Editors are relieved of the need to have global document formatting knowledge.
- A document can have multiple kinds of flowing text, each managed by its own editor. The different streams might be in two disjoint parts of the document or the streams might have a more intimate relationship as in a document that has a few lines of musical score intermixed with an analysis of that music.
- Blocks provide a uniform implementation of a number of interesting typographic features. It is believed the blocks model primitives can be used to achieve effects well beyond those described in this paper.

There are also some potential disadvantages of the blocks approach to document layout:

- The rigid interface between editors and the Blocks Manager may interfere with some typographic effects such as formatting text around an irregularly shaped figure.
- Performance is a concern for the same reason as above: the existence of strict interfaces between editors and page layout.
- General purpose mechanisms can be more complicated than special purpose mechanisms. Of course, this is balanced by the need to create a number of interacting special purpose mechanisms to achieve the same effect as the general purpose mechanism.

On balance, we believe that the blocks approach to page modelling is a good approach to building an extensible WYSIWYG editor. The blocks approach is well suited to a class of documents having a fairly regular structure, especially those in which the page layout is derived from the document contents (*e.g.*, books, technical reports). Its applicability to less regular documents (*e.g.*, newspapers, magazines, advertising copy) is less clear.

10. References

[Cham87] Chamberlin, D.D., Hasselmeir, H.F., Luniewski, A.W., Paris, D.P., Wade, B.W., and Zolliker, M.L. (1987). Quill: An Extensible System for Editing Documents of Mixed Type. In *Proceedings of the 21st Hawaii International Conference on System Sciences*. Washington, DC: IEEE Computer Society Press.

[Int86] *Interleaf Workstation Publishing Software User's Guide* (1986). Cambridge, MA: Interleaf, Inc.

[ISO86] *International Standard ISO 8879: Information Processing - Text and Office Systems - Standard Generalized Markup Language (SGML).* (1986). International Organization for Standardization.

[Xer87] *Ventura Publisher Edition Reference Guide* (1987). Xerox Corporation.

AN INTRODUCTION TO GARGOYLE:
AN INTERACTIVE ILLUSTRATION TOOL

KEN PIER, ERIC BIER, and MAUREEN STONE

Xerox Palo Alto Research Center

ABSTRACT
Gargoyle is an illustration tool for creating and editing two-dimensional graphic arts quality drawings. It provides an interactive, WYSIWYG, direct manipulation interface for a rich set of drawings; namely, any drawing expressible in the Xerox Interpress page description language. Graphical objects implemented in Gargoyle include complex outlines composed of lines and curves, scanned images, and text. Graphical object style parameters, such as line weight, line color, area fill, and text font, are also editable using Gargoyle. In addition, Gargoyle implements a new technique called snap-dragging for easily creating geometrically precise drawings. Snap-dragging uses a ruler and compass metaphor to equip the user with interactive aids for precision drawing. Gargoyle is one of several experimental document processing tools integrated into the Xerox Cedar programming environment. This paper provides a description of Gargoyle's user community, computing environment, imaging model, user interface, implementation goals, and techniques used to achieve those goals. Some images created with Gargoyle are included and the role of Gargoyle in the graphics research program at Xerox PARC is outlined.

1. Introduction

A high-quality document production system for a workstation requires a sophisticated and powerful illustration tool. Such a tool has many demands: it must work with a rich imaging model, use a graphical, highly interactive user interface, implement a way to easily create precise geometric relationships within and among graphical objects, produce graphics-arts-quality drawings, and integrate with other document processing tools in the workstation environment. The Gargoyle illustrator is our ongoing attempt to fulfill these requirements.

1.1. *Environment and related work*

In the Computer Science Laboratory of the Xerox Palo Alto Research Center (PARC) in Palo Alto, California, one research focus is software for electronic document processing. Research software runs on a network of high-performance personal workstations called Dorados [Pier83] in the Cedar experimental programming environment [Swinehart86]. Cedar provides an integrated platform for experiments in the creation, editing, transmission, storage and manipulation of documents in several media. Text, two- and three-dimensional graphics, scanned images, mathematics and computer algebra [Arnon87], voice [Zellweger88a], and active documents known as scripted documents [Zellweger88b] are media in our electronic documents.

Gargoyle fills the need for both a useful graphics editor and a vehicle for continuing research in graphics. Gargoyle is a testbed for experiments in shape and style editing, in graphical searching and replacement, in color definition and use, and in highly interactive user interfaces for complex systems. Gargoyle exploits advances in device independent graphics, printing, and computing environments.

The Gargoyle user community is composed of sophisticated, demanding users fluent in the use of interactive systems. Users range from computer science researchers and engineers to secretaries, graphic artists, and documentation specialists, all using Cedar on Dorados. Because Cedar users are accustomed to certain styles of interaction, particularly with the Cedar text editor, our user interface design takes these established conventions into account.

Gargoyle is the latest in a series of two-dimensional geometric graphics editors at Xerox. *Draw* [Baudelaire79] was a geometry editor for the Xerox Alto [Thacker82], the first personal workstation, in 1977. Draw implemented limited interactive editing of lines, curves, and text. Draw did not provide graphical feedback during interactive transformations and did not automatically refresh its background. *Griffin* [Baudelaire80], the next geometry and style editor, originally ran on the Alto in 1978 and later was ported to Cedar. Griffin is a curve and text editor, with a user interface similar to Draw and with filled areas, multiple curve types and graphical styles shared among objects. Griffin exposed a number of research issues including high speed incremental refresh, color definition, shape editing using mathematical transformations, and graphical style [Beach83]. *StarGraphics* [Lipkie82] followed in 1981 as part of the integrated text and graphics editor in the Xerox Star Information System. Star has an excellent user interface and a WYSIWYG ("what you see is what you get") display. StarGraphics includes points, lines, rectangles, triangles, open and closed curves, and text. Star objects are transformed interactively and exhibit rubberbanding while the transform is in progress. Star objects also have graphical style properties attached to them whose values can be changed by the user.

Gargoyle is comparable to Adobe Illustrator$^{(TM)}$[1] [Adobe87] in that both can produce arbitrary two-dimensional synthetic illustrations, but they differ in emphasis. Adobe Illustrator is optimized for manually converting scanned images into synthetic images, using techniques for quickly tracing the contours of a scanned image. Gargoyle can also trace, but is optimized instead for quickly creating geometrically

---

[1] Adobe Illustrator is a trademark of Adobe Systems, Inc.

precise objects and for precisely positioning, orienting, and sizing those objects. The user interface paradigms are also different. Adobe Illustrator uses a modal style, in which the user moves explicitly between modes (e.g., draw, scale, and rotate modes), invoking operations with a mouse and a set of option keys which may have different effects in different modes. Gargoyle uses a nearly modeless style of editing, relying on a three-button mouse and option keys to provide fast access to common operations. Gargoyle implements direct manipulation of graphical objects, with a single view of the entire scene which is always complete and accurate, even during interactive operations. Adobe Illustrator provides a split screen with an interactive section on one side next to an optional preview section which updates periodically.

1.2. *Imaging model*

Gargoyle is an *interactive interface* for editing the rich set of shapes and appearance parameters defined in the Xerox Interpress Electronic Printing Standard [Bushan86, Interpress86]. Interpress is a device-independent, high precision model for ideal images expressed in a *page description language.* Interpress page descriptions may include synthetic graphics, scanned images, text in many fonts, and many forms of color definition and application. The chief concepts in the Interpress imaging model are described in a 1982 paper by Warnock and Wyatt [Warnock82]. They introduce an intuitive, device-independent model of an imaging process which composes a complex image by superimposing simpler images in strict overlap order. The imaging model dictates how shapes are specified and how shapes and colors are combined. It loosely parallels the process used in silkscreening: pushing colored inks through a series of stencils onto an imaging surface. Ink laid down later in the process may obscure ink laid down earlier.

A rich imaging model challenges interactive editors. There are many parameters to be expressed and controlled via the user interface. A theoretically unlimited number of objects may compose a page and adequate user feedback and rendering performance challenges even the most powerful graphics workstations.

Gargoyle attempts to be a WYSIWYG editor for drawings; the illustration presented on the screen is a faithful representation of the image that will be printed. When a WYSIWYG display is coupled with a rich imaging model, rendering performance requirements are amplified and there is increased difficulty in using graphical feedback to show which objects are selected or in implementing precision drawing aids.

1.3. *Geometric precision*

Gargoyle makes creating geometrically precise drawings easy. Traditionally, geometrically precise editing has been accomplished with the use of grids [Lipkie82] or constraints [Borning79, Nelson85]. In grid-based editing, users manipulate curve control points that are constrained to lie on a grid of uniformly spaced points. In constraint-based systems, users achieve precision by actually specifying constraints to be maintained by the system for the user. For example, a line segment specified to be horizontal cannot be rotated by the user. Grids limit the space of objects that may be constructed to those whose control points lie on the grid. Constraints are difficult to specify and may be satisfied by the constraint maintenance system in completely unintended ways, such as collapsing a line into a point.

Gargoyle uses a new technique, called *snap-dragging*, which provides the best features of both grids and constraints without their drawbacks. Snap-dragging [Bier86] is briefly explained below. Snap-dragging causes precisely positioned lines and circles, called *alignment objects*, to be added to the scene by the system for use during interactive operations. Snap-dragging places further burdens on the user interface by requiring that alignment objects be drawn, by adding more user operations for creation and management of these objects, and by requiring real-time input handling and screen updates during interactive transformations.

2. Gargoyle functionality: problems and solutions

Our decision to build Gargoyle on top of a rich imaging model, to have it be largely WYSIWYG, to use snap-dragging as its major editing paradigm, and to integrate it with other tools in Cedar has raised a number of problems. These problems and our solutions to them are discussed in this section.

2.1. *Graphical objects and graphical style*

The Interpress imaging model provides for the specification of object *geometry* and object *style*. The geometry of an object is a description of its shape, such as a set of end points and control points for a given curve. The style of an object is a specification of how the geometry is to be rendered in the illustration. Elements of graphical style include stroke weight, treatment of stroke ends and joins, stroke pattern (such as dashed or dotted), stroke color, fill color for closed objects, and text font and transformation. Separation of geometry and style allows rendering of an illustration in a variety of ways to suit different needs. For example, white lines on a blue background are suitable for color slide presentations and black lines on a white background are suitable for printed matter [Beach83].

The first challenge presented by this rich imaging model is to provide ways to edit the different types of object geometry and the different style attributes.

Figure 1: *an open trajectory with four segments of different type; curve joints and control points shown as small white squares*

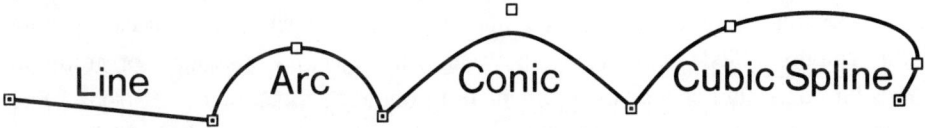

2.1.1. *Graphical object types and editing*

A Gargoyle *scene* contains all the graphical objects the user has created. These objects include curved paths, scanned images, and text.

Objects defined using paths are called *outlines*. An outline is a collection of trajectories. A *trajectory* is a collection of contiguous segments, and a *segment* is a curve specified by its endpoints, called *joints*, and its *control points*. Segment types include straight lines, circular arcs, conic sections, and several types of parameterized curves called splines, shown in Figure 1. Trajectories may be open (a path with two ends) or closed (a path with no ends; a closed path may be filled). The trajectories composing a single outline are rendered using wrap number or parity fill criteria, permitting filled shapes with cutouts to be constructed.

Full color, gray scale, or binary scanned images may be included in the scene. Text objects may be created in one of two ways: by pointing into the scene and typing text directly, or by selecting existing text in a text editing window and pointing out where a copy of that text should appear in the scene. Scanned images and text may be interactively translated, rotated, scaled, or skewed like any other graphical object. The impact of this transformability on the traditional notion of "text" in a certain "font" is discussed below.

In order to allow programmers to add new types of graphical objects to Gargoyle, we use an object-oriented programming style for the creation of new classes of graphical objects. The programmer must implement a set of simple procedures to specify the behavior of the new object class. Once this is done, the object participates fully in rendering, selection, transformation, gravity, generation of alignment objects, changing of style parameters such as color, and description in the Gargoyle file format. Existing special objects include *box* and *circle*, which respond to transformation commands by changing dimensions while retaining their essential shapes.

Editing classes of shapes requires operations to create, modify, position, and orient them, plus a set of commands for copying and grouping pieces into larger units. To create a new path, the user directly draws a trajectory composed of straight line segments into the scene, then specifies which curve type is desired. The new line segments are transformed to create the desired curve. Existing segments may simply be selected and converted to segments of any other type. Segments may be interactively transformed into new shapes; interactive operations include rubberbanding, translation, rotation, scaling, and skewing. Outlines may also be edited by adding or deleting joints and control points to segments, opening or closing trajectories, and grouping trajectories into outlines in which some trajectories may define cutouts, called *holes*, in an otherwise solid object. Commands for grouping pieces into units and changing a segment from one type to another (e.g., from a line segment to an arc) are done using pop-up menus. We use a special kind of pop-up menu called a pop-up button, discussed below.

The mouse is used to position control points, segments, trajectories, scanned images, and text objects. These positions can be specified precisely using snap-dragging.

2.1.2. *Graphical style and editing*
The elements of graphical style implemented in Gargoyle are:

- *stroke width:* a stroke of any width may be used while rendering segment geometry. Stroke width values are associated with individual segments.
- *stroke joins:* the joins between contiguous segments may be rendered as rounded, mitered, or beveled.
- *stroke ends:* ends of trajectories may be rendered as rounded, squared, or butted.
- *stroke pattern:* a dashed or dotted pattern may be specified to be used in rendering a segment. Dashed patterns may be arbitrary, possibly repeated, series of alternating opaque and transparent marks.
- *color:* segments, text, and filled areas may be rendered with any color. Solid colors may be chosen in several ways, as outlined below. Sampled colors are also available; a sampled color is specified by a pixel map (color, gray scale, or binary) which is used to tile the interior of an outline or clipping region.
- *fonts:* text may be rendered using an arbitrary affine transformation and filled with any solid color. Text font may be chosen from a large set of font families. Drop shadows for text are automatically created if desired.

The user must assign numerical values for stroke width, must specify stroke joins and stroke ends from a list of several available types, and must specify a font name from a large hierarchical name space of available fonts. The stroke join and stroke end types can be selected using a pop-up button. The stroke width can be specified by selecting a real number from anywhere on the Cedar desktop and clicking a pop-up button entry. Keyboard *accelerators* (mnemonic commands invoked using an option key and a single keystroke) are provided for specifying small integer stroke widths. Font names can be selected from anywhere on the Cedar desktop and set via a pop-up button. The user can keep a text file of favorite font names and select from that file.

A large number of colors can be printed on high-resolution color hardcopy devices.

People are generally not very good at describing colors. We provide a color naming scheme to get the user started. For example, the user can specify the color "vivid dark blue" or "lightish green" by typing the name and clicking a pop-up button. If this initial color is not quite right, the user can use a set of interactive sliders to smoothly mix a color in any of the RGB, CMY, HSV, or HSL color spaces.

Interpress uses fonts described by spline outlines. Font specifications include an affine transformation as well as a family and face. It is no longer adequate to describe fonts simply with a family name and a single scalar point size (e.g., TimesRoman 12). Text strings in any font may be rotated and/or scaled. Users may transform text to any orientation and size and then set the default text style by selecting the transformed text and clicking a pop-up button. Subsequent text entries will appear in the default style. If the user wants to examine or modify the transformation associated with a text string, the linear part of the transformation is printed out in the form [rotation 1: (degrees), scaling: (scaleX, scaleY), rotation 2: (degrees)]. Unless the text has been skewed, the second rotation will be 0. This form can be edited and used to define a new font transformation. This form is know as the Singular Value Decomposition [Golub83].

2.2. *WYSIWYG rendering*

Maintaining a faithful representation of a Gargoyle scene on the screen requires sophisticated rendering techniques for adequate performance and complicates the design of graphical feedback. Arbitrary collections of objects can be simultaneously transformed. When the transformation is complete, the new scene must be properly drawn. The repainting time should be small for small changes. To effect this, the bounding box of the changed region is computed and only those parts of objects that are in the bounding box are redrawn.

Simple bounding box culling is not enough to get good refresh performance when objects are being dragged or rubberbanded. For these operations, Gargoyle improves performance by scan-converting graphical objects into a collection of bitmaps before drawing the results on the screen. Because the Dorado is equipped with microcoded bitmap drawing operations (often called RasterOp [Newman79]) these bitmaps can be sent to the screen much more quickly than the objects can be scan converted. Two bitmaps are used. The first bitmap receives renderings of all of the objects and parts of objects that are not moving. The second bitmap receives renderings of all of the alignment lines and circles that are active. Each screen frame is then composed by writing the first bitmap to the screen, scan-converting all of the objects that are dragging or rubberbanding to the screen, and ORing the second bitmap on top to complete the frame. Additional speed can be gained by storing an individual bitmap for each moving object at its current size, rotation and skew. Other objects of that same size, rotation, and skew can be drawn using translated versions of the bitmap, instead of being scan converted. This cache of small bitmaps speeds up translation for all scenes and speeds up rotation and scaling in scenes that have translated copies of the same scene elements. For translation, it is possible to generate a new frame without doing any scan conversion at all.

Because the user can draw any shape as part of the Gargoyle scene, it is impossible to use graphical means to unambiguously indicate the state of the editing session. For instance, we need to show which objects are selected, which objects are used to trigger alignment objects, which objects are alignment objects themselves, and where the cursor is. We use a set of unlikely visible shapes, such as small black squares, to highlight selections and turn highlights off during dragging and pointing operations. When in doubt, the user can watch which highlights turn on and off to get a better idea of what is selected. If many objects are selected, selection highlighting is minimized to increase performance and reduce clutter on the screen. When an interactive selection operation is completed, the selected objects are highlighted and remain highlighted as long as they are selected. The cursor can be detected by moving the mouse. Alignment lines and circles are drawn with a special pattern and can be turned on or off collectively or individually.

The user receives textual feedback which describes the operation in progress as the cursor moves about the scene. Textual feedback appears just above the scene, near the user's line of sight. Textual feedback is vital for disambiguating the graphical object under the cursor in a crowded scene (e.g., for selection). When an operation actually completes, at the release of all mouse buttons and keyboard keys, textual feedback describes the operation performed. In addition, the user may open a typescript window containing a permanent record of completed operations and of responses to user queries about selected operands (e.g., ShowFont for text or ShowColor for a filled outline). As a general rule, any operand value that a user sets (e.g., SetFont or SetColor) will be displayed in text form in both the textual feedback line and the typescript. Given a textually specified value, Gargoyle can search the scene and select graphical objects with a matching value or set the values of selected objects to the specified value.

2.3. Snap-dragging

To allow users to precisely edit the geometric properties of objects, we provide a new interactive technique called snap-dragging [Bier86]. We review the essential properties of snap-dragging in this section and describe some of the associated performance and user interface problems.

Snap-dragging involves the cooperation of three geometric design techniques: gravity-active scene objects, ruler and compass construction techniques, and interactive transformations (e.g., rubberbanding, translation, rotation, and scaling). There is a

Figure 2: *the radius alignment menu with two active values*

Radius:	Get!	Add!	Delete!	1/18	1/9	1/8	1/4	**1/3**	1/2	2/3	3/4	1	**2**	4

software cursor in the scene called the *caret*. The caret is positioned by mouse motion, and its position in the scene is always one of the parameters for an interactive transformation. The caret is *gravity sensitive*; that is, if gravity is enabled and the caret moves near a *gravity-active* object, then the caret will snap onto the nearest point on that object. The caret can thus be accurately slid along the boundary of the object. Every graphical object in the scene is gravity active; that is, the caret will snap to the nearest point of any scene object it nears. The strength and type of this gravitational attraction is controlled by the user. In addition, a set of gravity-active lines and circles, called *alignment objects*, can be constructed and displayed. The type, placement, size, and orientation of alignment objects are controlled by the user. The user can achieve precise relationships between scene components by snapping the caret to alignment objects, scene objects, or the intersection points of all of these. Since translation, rotation, and scaling all follow the caret, these transformations can be done precisely just by placing the caret precisely. Objects following the caret are observed to move smoothly across the scene as the mouse directs the movement of the caret.

The challenges presented in implementing snap-dragging include creation, management, and display of alignment objects, providing ways to measure distances and angles in the scene to specify values for new alignment objects, integration of gravity into the user interface, and acceptable performance of the computationally intensive operations needed to perform snap-dragging during interactive transformations.

The user must specify sets of alignment values that are of interest. These values are a set of slopes, a set of radii, a set of angles, and a set of parallel line distances. It must be fast and convenient to turn alignment values on and off. Since Gargoyle cannot anticipate all of the values that will be of interest to users, we chose an extensible menu for managing alignment values. Alignment object menus are dynamic menus created and maintained for Gargoyle by the Cedar text editor. Figure 2 shows the radius alignment menu. These menus appear like a line of text, but each value is actually a screen button. Alignment values are activated or deactivated, causing alignment objects to appear or disappear, by clicking on the buttons in the menu. Any number of values may be active at one time. Activation is indicated by highlighting active values in boldface. A value may be added to any menu by typing a new value into an associated window and invoking Add!. All active values may be deleted from an alignment menu by invoking Delete!.

Once alignments are specified, the user selects a set of segments and control points as *triggers* for alignment objects by making the selected segments *hot*. Hot segments

Figure 3: *on the left, a line segment generating parallel distance lines at 0.5 inch and angle lines at 30 and 60 degrees to itself; on the right, an arc endpoint generating circles of radii 0.5 and 0.75 inch and slope lines of 45 and 90 degrees to the horizontal*

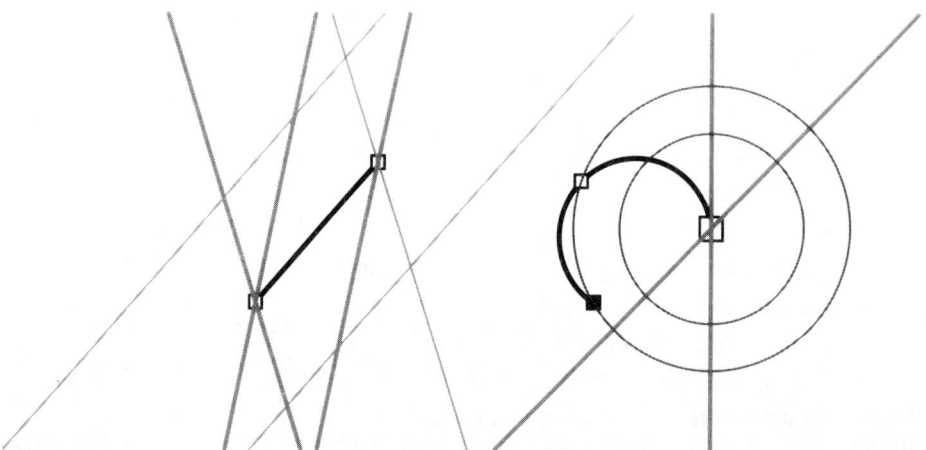

trigger alignment *angle lines* at enabled angles to the line through their endpoints, and pairs of *distance lines* at enabled distances from and parallel to the line through their endpoints. Hot joints or control points trigger *alignment circles* of enabled radii centered on the hot point and *slope lines* at enabled angles to the horizontal, passing through the hot point, as illustrated in Figure 3.

The user must be able to measure slopes, distances and angles in the scene and use the measured values to generate new alignment objects. Gargoyle constantly measures and updates the caret position as the user places the caret in the scene. This allows specification of any relevant dimension simply by pointing and using gravity and alignment objects for precise measurement. At any given time, Gargoyle displays the distance between the last two caret positions, the slope of the line between those positions, the relative angle of the last two measured slopes, and the perpendicular distance from the current caret position to the previously measured slope. Gargoyle displays this measurement information in the same windows used by the alignment menus to capture new values, so invoking Add! puts an alignment value of the measured dimension into an alignment menu. Selecting a segment and invoking Get! adds its length or slope as a value to an alignment menu.

Gargoyle maintains the currently active alignment objects. Whenever the alignment objects or triggers change, Gargoyle tries to incrementally update internal data structures rather than recalculating all alignment objects from scratch. Gargoyle also displays new alignment objects incrementally. Ordinarily there are only a few active radius values at any given time, so the circles are drawn very quickly by caching bitmaps for them and constructing the alignment object bitmap directly from the

Figure 4: *a portion of the Gargoyle control panel; pop-up buttons appear in italic typeface*

Gargoyle								
Scale	Rotate	Fit	Reset	Edge	Prev	CenterSel	FitSel	
~~Clear~~	~~Restore~~	~~Get~~	~~Store~~	Save	Merge	Stuff	IP Script	Help
Delete	Transform		Overlap	Curves	Shapes	Text	Fonts	Groups
Stroke	Color	Fill	Edit	Select	MakeHot	Units		

caches. During periods when the alignment objects are not changing, ORing this alignment object bitmap into the scene redraws all alignment objects without additional scan conversion.

During interactive transformation operations, the nearest point on the gravity-active object nearest the caret must be calculated many times per second for snap-dragging to work. Furthermore, intersection points of objects in the scene are calculated on the fly, as the caret nears a particular intersection point to which it might snap. Precalculating all the intersection points would have imposed a start-up delay for each interactive operation. Also, all objects carry within themselves their bounding box, used to quickly cull objects which cannot possibly be near enough to the caret to participate in snap-dragging at any given moment. Only objects whose bounding box contains or is near the caret are candidates for attracting it.

2.4. *Usability of the user interface*

Gargoyle's user interface must present a large number of user operations, partition the user operations into related sets, assign user actions to the operations, and be suitable for both frequent and infrequent users. Like other Cedar tools, Gargoyle is expected to be helpful, self-documenting, and to easily exchange data with other Cedar applications.

To begin, we need a way to present a large number of user operations in a small amount of screen space, suitable for both frequent and infrequent users. Categories of operations such as non-interactive transformations, overlap ordering, grouping of objects, and graphical style changes are represented at the top of a Gargoyle window in a control panel, using suggestive functional names, as seen in Figure 4. Each functional name is a *pop-up button*.

Cedar pop-up buttons combine several features in one user interface component. Most important, they are a solution to the problem of suiting the interface to both frequent and infrequent users. Even a former expert user, returning to a system infrequently, will be a novice until long unused skills return. Pop-up buttons are a combination of menus with accelerators, and the menus are used to document both themselves and the accelerators. If a user holds down any mouse button over a pop-

Figure 5: *the Edit pop-up button, popped*

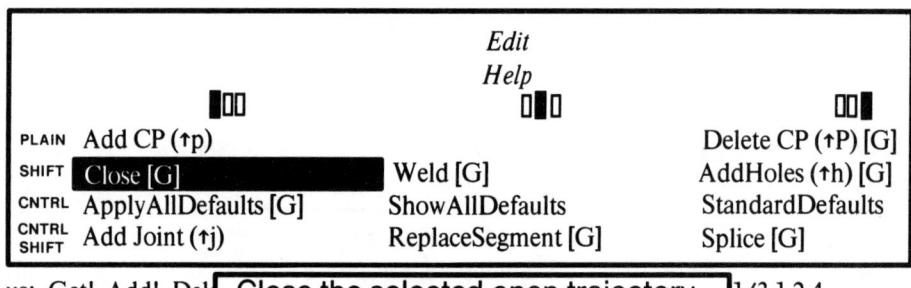

up, a menu of available operations appears; the Edit menu is shown in Figure 5. The user continues to hold down the mouse button while moving the cursor over each menu entry to select and highlight an entry. As each entry is highlighted, documentation for that entry appears immediately below the menu. When the mouse button is released, the highlighted operation is invoked and the menu disappears.

While pop-up buttons are our chief means for presenting a large set of commands to the user, using the menus can be unnecessarily slow. To remedy this, the user can tell from the arrangement of operations in a pop-up menu how to quickly invoke an operation, using a combination of mouse and keyboard keys, without popping up the menu and selecting the entry. For example, in the Edit menu, the three columns in the menu are labeled with small icons indicating the left, middle, and right mouse buttons respectively. The row labels indicate the combination of two option keys, called SHIFT and CNTRL, which may be held down independently or simultaneously. The row and column labels document a set of CNTRL/SHIFT/MouseButton actions that can be used to invoke operations without popping up the menu by quickly clicking over the pop-up button with the indicated option keys and mouse button. For example, the operation AddCP in the Edit menu can be invoked by quickly clicking the left mouse button over the Edit button. There is no need to wait for the menu to pop-up. Clicking the right mouse button with the keyboard keys SHIFT and CNTRL both held down will invoke the Splice command.

Users may pay no attention to the accelerated method of using pop-ups and always use the menus, or they may memorize accelerators to gain speed. Notice that this interface technique takes advantage of local repetition; a user may temporarily memorize a small set of accelerators for repeated use, then forget them and reacquire them as needed. The infrequent user need not remember operations or accelerators; the menus provide the needed documentation.

Some common menu operations can be invoked using single keystroke keyboard accelerators as well as through a pop-up. For instance, by holding down an option key and the "1" key, the user can set the stroke widths of selected objects to be 1.0 point wide. Keyboard accelerators are documented via both the Help menu and the pop-ups. For example, the Edit menu shows that the AddJoint operation may be invoked by typing CNTRL-j on the keyboard (in the menu, CNTRL is represented as ↑) as well as through the pop-up button.

Many operations are available only through the keyboard and mouse rather than through menus. Operations for creating, selecting, deselecting, and interactively transforming graphical objects require no menu based operations. Users employ a combination of mouse button clicks and keyboard control keys while the cursor is in the scene for these common operations. Documentation available via the Help pop-up button reminds the user of the mouse/key combinations; this documentation is permanently on the screen for repeated reference.

2.5. Integration and input/output

Gargoyle cooperates with the Cedar text editor (Tioga) to combine text and graphics into documents. More than simply a text editor, Tioga is an object-oriented editor/formatter and framework for document composition. Tioga creates tree-structured documents and manages non-textual node types which can carry arbitrary encoded information. Interpress nodes are one such node type. An Interpress master, regardless of source, can be integrated into a Tioga document and displayed or printed. Gargoyle generates Tioga nodes which contain the structured Gargoyle scene representation plus the Interpress description of the scene. Gargoyle can read such a node from a Tioga document to exactly recreate an editable scene.

Users interactively move selected Gargoyle objects into a Tioga document by simply pointing into the document at the desired insertion point and invoking the Gargoyle *stuff* operation. The converse operation is performed by selecting a Gargoyle node in a Tioga document and invoking the Gargoyle *merge* operation.

Gargoyle can read an Interpress master in one of two ways. The master may be read as a non-editable single entity, suitable for a background or filled box or for tracing; the master is merged into a scene as one graphical object. Alternately, the master may be read as a set of editable synthetic objects, in which case there will be a one-to-one correspondence between the drawing commands in the master and the editable objects created by Gargoyle. When Gargoyle writes its scene to an Interpress master, that master may then be transmitted to an Interpress printer for hardcopy or an Interpress preview program for display.

Figure 6: *PARC Car, by Steve Wallgren*

Figure 7: *SnapDragging, by Maureen Stone*

3. Conclusion

Gargoyle is a work in progress; neither its functionality nor its user interface is in final form. Current activities include more complete graphical hierarchy and alternate curve input and editing techniques. Future work will include research on techniques for easily creating symmetrical objects, management of large, complex scenes, and a rigorous redesign of the user interface based on statistics on user behavior and operation usage frequencies.

As the Gargoyle images in Figures 6 and 7 indicate, we have been successful at providing a high-quality tool for documentation graphics. The Interpress imaging model is a general purpose encoding of arbitrarily complex two-dimensional images, and Cedar provides a base for software dealing with these images interactively. Snap-dragging proves to be a workable mechanism for providing geometric precision in illustrations. The existing text editor framework makes it easy to integrate Gargoyle images both with text and with images from any other Interpress sources.

Acknowledgments

The authors would like to thank the other members of the CSL Systems and Imaging groups for providing the environment to make this work possible, with special thanks to Michael Plass and Doug Wyatt for their implementation of the Cedar imaging and Interpress packages.

References

[1] Adobe Illustrator$^{(TM)}$ User's Manual Version 1.0. (1987). Adobe Systems Inc.

[2] Arnon, D., Beach, R., McIsaac, K. & Waldspurger, C. (1988). CaminoReal: an interactive mathematical notebook. *Proceedings of the International Conference on Electronic Publishing, Document Manipulation and Typography* (EP88), Nice, France.

[3] Bushan, A. & Plass, M. (1986). The Interpress page and document description language. *IEEE Computer*, 19, 6, 72-76.

[4] Draw Manual. (1979). in *Alto User's Handbook*, Xerox Palo Alto Research Center, 97-128.

[5] Baudelaire, P. & Stone, M.C. (1980). Techniques for interactive raster graphics. *Computer Graphics*, 14, 3, 314-320.

[6] Beach, R.J. & Stone, M.C. (1983). Graphical style — toward high quality illustrations. *Computer Graphics*, 17, 3, 127-135.

[7] Bier, E.A. & Stone, M.C. (1986). Snap-dragging. *Computer Graphics*, 20, 4, 233-240.

[8] Borning, A. (1979). *Thinglab — a constraint oriented simulation laboratory*. Xerox Palo Alto Research Center, SSL-79-3.

[9] Golub, G.H. & VanLoan, C.F. (1983). *Matrix Computations*. John Hopkins University Press, Baltimore, MD.

[10] Xerox Corporation. (1986). *Interpress Electronic Printing Standard*, Version 3.0. XNSS

048601.

[11] Lipkie, D.E., Evans, S.R., Newlin, J.K. & Weissman, R.L. (1982). StarGraphics: an object-oriented implementation. *Computer Graphics*, **16**, 3, 115-124.

[12] Nelson, G. (1985). Juno, a constraint-based graphics system. *Computer Graphics*, **19**, 3, 235-243.

[13] Newman, W. & Sproull, R. (1979). *Principles of Interactive Computer Graphics*, McGraw-Hill Book Company.

[14] Pier, K.A. (1983). A retrospective on the Dorado, a high-performance personal computer. *Proceedings of the 10th International Symposium on Computer Architecture.*, SigArch/IEEE. Stockholm, 252-269.

[15] Swinehart, D.C., Zellweger, P., Beach, R.J. & Hagmann, R.B. (1986). A structural view of the Cedar programming environment, *ACM Transactions on Programming Languages and Systems*, **8**, 4, 419-490. Also available as Xerox PARC Technical Report CSL-86-1.

[16] Thacker, C.P., McCreight, E.M., Lampson, B.W., Sproull, R.F. & Boggs, D.R. (1982). Alto: a personal computer, in *Computer Structures: Principles and Examples*, eds. D.P. Siewiorek, C.G. Bell & A. Newell, McGraw-Hill Book Company.

[17] Warnock, J. & Wyatt, D.K. (1982). A device independent graphics imaging model for use with raster devices. *Computer Graphics* **16**, 3, 313-319.

[18] Zellweger, P. (1988). Active paths through multimedia documents. *Proceedings of the International Conference on Electronic Publishing, Document Manipulation and Typography* (EP88), Nice, France.

[19] Zellweger, P., Terry, D. & Swinehart, D. (1988). An overview of the Etherphone system and its applications. *Proceedings of 2nd IEEE Conference on Computer Workstations*, Santa Clara, CA.

FAXICOLOR : WORKSTATION FOR MIXED-MODE DOCUMENT COMPOSITION IN HOSPITAL ENVIRONMENT

RAFAEL DE SOUSA
LEE SHAOFENG
GILLES VAUCHER

Ecole Supérieure d'Electricité - Antenne de Rennes Avenue de la Boulais, B.P. 28, F-35511 Cesson-Sévigné, France

ABSTRACT

The FAXICOLOR workstation features an integrated image, text and graphics editor. FAXICOLOR processes images that are produced by medical equipments. These images have high quality resolution. Documents containing these images are structured in accordance with international standards. Producing documents with such a structure ensures powerful capabilities for communications. This paper describes the functions for image processing and document editing with FAXICOLOR. Futhermore, it explains the structure and the exchange protocol for FAXICOLOR documents.

1. FAXICOLOR Workstation

The SIRENE PACS, Picture Archiving and Communication System [Bir84], [Pac85], is designed in order to implement a radiology and hospital information system. The project started in 1985 at the CCETT[1] research center, in cooperation with the University of Rennes I and the Regional Hospital Center (CHR) of Rennes. Similar systems were announced by manufacturers such as IBM and GE (RIM - Radiology Information Management) and PHILIPS (MARCOM - Medical image ARchiving and COMmunication).

The SIRENE PACS [Sca87] is built on the local area network Carthage [Ren85]. It interconnects (figure 1) first of all radiology image sources (MRI - Magnetic Resonance Imaging, digital radiography, nuclear medicine, X-ray computer tomography), secondly an image and document archiving database, and lastly several workstations that process images and compose documents.

The major aim of this project is to enable medical doctors to analyse numerised radiological data (medical images) and to access the corresponding

---

[1] The CCETT - Centre Commun d'Etudes des Télécommunications et Télédiffusion is a French research center common to the P.T.T. and Télédiffusion de France.

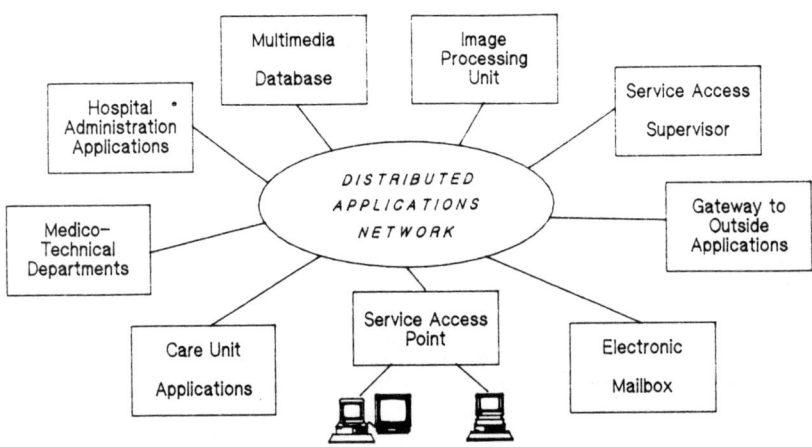

Figure 1: The SIRENE PACS

patient's informations stored in the database. Another purpose is to provide doctors with a whole set of tools to form and to store diagnoses according to image studies, radiological reports, and their own comments.

FAXICOLOR, a medium-sized workstation, was specially developed by ESE - Ecole Supérieure d'Electricité - and CCETT. It is designed for medical doctors and provides the necessary facilities for users to query the distant database to retrieve images and documents. It also provides a whole set of image processing and document composition facilities; it allows users to send composed or modified documents back to the database. The workstation has an alphanumerical screen devoted to the dialogue between the users and the SIRENE network database.

To process images, FAXICOLOR offers a wide range of digital manipulation capabilities, such as: optical filtering, histogram and density graphs, distance measuring, zooming, cine, frame, simultaneous display of studies and image comparison. Besides medical images, FAXICOLOR decodes and displays high or low resolution facsimile documents (the CCITT standard T.6) which are treated exactly as other medical images by the terminal.

For document manipulation, FAXICOLOR provides a set of functions and facilities which allow users to compose and manipulate electronic documents containing text, medical images from different sources, facsimiles, and graphics. This kind of documents are called mixed-mode documents. These electronic documents are stored in the SIRENE database and can be retrieved for further consultation or modification.

One important aspect in designing FAXICOLOR was to take into consideration the specific characteristics of final users. A doctor has been permanently advising troughout the whole development. In fact, medical doctors know well the nature of operations that can be done on medical images and have a particular "natural" manner to produce diagnostic documents, while they have dificulties in using a computer to perform these operations. Thus, the user interface in FAXICOLOR was implemented with an interaction style that is a metaphor of the doctors practices. Images and documents are presented to users in a high resolution display with a quality of reproduction closed to that of medical photographic equipments. A simple menu-oriented command language is provided for man-machine dialogue and a pointing device (mouse or tablet) is used to choose the commands in menus and to perform graphic operations over images. A team of specialists in ergonomy has reviewed the user interface design.

Another fundamental concern of FAXICOLOR and SIRENE is to comply with international standards. The communication interface is an application of the OSI model [Zim81]. The documents produced by FAXICOLOR are structured and exchanged in a format issued from the CCITT standard T73 in order to represent mixed-mode documents. Further development and adaptation of the system to other applications are greatly facilitated due to its standardized communication interface.

2. Image Processing

The image editor is an image kernel system which controls the image memory and image manipulations to help medical doctors in forming their diagnoses. The main issue encountered in the design of the editor is the diversity of image sources which produce different formats of images. The quality of images differs also from one another. When designing the terminal, one of the goals was to seek to accommodate diverse image types and to provide transparency for users. Another objective was to enhance image quality so as to enable doctors to analyse the images conveniently.

Besides the facilities that assemble images into a document together with text and graphs, this editor provides the following major functions :

Image display : each time the user calls for an image from the network, the image is immediately shown in the high resolution display which operates either in black and white mode with 256 resolution levels or in color (following medical requests, at present only the black and white mode is used for medical images). The images actually processed can have up to 1024 by

2048 pixels, a *scrol* function is provided to explore the whole image. A *zoom* function can be used to reduce or to enlarge an image. A cut function provides allowance to isolate a rectangular part of an image. A menu is shown beside the image to guide the user to perform all possible operations. The users can get the original form of a modified image at any time. A selection mechanism is provided permitting users to choose the image they want to observe and to modify.

Image comparison : comparing two similar images taken at different times from the same patient allows doctors to evaluate the evolution of the diseases. The comparison is made by calculating the difference in color levels for each pair of corresponding pixels in the two images. The result of the comparison is a new image on which other operations can be performed to enhance quality.

Simultaneous display of up to sixteen images : this is another method used by doctors to analyse groups of images. This method consists in reducing and placing images besides each other to obtain an output image where one can see all important details of a patient disease such as a summary of a disease's ovolution which can later be put into a document with some text comments.

Cine : sequential display of a number of images. Some radiological analyses are performed by realizing time sequential images of the human organs (example : the images of the brain taken while a nuclear fluid circulates in the cerebral vascular system). Then time dependent characteristics of the organs can be observed with the cine function. The users are at liberty to choose the correct speed of display.

Histogram and density calculations : statistics of color levels inside images that are presented in graphic form. The user draws within an image the outline of a zone in which he is interested, the workstation then performs the histogram calculation on this zone and displays the resulting graph. The latter helps the users to enhance the quality of medical images by means of computer aided *optical equalization and filtering*. To perform these last two operations, the workstation displays a graph representing the filtering parameters that are related to the contrast used to visualize the image. The shape of this graph can be modified by the user with the pointing device. The modification of the graph shape corresponds to the simultaneous modification of the filtering parameters, i.e contrast, for image display. This highly interactive operation allows the research of lesions of human tissues. The equalization graph and the histogram graph can be put into a document with the image.

3. Document Composition

3.1. Overview

The documents produced by doctors in a medical environment have just a few pages containing radiology images associated to the corresponding diagnosis (figure 2). Thus, FAXICOLOR documents have up to five pages where user can define rectangular blocks. These blocks can be filled with images, graphics or text.

While the document is being composed, a menu is displayed on the current page of the document. All functions of document composition are activated by a pointing device. In the same way, the pointing device is used to define block positions in the pages and to draw graphics. The keyboard is used to enter a text into a block within a page of document and to command text formatting operations.

The commands for document composition allow the creation and the modification of pages, blocks and contents. Using the communication facilities of the workstation, it is possible to insert one document into another.

Besides the facilities for copying and pasting blocks within a given document, the document editor furnishes a set of functions for manipulating block contents. The text edition facilities include a large group of usual functions, such as justification, tabulation, etc. For graphics, the workstation provides a pen, an eraser and facilities for drawing simple geometric figures such as lines, circles, rectangles and irregular polygons. All image manipulations (section 2) are available during document edition.

3.2. Document structure

FAXICOLOR offers users the possibility of creating and modifing mixed-mode documents. A mixed-mode document is defined as a document containing *contents coded with different techniques* such as facsimile codes, raster graphics codes or character codes, and *an identified structure* enabling document recognition, rebuild and reedition.

The concept of mixed-mode documents is used in the definition of international standards for document processing and communication such as the CCITT reccomendations T73 [T7384] and T400 [Dta86] or the ISO 8632 series for ODA: Office Document Architecture that are well discussed in [Jol86].

The document representation in FAXICOLOR is based on T73 recommendations but complementary definitions have been added to establish an image content architecture. FAXICOLOR documents have a logical structure that meets the needs of diagnosis composition. The lay-out structure is

```
┌─────────────────────────────────────────────────────────────┐
│              PATIENT: Mr. SMITH John, 27 years old          │
├─────────────────────────────────────────────────────────────┤
│                                                             │
│   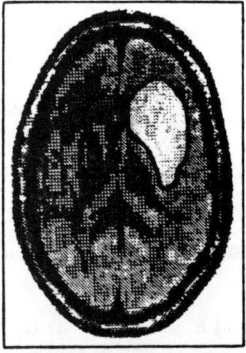   REPORT: M.R.I. and Nuclear Medicine studies.
│                                                             │
│              DATE: February 28, 1987.                       │
│                                                             │
│              REASONS of STUDY: Recent appearence of epileptic
│                                crisis. Normal neurological  │
│                                study. Previous history      │
│                                unknown.                     │
│                                                             │
│              DIAGNOSIS: M.R.I. study shows a lesion on the  │
│                         right fronto-temporal lobe with     │
│                         little mass effects upon ventricular│
│                         system.                             │
│   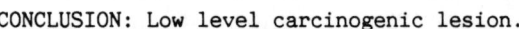   Nuclear Medicine study of Carotid  │
│                         vascular system shows that vascular │
│                         tissues are not affected.           │
│                                                             │
│              CONCLUSION: Low level carcinogenic lesion.     │
│                          Chemotherapy to be performed.      │
│                          Lesion evolution to be followed with
│                          M.R.I. studies.                    │
├─────────────────────────────────────────────────────────────┤
│                                                             │
│   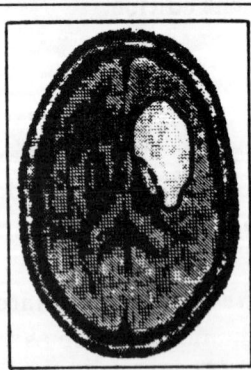   REPORT: M.R.I. study.              │
│                                                             │
│              DATE: March 20, 1987.                          │
│                                                             │
│              REASONS of STUDY: Carcinogenic lesion evolution.
│                                                             │
│              DIAGNOSIS: Rapid expansion of the lesion. Mass │
│                         effects upon ventricular system have│
│                         become critical.                    │
│                                                             │
│              CONCLUSION: Chemotherapy is inefficacious. It is
│                          necessary to perform a surgery.    │
└─────────────────────────────────────────────────────────────┘
```

Figure 2: A Diagnostic Document

a hierarchy containing a document descriptor, up to five page descriptors, up to thirty-two block descriptors per page and the associated content units. On the other hand, the generic descriptors (such as a page model) that are defined in T73 to avoid redundances are not used in FAXICOLOR. In fact, SIRENE documents are diagnoses with a simple structure and so there is no need for generic descriptors.

The document structure is described in terms of a tree. The nodes in a given tree structure represent the objects of the document structure. The tree leaves are block descriptors. The blocks in each page form an ordered list. The root of a block list is a page descriptor. The block is the only object to which a content can be assigned. Page descriptors are arranged in page number order. The root of the page list is the document descriptor.

3.3. Document exchange

To allow standard document analysis and recognition, FAXICOLOR documents are exchanged and archived in a format that contains a sub-set of the capabilities specified in the CCITT Recommendation T73 (now completed in the T400 series). This exchange format is called TIF7 according to term definitions in Recommendation T73.

Although there was already a mixed-mode exchange format (TIF1) defined within the Recommendation T73, it was necessary to create TIF7 because of specific characteristics of both FAXICOLOR and SIRENE. TIF7 includes the following features not present on TIF1: *a new resolution value of 100 points/inch for document reproduction, a bitmap code without compression* for medical images and a *bitmap code with compression* for graphics. These features have been introduced for purposes of reproduction and transmission of images and graphic contents in the documents produced by FAXICOLOR.

The set of fundamental objects of a document to be structured and exchanged in format TIF7 are one *Document Profile Descriptor* and the following *Specific Layout Object Descriptors*: one *document descriptor*, one or more *page descriptors, block descriptors, content units* (text, image, graphics).

The document descriptors of structured documents are transmitted in accordance with their position in the document tree, that is, in accordance with the hierarchy in the document structure. The protocol elements representing specific objects (Document, Page and Block Descriptors) follow the Document Profile Descriptor. Each Content Unit follows immediately the associated Block Descriptor.

The document structure is transmitted using the CCITT Recommendation X409: Presentation Transfer Syntax and Notation. The standard notation defined in X409 is a formal description method that allows complex data structures to be specified in terms of elementary data types such as integers, octets and character strings. In fact complex structures are divided into elementary pieces having three components: a *type*, a *length* and a *value*; so that they are called TLV structures. The effective content of the TLV is placed in its component "value"; the class and the length of the information in the content are placed respectively in the components "type" and "length". The content of a TLV can be another TLV.

4. Conclusion

The whole software has been delivered in April 1987, it is written in C language and contains 46,000 lines of code. FAXICOLOR has been installed, with the SIRENE PACS, in the CHR hospital in Rennes by the end of 1987. The software is considered portable across UNIX systems having a display memory with each pixel accessible through word addressing capabilities of the host processor.

A group of medical doctors from the CHR hospital has evaluated the workstation before its final installation. Their evaluation shows that doctors are satisfied with the terminal capabilities. Doctors did not ask for any modifications of the software functions or of the user interface.

An expert market analysis has been done to evaluate the fields of application and the commercial future of FAXICOLOR. The analysis shows that there is an important market in the USA. In Europe, the medium-term prospects are very optimistic.

The present software version is adequate to play the role of image processor in the radiology platform within hospitals. Today the workstation prototype is relatively expensive due to its hardware structure. Some efforts are still to be done by means of compacting the hardware composition in order to reduce the terminal costs, so as to make it accessible to private medical doctors. A possible solution is to transplant the software onto a Personal Computer to form a low cost workstation based on a PC.

Although FAXICOLOR, along with the whole SIRENE system, is designed for medical purposes, its communication possibilities and its image and document processing capabilities interest other activity fields such as tourism, museums, communication within enterprises and communities, estate agencies. FAXICOLOR also attracts the attention of cartoon producers.

Using FAXICOLOR as a terminal connected to the French Satellite Network TELECOM1 for image processing is a project well under way.

5. Acknowledgements

We took the responsibility for writing this description of the FAXICOLOR workstation. But credit for the creation of the system goes also to other people working in the framework of SIRENE. Maryse Launay at CCETT and some ESE students initially tested the hardware and made some tools to evaluate user needs. Boumedienne Mahieddine contributed to the realization of the file transfer services and a CCETT team made basic communication facilities for the Carthage Network.

References

[Bir84] D.A. Birkner. Design considerations for a user oriented pacs. In *IEEE Proceedings on Medical Images and Icons (MEDPACS)*, pages 515, 89–102, 1984.

[Dta86] *Draft Recommendation T4xa, Document Transfert Architecture - General Principles, Document Architecture, Application Rules.* Geneva, Switzerland: CCITT, 1986.

[Jol86] V. Joloboff. Trends and standards in document representation. In van Vliet J.C., editor, *Text Processing and Document Manipulation*, pages 107–124, Cambridge University Press, 1986.

[Pac85] *Third International Conference on Picture Archiving and Communication System (PACS 3) for Medical Applications.* 1985. Schneider, R. Dwyer, S.J. ed. Proc. SPIE 536.

[Ren85] R. Renoulin. Evolution of a local area network from office automation applications to picture archiving and communication system in a hospital environment. In *EFOCLAN85 : Third European Fiber Optic Communications and Local Area Networks Exposition*, 1985.

[Sca87] J.M. Scarabin, et al. *The SIRENE Project, Computer Assisting Radiology (CARS).* Berlin, FRG., 1987.

[T7384] *Recommendation T73 - Document Interchange Protocol for the Telematic Services.* Geneva, Switzerland: CCITT, 1984.

[Zim81] H. Zimmermann. Progression of the osi reference model and its applications. In *Proc. of the NTC 81*, 1981. F8.1.1-F8.1.6.

VIDURA - AN INTERACTIVE MULTILINGUAL PUBLISHING SYSTEM - SPECIFICATION & DESIGN

SATYAJIT NATH, SUMANTA N. PATTANAIK and S.P. MUDUR

National Centre for Software Technology, Bombay, India

ABSTRACT

There are a large number of languages, many with their own distinct scripts, in current use in India. There are no real standards yet for Indian language text input, editing, etc. Word processing in Indian languages is yet to take off. Design of a publishing system for Indian languages requires specification right from text input, to text editing to page composition and printing. This paper presents the specification and design of an interactive multilingual publishing system for handling many of the Indian scripts including the Roman script. The system is being developed for the Department of Arts of the Government of India. Distinctive features and specific composition logic of the Indian scripts are briefly discussed first. Discussed next are the problems and inadequacies of extending commercially available desk-top publishing systems for handling context-sensitive scripts dominant in India. Then a unique keyboard input and text encoding scheme compatible with ASCII is presented followed by the publishing system specification with some design details. Unlike the available systems which are based on the 2D layout paradigm, throughout this system specification, the text editing paradigm is used to model the document and the user interface, even for the page make up task. This has also lead to a simple consistent user model for all the tasks of document input, editing and page composition, and also a single integrated representation for a document complete with layout attributes.

1. Introduction

Electronic Publishing has evolved starting with batch oriented text formatters to screen editors, word processors, turnkey photocomposing systems, sophisticated typesetting packages and now interactive publishing systems [Furuta82, Kernighan82, Knuth84, Mudur79, Reid80]. One of the hottest topics in computers is desk-top publishing and there is a plethora of new low cost systems claiming the ability to produce publication quality documents [Alsop87, Holmes87]. Desk-top publishing gives one complete control over the creation of a printed document. One can now key in text, edit text, draw illustrations, include photographs, design page layouts and also print a finished document with a relatively small and inexpensive computer and laser printer.

There are a few features which together distinguish desk-top publishing from the other electronic publishing tools such as wordprocessors, typesetting packages, etc. [Seybold87]. Firstly, one can compose text in a manner that comes close to the requirements of typesetting. Secondly, the WYSIWYG bit mapped screen is supported and one can perform the composition task with interactive commands. Thirdly, they include a pagination or area composition program, letting one include graphics and output illustrative matter along with the text. They also provide reasonably good editing tools of the kind offered by the best word processors, to make textual changes interactively, not merely to uncomposed text, but to text in the process of interactive composition. Lastly, they support printing on a medium to high resolution raster printing device for text and graphics preferably interfacing via a page description language like PostScript[1]. As of today, very few commercially available desk-top publishing systems provide all these features.

In India, in current use, there are 16 different languages and hundreds of dialects with many of these languages having distinct scripts of their own. The English language, written in the Roman script, is also widely used, particularly for most official correspondence and higher education in science and technology. This has been largely due to the rapid advances that printing technology has made when dealing with the Roman script. Electronic publishing in Indian scripts is still in its infancy. When digital typesetting systems began to be imported for English language printing they evoked considerable amount of interest amongst academics from computer science as well as graphic arts.[Mudur80, Sinha84]. Considerable amount of preliminary work got done for adapting this technology to the Indian scripts. Typesetting and typefont design systems were indigenously developed. Even TEX and METAFONT [Knuth79] were used for experimental purposes with encouraging results [Ghosh83]. However, the commercially available systems are all based on traditions of the movable type and though very well suited to handle the Roman script are quite unsatisfactory and problematic when extended to handle the context sensitive scripts dominant in India [MacKay86]. For none of these scripts adapt themselves amicably to matrix bound character designs. What is really needed are electronic publishing systems specifically designed and developed to handle the Indian scripts and their specific graphic and composition requirements. Fortunately, most of the Indian scripts are derived from the Sanskrit script, Devanagari, and can be handled by the same logical mechanisms.

---

1   PostScript is a trademark of Adobe Systems Inc.

One important point to note here is that electronic publishing is really not a new concept for the Roman script. Established standards exist for handling of text in this script including editors and wordprocessors. Available publishing systems are designed to and very often rely heavily on being able to incorporate text created by other systems. The centre piece of these publishing systems is thus the pagination or area composition software. On the other hand, electronic publishing of Indian language texts has yet to take off. There are no standards yet for keyboard input, text encoding, text editing, etc. Word processing programs available are very few and usually quite dismal in performance. There do exist manual typewriters. Their design is based more on graphical primitives and less on the known alphabets of the languages. Composing graphic primitives into letter shapes is the burden of the typist. It is well understood that such a layout is unsuited for computer input mechanisms [DoE86]. One immediate implication of this is that whereas the designer of a publishing system for the Roman script has to concentrate only on the page make-up task, for Indian languages the designer has to worry about specifications for keyboard input mechanisms, to text editing to page composition and printing. There is however one positive aspect to this entire design task, which is that it is now possible with some care to base the system design on efficient and consistent models for document maintenance and user interface. This, in our opinion, is something that the available Roman script publishing systems have been unable to do. The rest of this paper describes the specification and some design details of an interactive publishing system, Vidura, specifically designed to handle Indian scripts including the Roman script.

2. Distinctive Features of Indian Scripts

In the Roman script, as is used for English, the phonetic form of words in the language, basically pronunciation, is ambiguous (the but-put problem) i.e., there is no exact match between phonemes and orthographic representations. This information is based on arbitrary historical rules and is memorized by people using the language. Other European languages add some diacritical marks to represent this information. Even then, ambiguity is not totally eliminated. However, due to this fortuitous reason, in the Roman script, there is no Context-Sensitive composition, except for adding diacritical marks. Unmodified characters from the base alphabet are always added linearly to the right. Thus, composition of syllables and consequently of words is strictly a process of juxtaposing alphabet symbols in a horizontal direction. In Devanagari and related Indian languages, a phoneme is directly represented in a unique graphical form. The basic graphical unit in these Indian scripts is the AKSHARA. Aksharas are added linearly to form words and words are similarly added linearly to form lines. In this respect, composition rules in Devanagari and Roman are identical. But, the most important difference lies in the rules governing the graphic form of Aksharas. Aksharas are formed out of a basic alphabet consisting of 34 CONSONANTS (C), 2 CONSONANT MODIFIERS (Cm), 14 VOWELS (V) and 3 VOWEL MODIFIERS (Vm). Some South Indian languages have more than 14 vowels.

An Akshara could be of two types:

- a sequence of one or more consonants, each optionally followed by a consonant modifier, followed by a vowel, optionally followed by a vowel modifier, i.e. C [Cm] [C [Cm] ... C [Cm]] V [Vm].

- a lone vowel, optionally followed by a vowel modifier, i.e. V [Vm].

Figure 1: *the basic alphabet set and various graphical forms*

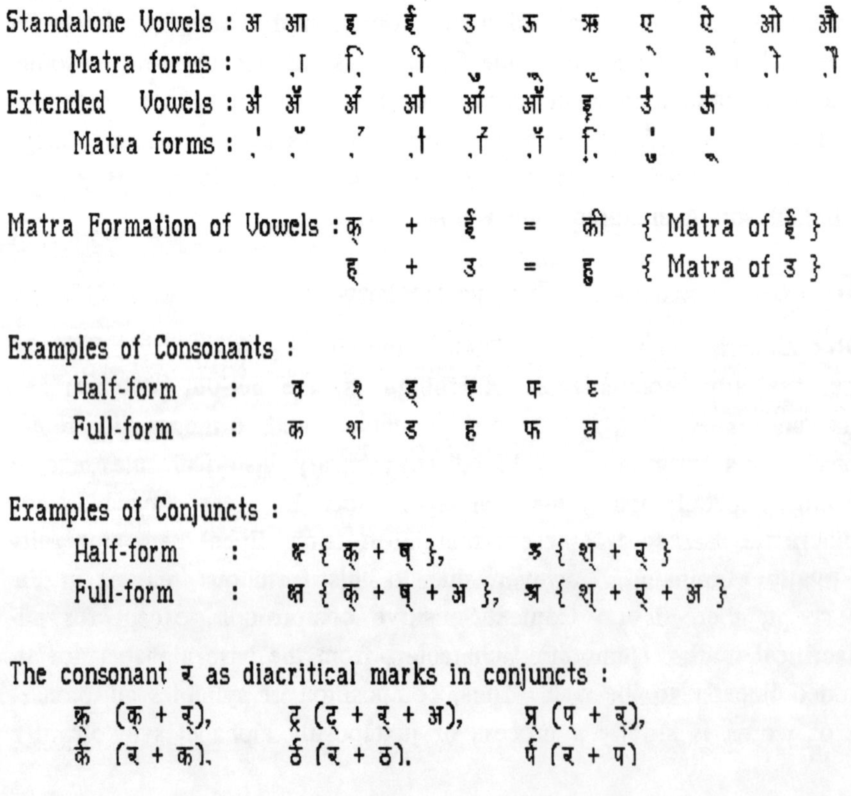

Standalone Vowels : अ आ इ ई उ ऊ ऋ ए ऐ ओ औ
Matra forms : ा ि ी ु ू ृ े ै ो ौ
Extended Vowels : अॆ अँ अं ऑ ऑ ऑ ॠ ॡ ॡ
Matra forms : ॆ ँ ं ॉ ॉ ॉ ॄ ॢ ॣ

Matra Formation of Vowels : क् + ई = की { Matra of ई }
                            ह् + उ = हु { Matra of उ }

Examples of Consonants :
    Half-form   :   क् श् ड् ह् फ् ब्
    Full-form   :   क   श   ड   ह   फ   ब

Examples of Conjuncts :
    Half-form   :   क्ष् { क् + ष् },   श्र् { श् + र् }
    Full-form   :   क्ष { क् + ष् + अ },   श्र { श् + र् + अ }

The consonant र as diacritical marks in conjuncts :
    क्र (क् + र),   द्र (द् + र + अ),   प्र (प् + र),
    र्क (र + क).   र्ठ (र + ठ).   र्प (र + प)

The sequence of consonants in a Type-I Akshara results in different graphic forms depending on the consonants involved. Some consonants combine to form completely new graphic forms called CONJUNCTs (Samyuktaksharas). Other consonants combine linearly as a simple juxtaposition of their HALF-FORMs.[1] In any given Type-I Akshara, one or more sub-sequences of consonants may result in conjuncts. Half-forms and conjuncts combine linearly and are almost always restricted to the X-height region.

The graphical form of a lone vowel in a Type-II Akshara is absolutely different from that of the vowel in a Type-I Akshara which has consonants immediately preceding it. In the latter case, the vowel takes the form of a MATRA (a diacritical mark) which attaches to the consonant; whereas in the former a stand-alone graphic form results. Unlike in the Roman script where diacritical marks usually appear in the ascender or descender region of a letter, MATRAs in Indian scripts and vowel/consonant modifiers may appear even in the X-height region of a letter. In fact, some MATRAs may occur in all regions and even to the left of the preceding consonant sequence. Figure 1 shows the basic alphabet set and the various graphical forms. A one-to-one correspondence between an alphabetic character and a type cannot be assumed. This is true also for diacritical marks on Roman letters. But whereas this is an exception in the Roman script, for Indian scripts it is the general rule. As pointed out earlier, it is extremely difficult to work with composition logic that is based on matrix bound character graphics unless an extremely large graphic character set is maintained. This, however, introduces its own incumbent problems of keyboarding and encoding because it is not possible to restrict the set to say, within 256 or so. Kern tables, accent marks and ligatures - some of the mechanisms available in today's systems - are being used for handling Indian scripts. The resulting solutions are not only cumbersome, inefficient and limited in many ways but also result often in graphically unsatisfactory output.

3. The Input Mechanism and Character Encoding

As suggested earlier, the phonetic division of Indian alphabets into vowels, consonants and their modifiers serves as a common base for all Indian scripts. The methodology of combining these basic groups to form syllables is governed by a set of well-defined rules, laid down during the time of Panini, the great grammarian and linguist. The basic principle is to com-

---

1   Note: In fact this is the only case in which Akshara composition has rules similar to those of Roman.

pletely distinguish between vowel sounds and consonant sounds. Therefore, to vocalize a syllable, one either pronounces a pure vowel sound or a sequence of pure consonant sounds followed by a vowel sound. The consonant modifiers serve to modify the consonant sounds and the vowel modifiers do the same for vowels. On this basis we have described aksharas as Type-I or Type-II. Hence, given a sequence of characters denoting pure consonants and vowels we can unambiguously compute their partitioning into a sequence of Type-I and Type-II aksharas by going through the sequence one at a time from start to end. Figure 2 shows the PC keyboard layout. We have taken great care to ensure that we only replace the Roman script key positions of the QWERTY keyboard. For ease of use we have also provided frequently used conjuncts and very infrequently used vowels and modifiers in the ALT position of the keyboard. For a detailed analysis of this approach, see [Pattanaik87].

Figure 2: *the PC keyboard layout*

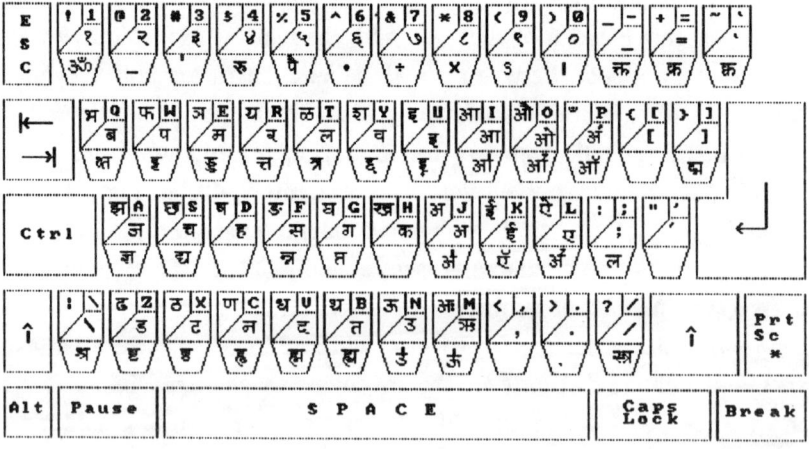

The phonetic scheme used for inputting from the keyboard is also used for representing text in the computer. Although most Indian languages follow the generic rules of composition of Aksharas described above, the graphical forms for aksharas as well as composition rules for individual MATRAs and modifiers vary from one language to another. Thus, to cite an example, a vowel MATRA which attaches in the super level of the Akshara in Devanagari might attach in the ascender X-height level in Assamese (ae-kaar). Such variations show that though Aksharas, in principle, are formed exactly in the same manner in all these languages, the final graphic form may be widely varying. One can therefore, think of a common representation which will encompass all these languages and be independent of the final graphic form of the aksharas.

There are two aspects to the task of assigning codes to the basic script primitives. Since implementation is being carried out on a machine which uses ASCII for the Roman script, it is essential that no damage be done to this system while adding our codes. Secondly, the codes must be assigned in such a way that the dictionary sorting order for Devanagari is maintained. Figure 3 shows the encoding for Devanagari. The same encoding applies to all Indian scripts. For multiple languages we use nested SI and SO codes with a single additional byte to denote the language. Note that the 7 bit ASCII codes for Roman have been left untouched.

Figure 3: *encoding for Devanagari*

L/H	2	3	4	5	6	7	-	10	11	12	13	14	15
0:	SP	0	@	P	`	p		SP	०	@	औ	`	भ़
1:	!	1	A	Q	a	q		!	१	9	.	झ़	म्
2:	"	2	B	R	b	r		"	२	ऽ	..	ञ़	य्
3:	#	3	C	S	c	s		#	३	ॲ	क़्	ड़	ऱ्
4:	$	4	D	T	d	t		$	४	ॲं	ख़	ठ़	ल्
5:	%	5	E	U	e	u		%	५	अः	ग़्	ड़	ळ
6:	&	6	F	V	f	v		&	६	अ	ब़्	ढ़	व्
7:	'	7	G	W	g	w		'	७	आ	ङ़्	ण्	श्
8:	(	8	H	X	h	x		(	८	इ	च़्	त्	ष्
9:	)	9	I	Y	i	y		)	९	ई	छ़्	थ्	स्
10:	*	:	J	Z	j	z		*	:	उ	ज़्	द्	ह्
11:	+	;	K	[	k	{		+	;	ऊ	[	ध्	{
12:	,	<	L	\	l	|		,	<	ॠ	\	न्	|
13:	-	=	M	]	m	}		-	=	ए	]	प्	}
14:	.	>	N	^	n	~		.	>	ऐ	^	फ़	~
15:	/	?	O	_	o	DEL		/	?	ओ	_	ब़	DEL

As mentioned earlier, an akshara could be a sequence of one or more characters. For interactive display purposes, intermediate graphic forms of aksharas have to be displayed. With every new character appended to or deleted from (during editing) an akshara, the graphic form displayed has to be updated. The akshara structure can be elegantly represented by a tree. Each edge in a tree represents a coded primitive and each node represents a graphic symbol to be displayed [Mudur80]. Thus any Indian language can be regarded as a set of akshara trees [1]. Therefore, in the simplest case, an algorithm for displaying aksharas will "walk through" appropriate trees in the set by following edges governed by the code sequence and displaying graphic forms whenever a leaf node is reached. In the case of interactive display, the algorithm will display the graphic form for each node at every level.

Conceptually, this scheme is ideal for the task. However, from an implementation point of view, it requires a lot of storage. This happens because, in many cases, there are simple rules of graphic composition for a group of aksharas and this information is not utilized in this scheme. For example, addition of a vowel to a consonant causes the pure consonant form to change to the full form with the vowel MATRA getting attached to it. Similarly, addition of a consonant to a consonant may cause either the pure consonant changing to the half form and the new consonant taking the pure form, or the pure consonant changing to a pure conjunct form. In the tree scheme, for each akshara, with one consonant and one vowel, there would be a separate tree, i.e., a total of 36 x 12 trees. An alternative solution is to classify various types of aksharas and have separate procedures for displaying them. This scheme has lower memory requirements but is computationally expensive. Depending upon what is more important, speed or storage, a choice has to be made between the two schemes. In an interactive system, real-time display is very important. Hence we have adopted the former by flattening out the set of trees into a 2D table accessed by a pair of consecutive primitive codes.

4. The Usage Paradigm For Vidura

With emphasis on bit mapped multi-window graphics, pop-up or drop-down menus, icon driven interfaces and mouse-based pointing and positioning, the two dimensional layout paradigm as used for engineering draughting, interior design layout, etc., seemed natural and fashionable to choose as a paradigm for page composition. And this is what all systems have done. It has a lot of high-tech appeal too for the lay user. However, we do not at all believe that this is the ideal paradigm for publishing. In fact, on rectangular pages, horizontal and vertical alignments are crucial both aesthetics as well as readability wise. Hence, arbitrary dragging of paragraphs within a

---

[1] A matter of interest is that the Roman script is a special case in this structure - it is a set of trees with only one node in each tree.

page and snapping to grids are far too general, unconstrained and somewhat unnatural operations for page composition or column setting. For example, without elaborate geometric interference checks, one cannot ensure that matter is being set with proper placement and no unintended superimposition. Another undesired side effect of this is that most publishing systems do not focus at all on the creation of the matter (text and graphics) in the document. Some limited capabilities are included without properly integrating these into the system, for it is assumed that text and graphic elements will be imported during the time of composition. As a result, most of the systems do not properly handle large publications, cannot reflect edit changes or perform global edits or do h & j etc., essentially tasks which are handled elegantly and efficiently by many screen editors and word processors.

Considering the fact that more than a substantive part of the total task of publishing a document happens to be creation and editing of the matter that goes in, and additionally, the earlier observation, that electronic document creation tools have only now begun to emerge for Indian scripts, we decided when working on Vidura that we shall base the specification on the text editing paradigm. For, this paradigm is simple and easy to understand. Also formal specifications have been worked upon [Sufrin82]. Below we shall informally elaborate on this paradigm before discussing in some detail the design specification and how this paradigm has had its influence.

In the text editing paradigm, typically we have edit and display mechanisms.

- Editing is always described around a current point of intereset, the cursor. Editing operations constitute moves, inserts, replaces and deletes. All these operations are defined over a hierarchical structure of syntactic constructs from the cursor point. Typical syntactic constructs in editing are: characters, words, lines, paragraphs, pages, blocks and the document itself.

- The display mechanism can be likened to one that enables looking at the document through a movable window which locates itself so as to keep the cursor in view. The matter within a window is projected into a two-dimensional region with typographic attributes taking effect wherever applicable.

5. Vidura Specifications

Vidura specifications are entirely based on the one single paradigm of text editing.[1] This has resulted in a consistent, simple, elegant and powerful user interface and an integrated document structure. Four key design concepts that have facilitated this are - (a) a notional composite cursor with typographic attributes, (b) nested typographic and composition attributes using a block structured scope rule, (c) A hierarchical box structure for generating composed pages, and (d) composition style macros.

The document is modelled simply as a sequence of multi-lingual letters or glyphs (Indian script aksharas, Roman script letters, ASCII symbols, etc.), with composition and typographic control attributes associated with some subsequences and with some positions (between two glyphs) in the sequence. At any instant of time there is a single point of interest, i.e., the cursor. It always lies between two glyphs. The cursor is always associated with a complete setting of typographic attributes. Attribute settings are scoped and nested (block structured) [Mudur79]. That is, they apply over some contiguous subsequence of the document. There are three ways in which attribute settings get associated with the cursor. One, when the cursor is explicitly moved into or out of an attribute scope. Another, when a new attribute setting is inserted at the current cursor position. This begins a new attribute scope which has the cursor within it but nothing else. As letters are inserted they take on the typographic attributes of the cursor and become part of the current scope. And a third, when there is deletion of text that results in an attribute setting with empty scope (no text or the cursor) or when there is no text separating nested settings. The cursor can be moved over syntactic units in the document. The cursor may lie anywhere within a syntactic unit other than an akshara or letter. Standard move and delete operations, as in any other wordprocessor, are available. Because of the aksharas being distinct glyphs, a special DELETE key is needed for intra-akshara editing.

The display mechanism is the one which outputs the matter in the document in the form of composed pages. A subtle but fundamentally important difference from many of the available systems must be noted here. The basic idea is to have one or more movable windows defined over the document and project these suitably onto the regions in a page as against the approach in existing systems of importing text or other matter into a region

---

[1] In fact we have also used this paradigm for drawing and editing of illustrations; but that we shall be describing elsewhere.

in a page. The parameters of the projection define a composition style. It is clear that in this mechanism one can support predefined composition styles, a very useful and powerful facility that is commonly available in large type setting packages operating in batch mode and in very few interactive publishing packages [Holmes87, Mudur82].

A document is displayed as a sequence of non-overlapping pages. A page is the largest possible box. It may be tessellated into smaller non-overlapping boxes which may also be tessellated into smaller non-overlapping boxes. The document display structure is therefore hierarchical. Pages are identified by a page number while each box within could have a unique name - *header , footer, footnote, caption,* etc . Except the page, all boxes have a type: text, image or empty. Empty boxes are white space in the page. A box has a default attribute setting associated which is applicable to matter that is set into the box. All child boxes inherit attributes from their parent unless they are explicitly altered. The text box attributes are classified into types like dimensions, stretchability (size of a box depends on its contents), matter permanency (useful for running heads, etc.), layout parameters and typographic parameters. For detailed design specifications and user interface description, see [Nath87].

6. Implementation Status

The Vidura multilingual publishing system is being developed to operate on an IBM PC/AT with a medium resolution graphics screen and supporting at present PostScript printers, many dot matrix printers (for draft copies) and the DEC LN03 laser printers. Initially the Roman and Devanagari scripts will be incorporated. A PostScript interpreter has been developed and supports dot-matrix printers and the DEC LN03 laser printer. Digital typeface design too is in progress. A prototype of the Vidura system is expected to be demonstrated towards the end of 1987.

Acknowledgements

We are extremely grateful to Prof. R.K. Joshi, IIT, Bombay, for his involvement in all the linguistic aspects of this work, particularly the keyboard layout and the typeface design. His enthusiasm as well as his own love, his Deshascript, a common script for all Indian languages, have been strong motivating forces. We thank the Indira Gandhi National Centre for Arts for supporting the total development of Vidura. We are also grateful to Dr. S. Ramani, Director, National Centre for Software Technology, for his support and encouragement. We are grateful to Shri V. Padmanabhan for all his efforts in ensuring that this manuscript gets produced in time.

References

[1] Alsop Stewart, DeskTop Publishing Without Hype, *PC MAGAZINE*, 111-156, Feb.10, 1987.

[2] Dept. of Electronics, Govt. of India, Report of the Committee for Standardization of Keyboard Layout for Indian Script based Computers, *Electronics - Information & Planning*, **14**, 1, Oct. 1986, 3-18.

[3] Furuta Richard, Jeffrey Scofield and Alan Shaw, Document Formatting Systems: Survey, Concepts, and Issues. In *DOCUMENT PREPARATION SYSTEMS*, eds. J.Nievergelt et al, North Holland Publishing Company, 1982.

[4] Ghosh P.K., *An Approach to Type Design And Text Composition in Indian Scripts*, Report No. STAN-CS-83-965, Stanford University, April 1983.

[5] Holmes Thom, Make My Page!, *BYTE*, **12**, 5, 159-166.

[6] Kernighan Brian W., Michael E. Lesk, UNIX Document Preparation. In *DOCUMENT PREPARATION SYSTEMS*, eds. J. Nievergelt et al, North Holland Publishing Company, 1982.

[7] Knuth D.E., *TEX and METAFONT: New Directions in Typesetting*, Digital Press, 1979.

[8] Knuth D.E., *The TEX Book*, Reading, MA: Addison-Wesley, 1984.

[9] MacKay Pierre A., Typesetting Problem Scripts, *BYTE*, **11**, 2, 201-218.

[10] Mudur S.P., A.W. Narwekar, Abha Moitra, Design of Software for Text Composition, *Software - Practice and Experience*, **9**, 313-323.

[11] Mudur S.P., R. Sujatha, Three Systems for Typesetting - A Survey, *Computer Science and Informatics*, **12**, 1, 3-9.

[12] Mudur S.P., L.S. Wankankar, P.K. Ghosh, *Design Information Report on Text Composition in Devanagari, RIND Report*, Research Institute for Newspaper Development, Madras, Sep. 1980.

[13] Nath Satyajit, S.P. Mudur, *Vidura Functional Specifications and User Interface*, Internal Design Report, Graphics & CAD Division, NCST, 1987.

[14] Pattanaik Sumanta N., Satyajit Nath, S.P. Mudur, Computer Processing of Indian Scripts - A Pure Consonant Approach, In *Proc. of Computer Assisted Language Processing Seminar*, Delhi, Sep. 1987.

[15] Reid Brian, *SCRIBE - A Document Specification Language and its Compiler*, Ph.D. Thesis, Dept. of Computer Science, Carnegie Mellon University, 1980.

[16] Seybold John W., The Desktop-Publishing Phenomenon, *BYTE*, **12**, 5, 149-154.

[17] Sinha R.M.K., Computer Processing of Indian Languages and Scripts - Potentialities and Problems, *Journal of Institute of Electronics & Telecommunication Engineers (India)*, **30**, 6.

[18] Sufrin Bernard, Formal Specification of a Display - Oriented Text Editor, *Science of Computer Programming*, 1982, 1, 157-202.

SYNTHESIS OF PRINT-QUALITY CURSIVE SCRIPT BASED ON A MODEL OF THE HUMAN HANDWRITING MECHANISM

E.H. DOOIJES
Department of Computer Science, University of Amsterdam

ABSTRACT

We propose a technique for the generation of quasi-calligraphic script, suitable for application in high-quality book printing. This technique, named Heliscript, is based upon a simple model of the human handwriting mechanism.

1. Introduction.

Most of the recent literature on digital typography deals with the design and generation of detached letterforms, to be put together into lines of text essentially in the fashion of Gutenberg. Examples are [Bigelow83, Coueignoux85, Flowers84, Knuth79]. In this paper, on the contrary, we propose a technique for the generation of running, quasi-calligraphic script from keyboard input, based upon the imitation of the handwriting process. The epitheton 'quasi-calligraphic' refers to the intended application of this technique in high-quality book printing. We expect our system to produce script with a more natural appearance than is possible with detached-type fonts, while allowing for variations in size, style, letter spacing and output device resolution without requiring the complete redesign of the basic character set. Also transformations like mapping onto a curved baseline could be performed easily.

While the proposed method may have interesting applications in Western typography, a more obvious target is the essentially calligraphic Arabic script. A recent review of the peculiarities of Arabic text processing is given in [Becker87]. Indeed, our ultimate objective is the construction of an Arabic text composer. In the present paper we will however restrict our attention to Latin script, as the problems encountered there are relevant for Arabic as well. Features of our system of relevance for handwriting motorics research are discussed in [Dooijes87].

For the design of digital typefaces two different, and in a sense complementary methods are in vogue. With the first of these, the letter is defined by its outlines. With the second method, instead, a letter is considered as being drawn with a pen or brush having a fixed or varying profile. The letterform is determined by the dot pattern representing the brush, together with the trajectory of the brush's center. In keeping with the writing imitation principle, our technique is based on this approach.

With script synthesis, a number of problems is encountered not present with typeface construction. Obviously, one of these is the need to construct a continuous brush trajectory, corresponding to a contiguous *sequence* of letters. Furthermore, in script the form of a letter is generally affected by its predecessor and successor; also it is not possible to ensure that a letter's position with respect to the raster is always the same. Therefore, rasterization has to be performed 'on the fly' in contrast with the detached-type situation, where each letter has to be rasterized only once (for a given resolution of the output device). As a further consequence, procedures have to be included in the system for automated 'tuning' of the resulting dot patterns, whereas in typeface design the artist has the option of correcting these patterns manually.

In this paper we will mainly deal with the first issue: the design, representation and interconnection of the virtual pen trajectories of separate letters.

2. Problems with the synthesis of letters and their connectors.

In this section, we review a number of typical problems encountered in the design and representation of separate script letters, and in the synthesis of the pen trajectory. First, it is essential for our purpose that any single letter can be defined without the explicit constraint that its trajectory match that of potentially adjacent letters. Instead, each letter has to comply automatically with its neighbours. A closely related problem is that the precise extent of a script letter is hard to define: a letter has *compliance regions* at both ends. The influence of the adjacent letters on the shape of a given letter is taken to be confined to these (non-overlapping) regions. Non-overlap implies, of course, that a letter is influenced by its nearest neighbours only.

It turns out that these peculiarities are not easily dealt with in a straightforward way by any of the highly developed techniques for freehand curve design known from the CAD literature [Fournier85, Pavlidis83, Plass83]. As an illustration we sketch here one of our early attempts, based on the representation of the pen trajectory as a polygon-guided cubic B-spline curve. (For a survey of B-spline theory and terminology, see [Boehm84]). This parametric representation allows to construct in a simple way a continuous pen trajectory from a number of single-letter trajectories. This stems from the fact that a B-spline curve is invariant under linear transformations of its associated knot vector. Thus, a two-letter trajectory, including the connector in between, can in principle be constructed by simply shifting both the guiding polygon and the knot vector of the second letter to their appropriate positions in XY and parameter space, respectively; whereafter a new spline curve is computed, defined by the combined knot vectors and guiding polygons.

Unfortunately, as it appears by experimentation, this approach is hampered by a number of serious imperfections, which can be summarized as follows. First, with the spline continuation technique described above it is certainly possible to obtain 'pleasing' curves, due to the inherent smoothness properties of splines in general. However it is hard to invent *uniformly* applicable constraints which could provide these curves with a *natural* appearance as well. The uniformity issue arises from the necessity to compute any letter pair's connector 'on the fly', and under varying conditions of scaling or similar transformations of the basic letterforms.

Furthermore, though for the method discussed here the extents of the compliance regions are in a simple way related to the knot or guiding point densities at both ends of a letter, these quantities are not easily accessible for handling by the designer.

We remark in passing that our objective -the construction of natural-looking script- could be approached, in principle, from a radically different point of view. Research in the motoric aspects of real handwriting has made it plausible that the pen movements resulting in the production of cursive script are brought about by the action of simply coded 'motor programs' controlling the neuromuscular apparatus involved in writing [Denier65]. Thus, emulation of this system seems a natural way to obtain the desired result. Unfortunately, derivation of the motor program needed for constructing a given letter or letter sequence turns out to be a hard problem [Dooijes84], particularly if the result has to fulfil typographical criteria.

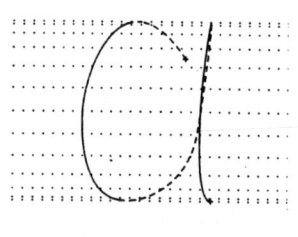

Figure 1: Simple example; subdivisons at 15° intervals.

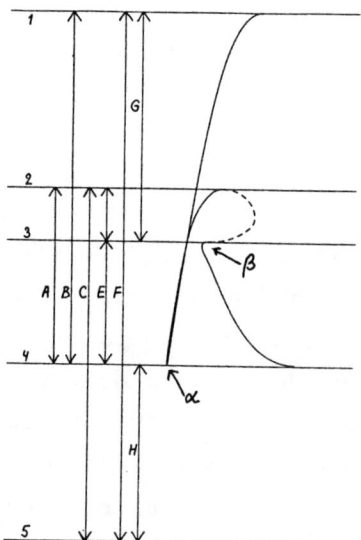

Figure 2: complex letter; levels (1-5) and cylinders (A-H).

3. The Heliscript approach.

Our new approach is based on the observation [Dooijes84] that in natural writing the pen tip's movement can be described as a loop-like motion of varying extent and sense of rotation, superimposed on a horizontal motion which -when observed over the extent of a full word- can be described as uniform to a good approximation. For later reference we call this uniform component the *progression*. The principle of our technique can be understood best by neglecting, for the time being, that the loops appear in various vertical amplitudes.

Now it is conceivable that a script-like pattern can be obtained by orthogonally projecting onto a flat surface a suitably designed *three-dimensional* helical curve, imbedded in the surface of a circular cylinder whose axis is parallel to the viewing surface. Simple letters (like *a*, see figure 1) can be obtained by modulating the pitch of the helix. It is immediately apparent, that the vertical extent of letters defined this way is constrained in a natural way, and that slope discontinuities in the two-dimensional projection just disappear in the helical representation. As we will show later on, this representation also allows the automatic construction of perfectly

Figure 3: Cross-section of cylinder set.

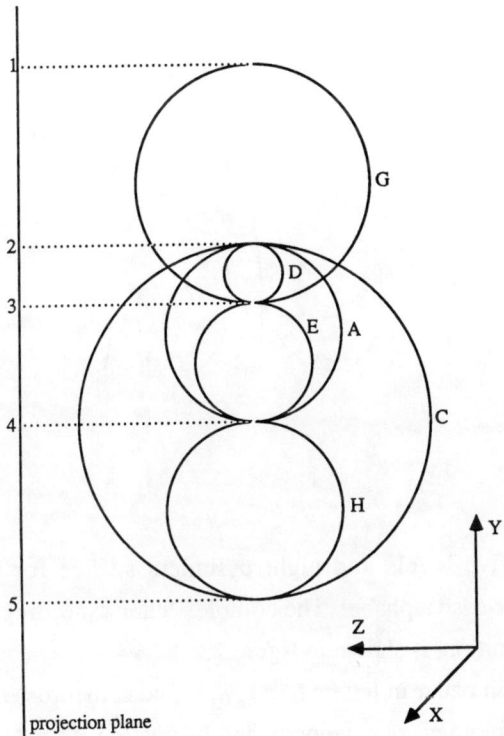

natural looking connectors between letters.

To be useful for the construction of letters more complex than the one shown in figure 1, our technique has to be extended to accomodate a) cylinders of various diameters and b) reversals of the sense of rotation associated with the helix. Cylinders of different diameters can be combined without undue discontinuities in the helix or its projection, by having them share a describing line lying in the same plane -parallel to the viewing plane- as their axes. Figure 3 shows a cross-section through the set of cylinders. For clarity some of the cylinders are omitted in this diagram. The projections of the cylinders onto the viewing plane define the set of levels denoted 1 through 5 in figures 2 and 3. Each of the level pairs A through H corresponds to a cylinder.

Figure 4: Inflecting connector. Figure 5: Non-inflecting connector.

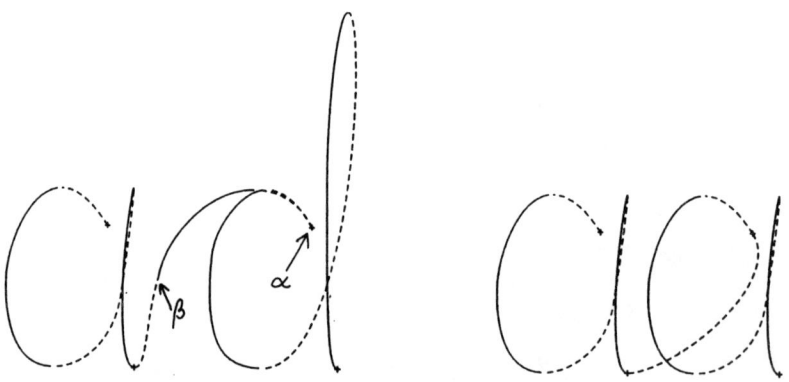

Experimentation shows that five levels and eight cylinders suffice for the definition of an experimental lower-case alphabet. The complex letter *k*, needing all except one of the levels for its definition, is shown in figure 2.

Reversals of the sense of rotation occur in letters like *k*, *n*, *s*, and sometimes in a connector. There exist, in our terminology, zero-velocity and S-type reversals. Only the first type involves a slope discontinuity in the helical curve (for instance, at the points marked α in figures 2 and 4). S-type reversals (corresponding to inflexion points in the projected curve; β in figures 2 and 4) are accomplished by making a transition to a cylinder tangent to the original one either in a vertical or in a horizontal plane through its axis. In the latter case, illustrated by β in figure 4, the transition can be imagined to be made onto an identical cylinder lying before of behind the original one, as seen in the projection direction (see figure 6).

Like the classical method described in the previous section, the present approach depends on B-splines, in view of their advantages in the interactive design of the letter forms. However, rather than working with three-dimensional spline curves constrained to lie on a cylinder (which is possible, at least in principle), we employ a *one-dimensional* B-spline-based function p(t) governing the pitch of the helix (pitch-function, for short).

Figure 6: S-type reversal of rotation sense ('horizontal' case).

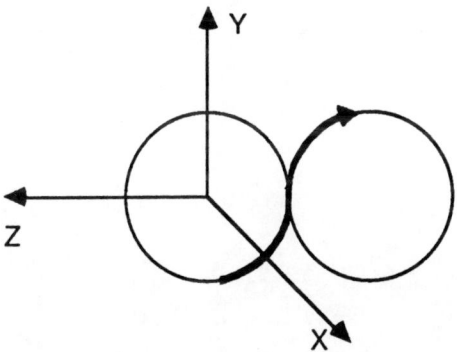

Connectors are computed simply as one-dimensional patches between the pitch-functions of the letters to be concatenated. Evidently, this can be done only after the correct inter-letter distances have been established, as explained in section 4. Connectors come in two types; one involving an inflexion (figure 4), the other not (figures 5 and 7). Which type is actually used depends on the boundary conditions imposed by the particular letter combination, and sometimes on the space between the letters, as illustrated by the *a-a* and *a-d* pairs shown. The space between both *a*'s in figure 5 is too small to permit an inflecting connector whose X-component also meets the requirement of being a monotonous function of pseudo-time (see the next section).

Notice in figure 7 that the connector forms an integral part of the letters it connects. In this way the problem of defining and implementing compliance regions is almost completely avoided. Upstrokes at the beginning of a word are obtained by means of a preceding invisible 'null' character.

4. Parametrization.

An interesting feature of this method is that the parametrization of the planar letter curve is comparable to that found in real handwriting where time is the parameter. To see this, consider the simple cylindrical helix H (figure 8a) which can be represented parametrically by the following triple of equations:

Figure 7: Connector as a part of a letter.

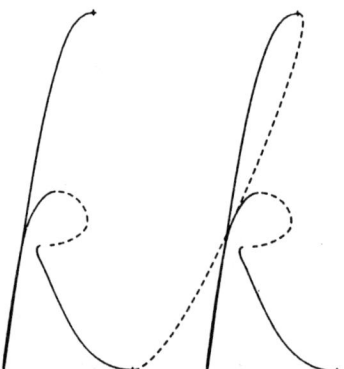

x(t) = p(t); y(t) = R.cos(t); z(t) = R.sin(t);
where p(t) is the pitch defining function. The parameter t is chosen to equal the cumulative polar angle associated with the point (x,y,z); see figure 8b. Since the projection plane is parallel to the XY plane, the definition of the planar projection curve is obtained by just leaving out the Z component from the helix definition. If we put, for instance, p(t) = r.sin(t), the projection curve is a closed ellipsoid, its excentricity being defined by the ratio r / R.

If the curve is to depict a letter, which is a non-closed loop in general, p(t) should include both an oscillatory and a *drift* component. Now, if we associate the parameter t with time, the functions x(t) and y(t) representing a sequence of letters are almost sinusoidal signals just like the components of the pen motion in real handwriting; see figure 9. Of course, actually there is no connection between t and real time; hence we refer to t as the pseudo-time parameter.

The chosen type of parametrization is a helpful feature, as it acts as a bridge between the (typo)graphical and biophysical aspects of script production. Consequently, it enables us to invoke the known temporal characteristics of real handwriting as a guide in design issues. For example, in our prototype system the length of the connector between a pair of letters is computed such as to maintain the

Figure 8a,b: Cylinder with coordinate system XYZ, polar angle t.

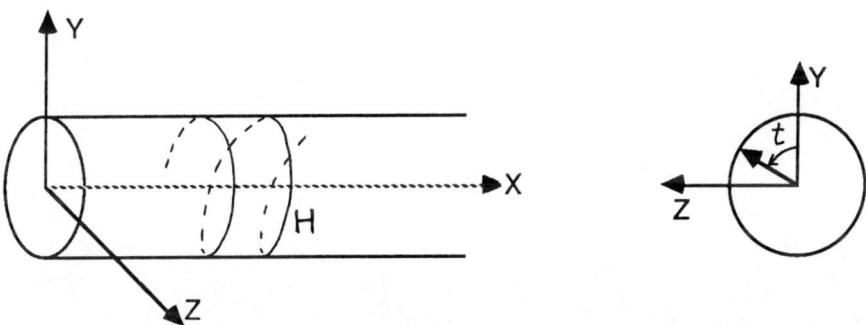

over-all time-linearity of the progression, taking into account the time durations and widths of both letters under consideration.

5. Rendition of completed words.

Once the brush trajectory for a given word has been computed, the word can be painted to the raster-oriented output device, typically a laser printer.

In order to trace out the brush trajectory evenly is the brush should be advanced with equal increments of curve length. To do so efficiently a simple relationship (ideally a linear one) between curve length and curve parameter is required. As has been shown in the previous section, the parametrization provided by Heliscript is not linear. However it is simple enough to permit brush location without expensive iterative calculations. This is a clear advantage over common spline-based techniques for freehand curve design.

Unfortunately, this straightforward painting method is unduly time consuming: every pixel in the word pattern is visited many times without any result once it has been turned on. This problem is particularly apparent with high-resolution output devices.

In contrast with brushing, the representation of a word-pattern by its outlines enables the use of more efficient algorithms for region filling. Gosh and Mudur [Gosh84] advocate this approach, showing how it can be used also to simulate

Figure 9: X (heavy trace) and Y (light trace) as functions of pseudo-time.

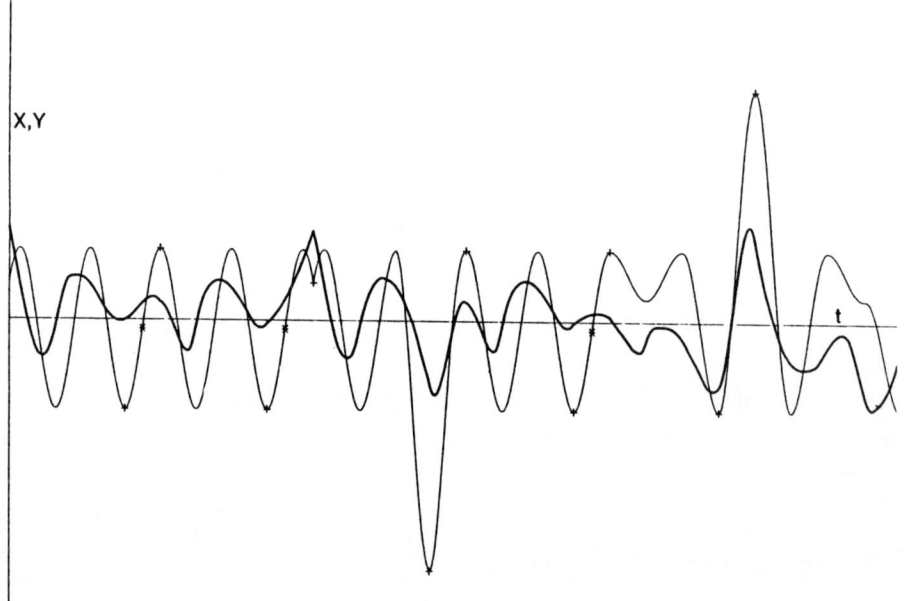

changes in the brush profile like those caused by writing-pressure variations. However, as discussed in [Dooijes86], the required step from brush trajectory to contour line representation is by no means trivial. Presently we are investigating a hybrid approach [Dooijes88].

The final problem discussed here is the 'fine tuning' of the dot pattern resulting from the previous step. It has been pointed out in the Introduction that this has to be done according to a general rule or algorithm, without the intervention of the designer. It is a common supposition [Coueignoux85, MacKay84] that this is all but impossible, at least for the case of Latin typefaces rendered at medium resolution (300 dots per inch, typical for a first-generation laser printer). However, work by Casey et al. [Casey82] and Hersch [Hersch87] gives rise to a more optimistic view on this issue. With modern high-resolution laser printers and photocomposers (1200 dots per inch and up) the problem is virtually non-existent.

To give an impression of the result, in figure 10 the 'brushed' version of *augurk* is shown as rendered on a low-resolution matrix printer, without any corrections.

Figure 10: Result of brushing the pen trajectory.

6. Explanation of the figures.
The illustrations going with this paper are only meant to illustrate the principles set out in the previous sections; no claims are made as to their esthetic value.

In figure 1 subdivisions are drawn corresponding to 15 degrees intervals on cylinder A. Dotted segments of the pen trajectory denote those parts of the three-dimensional helical curve which are 'hidden' behind the cylinder. In figures 4, 5 and 7 the body of a letter is delimited with + marks, to make it distinguishable from the connector.

The X and Y components of the Dutch word *augurk* are shown in figure 9 as functions of pseudo-time. For clarity, the linear progression component has been subtracted from the X-component. A + mark indicates a letter/connector boundary, while * denotes a reversal of the rotation sense halfway an inflecting connector.

7. Conclusion.
We presented a novel approach to the synthesis of quasi-calligraphic script. Evidently, there are more aspects to our project. The development of user interfaces, both for the alphabet designer and the end user is not considered in this paper. The same is true for various text-processing aspects, such as the design of an editor.

At the time of writing, a demonstration system producing texts (in lower case only) on a pen plotter has been completed; work is in progress on a laser printer rendition algorithm.

Acknowledgement.
This research is partly supported by IBM-Nederland N.V.

References.
[1] J.D. Becker: Arabic word processing. Comm. ACM **30** (1987) 600-610.
[2] C. Bigelow and D. Day: Digital typography. Scientific American **248** (1983) no.8 p.94.
[3] W. Boehm, G. Farin and J. Kahman: A survey of curve and surface methods in CAGD. Computer Aided Geometrical Design **1** (1984) 1-60.
[4] R.G. Casey, T.D.Friedman and K.Y. Wong: Automatic scaling of digital print fonts. IBM J. of Research and Development **26** (1982) 657-666.
[5] P. Coueignoux: Character generation and display. In: R.A. Earnshaw (ed): Fundamental Algorithms for Computer Graphics. NATO ASI Series F vol.17, Springer 1985.
[6] J.J. Denier van der Gon, J.Ph. Thuring: The guiding of human handwriting movements. Kybernetik **2** (1965) 145-148.
[7] E.H. Dooijes: Analysis of Handwriting Movements. PhD thesis, University of Amsterdam 1984.
[8] E.H. Dooijes: Digital Synthesis of Calligraphic Script. Proc. Eurographics 1986, A.D. Requicha (ed.), North-Holland 1986; pp 53-57.
[9] E.H. Dooijes: The Heliscript technique for the digital synthesis of quasi-calligraphic script. Report FVI 87-12, Computer Science Department, University of Amsterdam. To appear in: Proc. 3rd Int. Symp. on Handwriting and Computer Applications (Montreal 1987), North-Holland 1988.
[10] E.H. Dooijes: Efficient rasterization of complex brush trajectories. In preparation, 1988.
[11] J. Flowers, Digital type manufacture: an interactive approach. IEEE Computer **17** (1984) no.5 p.40.

[12] A. Fournier, B.A. Barsky: Geometric continuity with interpolating Bezier curves. In: N. Magnenat-Thalmann, D. Thalman (eds): Computer Generated Images. Springer 1985.

[13] P.K. Gosh and S.P. Mudur, The brush-trajectory approach to figure specification: some algebraic solutions. ACM Tr. on Computer Graphics **3** (1984) 110-134.

[14] R.D. Hersch: Character generation under grid constraints. Proc. Siggraph '87, Computer Graphics **21** (1987) no.5 p.243-252.

[15] J. Hoschek, Offset curves in the plane. Computer-aided Design **17** (1985) 77-82.

[16] D. Knuth: Mathematical typography. Bulletin of the American Mathematical Society **1** (1979) 337-372.

[17] P.A. MacKay, TEX coming of age. In J.J.H.Miller (ed.): Protext I, Proc. First Int. Conf. on Text Processing Systems, Boole Press 1984.

[18] T. Pavlidis: Curve fitting with conic splines. ACM Trans. on Graphics **2** (1983) 1-31.

[19] M. Plass, M. Stone: Curve-fitting with piecewise parametric cubics. Proc. Siggraph 1983, pp 229-239.

CHINESE CHARACTER PROCESSING SYSTEM BASED ON CHARACTER-ROOT COMBINATION AND GRAPHIC PROCESSING

FAN CUN-CHANG*, PAOLO ZINI**

* Shanghai Institute of Ceramics, Chinese Academy of Science, Shanghai, China
** CNUCE, Institute of CNR, Pisa, Italy

ABSTRACT

This paper deals with the problem of Chinese character processing. An introductory description is given. The existing solutions are discussed and their limitations pointed out. A new system for Chinese character processing based on character-root combination and graphic processing is proposed. A prototype implementation based on a microcomputer system is described. The memory size occupied is small and can fit even in a personal computer. The input rules are simple and can be easily accepted by untrained users. With 330 Chinese character-roots and a few combination rules the system can produce more than 8,000 Chinese characters

1. Introduction

The first consideration to be made before starting on a project of this kind is the difference in composition of a Chinese character (in the sense of a word) and that of a word in any Western language. In the latter case, all words are formed by the composition of alphabets taken from a list of a few dozen. Chinese characters can, at most, be split up into minor radicals generally known as character-roots. From the phonetics point of view, the pronunciation of a word in Western languages depends largely on the characters with which the word is spelt; in Chinese, there is little dependence of the pronunciation of a character on the character-roots composing it. Moreover, it often happens that a number of quite different characters may have the same pronunciation.

The structure of Chinese characters is very complex. Character-roots have variable positions in different characters. Different compositions of the same character-roots may produce distinct characters. So the problem of writing Chinese characters with a computing system is quite complex.

The "Kang Xi Dictionary" edited in 1716 contains more than 47,000 characters. The authoritative "Chinese Dictionary" edited in 1915 includes more than

48,000 characters. At present, the number of commonly used Chinese characters is about 5,000 to 8,000 [1, 2, 3].

Chinese character information processing is becoming an important subject in the field of computer science, and in the last ten years, an ever increasing number of computer scientists are involved in this subject.

1.1 *State of the art*

Research has been done on many methods to generate Chinese characters on the computer [4-8]. A commonly used method is to have a Chinese character library in memory, where the characters are stored in dot-matrix patterns. A special coding scheme is adopted to address the characters.

A great variety of coding schemes are in use.

- The "Standard code" is based on the standard telegraph code of Chinese characters used in China for telegraph transmission [9]. Each character is coded with four decimal digits, and it is difficult for the ordinary person to be familiar with these "meaningless" codes.

- The "Big Keyboard" is derived from the big character case of Chinese character typewriters [4]. The code character in this case is the character itself. The big keyboard is compactly laid out in order to reduce its size, and the keys are labelled with the respective Chinese characters. By touching a key with a pencil-like probe the corresponding character is displayed.

The "Big Keyboard" is more easily accepted by users, as they can look up the big keyboard and, however slowly, finally find the character they want. The keys have their definite meanings. The drawback is that it is a tedious job for the average users to pick a character up from more than 2,000 characters. Besides, it is very difficult to produce characters which do not exist on the keyboard or in the memory.

- The "Pinyin Code" is based on the standard pronunciation of Chinese characters expressed by an alphabet similar to the English one. However, under the same Pinyin code there may be several Chinese characters. Other complementary actions must be taken to eliminate the ambiguity [7]. Normally the code of the radical or of the character-root may be added, then we obtain a scheme which combines pronunciation with form.

This method can reduce the number of keys to 300, or a standard keyboard may even be used, but the input rules are not simple. Besides, people who are not familiar with the Standard Chinese Pronunciation would find this method difficult to apply.

– Coding according to character form seems at this point more acceptable. The components of the characters, or the character-roots, are studied and employed in character processing system.

The "Double character-root code" Chinese character input system developed by the Shanghai Jiaotong University is a typical example. It is popular among users thanks to its audio-visual format and simple rules [10].

– The combination of character-root with pronunciation also seems adoptable. "Seeing Character is Knowing Code", proposed by Dr. Zhi Bing-yi, is a famous coding scheme of this type [10]. The code of the character is the combination of the first letter of the Pinyin code of the character-roots composing it.

The "Ink jet printer for Chinese characters" developed by the Olympia Company adopts this kind of code, and the input keyboard is just a standard one. Of course, the practical input rules are not simple.

In general, all these methods use a character library and a large size of memory would be needed. With 4,000 Chinese characters in 32x32 dot-matrix pattern, the library would occupy about 500k bytes. This is a disadvantage which should not be ignored.

Graphic processing is another way to realize the Chinese character processing [6]. However, in the past the required hardware and software were considered comparatively complex and only few people were interested in it.

2. Our Approach

We believe that we must first consider the needs and characteristics of the potential users of a Chinese writing system before making any attempt to find a solution to the Chinese writing problem. After this evaluation we can try to analyze the problem by following as much as possible the "natural" way. Practically we believe that the application must work according to man needs and not viceversa. We have analyzed the method of Chinese writing used in Chinese schools to deduce the "mental" approach of Chinese people to writing and tried to design our Chinese writing system according to that; the results obtained are promising.

2.1 *The requirements*

There is a high number of potential users of this system in offices, in mass media, in printing, in libraries and in all jobs where information retrieval is requested. In these environments, complex machines requiring trained and skilled users are difficult to use and are often not accepted.

From the hardware point of view, most of the above mentioned applications need writing systems, terminals for medium or large size computers, and above all, personal computers.

On the basis of these considerations and after an examination of the existing solutions and their limitations, we deduce some basic requirements.

- The method, which has to be used on equipment of mass production, must be very cheap;

- the keyboard must be of a simple and compact structure. Keyboards with over 200 physical keys are expensive and require long training periods.

- the system should be able to produce at least the 8,000 characters which form the basic Chinese vocabulary, and should, moreover, offer possibilities of future expansion;

- the coding system should be simple and intuitive so that a "normal" user with no particular training does not encounter great difficulties.

2.2 "School" method on Chinese writing

Let us now consider the approach commonly adopted in most Chinese schools to teach children Chinese writing, and point out some interesting aspects of this method.

Each character is contained graphically in a rectangular of a fixed dimension and is considered as a single unit. However, every character is made up of one or more components, which may be defined as character-roots, each occupying a certain position in the rectangular according to a series of combination rules. The character-roots forming a character may acquire another meaning in another character if their position is changed (see Fig. 1a). It can be noticed that a character formed by some "simple" character-roots may appear as a "complex" char-

Figure 1

呗　　　员　　　呆　　　杏
口贝　　口贝　　口木　　木口

匾　　　矮　　　逝　　　薄
匚扁　　矢委　　辶折　　艹溥
户冊　　禾女　　扌斤　　氵尃
　　　　　　　　　　　　甫寸

新　　　斑　　　晏　　　鸳
亲斤　　王文王　日宀女　㐈鸟
立木　　　　　　　　　　夕巴鸟一

acter-root in another character. This concept of "complex" character-roots is exploited in our system to facilitate the combination process (see Fig. 1b). A more detailed explanation will be given later.

A closer study reveals that some character-roots are graphically modified versions of other character-roots. This is done by adding or cancelling one part or one stroke of the "mother" character-root(s) (see Fig. 2).

Figure 2

At this point, we can say that by a repetitive composition process of the character-roots, different layers of complexity in root construction are possible; i.e., we may obtain a more or less complex character-root with a greater or smaller number of simple character-roots. We have preferred to take the school level as our standard, as this is the most representative one for the ordinary person.

At this level, the combination possibilities which are to be considered as combination rules in our system are few: the roots may appear side by side, or one on top of the other, or one root may be "enveloped" in another. In these combination procedures, the roots may be compressed or they may change their dimensions according to the case, while maintaining their graphic structure.

2.3 *The algorithm*
On the basis of the previous analysis, we have developed an algorithm which uses a table of character-roots, some composition operators and some modifying operators, or simply modifiers. A table of 330 roots has been obtained from the Chinese Dictionary. If we attempt to derive a specific combination rule for each type (the graphic arrangement) of character, we would have too many rules for any practical application. We have chosen instead the idea of repeated applications of composition operators, storing the intermediate result of the composition in a temporary memory. This "temporary root" can be used again in further compositions with other simple or "complex" roots. Only the final result will appear on the screen and the composition operators behave practically like arithmetic operators. The composition operators adopted are those described in the previous section, namely side by side combination, stacking and enveloping.

In order to simplify the table of character-roots and to adhere as much as possible to the school standard, we have provided a series of modifiers which, as it has been mentioned above, are used to add, cancel or change a stroke or a part of one character-root to form another (see Fig. 2). These modifiers not only reduce the size of the table, but also solve some graphic problems whose solution would otherwise be impossible. To expand the capability of the algorithm other operators or modifiers can be added, each operator requiring only a few more statements for its implementation.

The character-roots cannot be stored in dot matrix form because they are subject to complex dimensional changes not easily performable in this form. So we have preferred to store and manipulate character-roots as graphic vectors so that a change in dimension is simply a multiplication by a size factor. Moreover, the small size of roots table makes it possible to use multiple roots tables to change the "character font", i.e., the graphic aspect of the characters.

The resulting keyboard will generate about 350 root codes and a few operators. The keys are labelled with the corresponding root and they have a more "direct" impact on the user, since they are a part of a Chinese character, and not simply "meaningless" codes.

The problem remains as to whether it is compulsory for a user to always insert the operators together with the root, or whether these operators could become implicit if the roots are typed in a certain sequence.

After a first analysis of the dictionary, we discovered that in most cases, certain character-roots in a given sequence can result in one and only one "meaningful" character. Only a very limited number of sequences of character-roots can produce different possibilities of characters, the so-called ambiguous cases, which can easily be singled out during program writing.

Probably the best compromise is that of using a parser for the common cases and specified operators for the ambiguous ones. However, the analyses done up to now are not sufficiently thorough for us to define a context free grammar for the method [12, 14].

3. Implementation

To verify the functionality of the method an experimental implementation has been carried out. The prototype uses a graphic terminal Tektronix 4013 and a microcomputer ONIX 8002 using the UNIX V7 operating system. The tools are not chosen for any particular reasons but simply because they are available at the center where the authors are working.

The first version of this prototype shows that the method is simple enough to be easily adapted to simpler microcomputers without any loss of efficiency. The display screen used is a graphic storage tube, but the same features can be found on several other cheaper personal computers. -

3.1 The graphic representation

As we have stated before, the roots change their dimensions relatively to the position and space they occupy in the final character. This is done with the graphic vector representation of the roots. The root is represented by a sequence of pairs of coordinates each of which specifies respectively the start and the end of every graphic segment of the root. The sequence is ended by a terminator symbol. Optional information is located after the terminator, to be used for some composition or modification operations, like the "envelope" composition, in which the information will be the size of the "box". If the root has modified versions the additional information will be the modification to be applied. The roots table holds 330 roots and its size is about 15 kbytes; an optimized organization of the table can reduce its size to less than 5 kbytes. The total size of the object code is about 40 kbytes.

3.2 The keyboard

The keyboard (a prototipe has been implemented) has about 120 physical keys for the roots, a couple of keys for shifts, about 10 keys for composition or modification operators plus all the classical function keys of a keyboard (carriage return, line feed, backspace etc.). The roots have been encoded, in an absolutely arbitrary way, by using pairs of lowercase ASCII characters; the operators are encoded with other ASCII characters and space is used as a character terminator symbol. This means that a Chinese text is encoded as a sequence of ASCII characters and is fully compatible with all operating systems.

A lexical-analyzer [12, 13] program translates these pairs into roots table addresses and the symbol representing the operators into special codes. The output of the lexical-analyzer is the input of the program which implements the algorithm described in the next section.

3.3 The algorithm implementation

The algorithm is implemented by a program written in the C language [11]. It accepts as input strings of roots, composition operators, modifiers, and terminators. The operators can be unary or binary and are all postfixed, so that the input string looks like an equation expressed in reverse Polish notation. A stack is used to hold the roots and the "composed" roots resulting from previous composition operations. The program scans the input string and, when a root is found, its vector representation is pushed into the stack. When a unary operator is found, the last pushed root is popped out, the operation is performed on it and the resulting root is again pushed into the stack. Analogously, when a binary operator is found, the two last pushed roots are popped out, the operator applied and the resulting "complex" root pushed into the stack. When the terminator is found, the stack is scanned: if the stack contains only one root it is displayed by a standard graphic package, otherwise the roots contained in the stack are composed

according to the final composition rule and the resulting character is displayed. In our prototype, the final default operator is a "side by side" composition operator, and can compose up to three roots. In case of vertical composition; i.e. stacking, the final composition operator must be specified.
The basic operators are:

—side by side composition
—stacked composition
—enveloped composition
—modify by suppression of one stroke
—modify by addition of one stroke
—modify by replacement of one stroke with one or more different strokes.

To simplify the writing we have added one more operator for a special composition (Fig. 3). This operator is not actually necessary as the same result can be obtained by using two basic operators. However, it implements a usual construction of Chinese writing. The implementation of composition operators is not complex; each operator requires only a few statements, and each operator executes only compressions (multiplication by coefficient), shifts (sum of a constant), and merging of vectors of coordinates representing the roots into a single vector.

Figure 3

This implementation has proven to be rather powerful and relatively easy to use: all the 8,477 characters listed in The XINHUA Dictionary have been written out in different sizes and the needs of general Chinese character processing purposes are met.

3.4 *Plans of future development.*
We believe that it is necessary to first test the applicability of this method to small computers. Our schedule covers a second personal-computer based prototype. During its implementation, due consideration will be taken of the implementation cost of necessary graphic functions. As to the algorithm, the composition rules are very simple, but the elimination of the explicit specifications makes the system even simpler.
It is therefore our intention to continue our research on a parser capable of deducing composition rules from the sequences of the roots, without specifying the operators.

4. Requirements Matching

At its present stage, the prototype seems to be very interesting and easy to implement.

The present version of the prototype was completed after 5 months of work. Most of the time was spent on preparing the roots table. The keyboard implemented has a relatively limited number of keys and seems to be quite easy for the typical user and relatively cheap.

The method of composition, being very close to the method of hand writing, seems to be simple and linear to understand, and does not request any previous knowledge of meaningless codes or of the exact pronunciation of the characters.

The simplicity of the system itself provides possibilities of producing different sizes (by specifying a parameter) (see Appendix) and different types of graphic characters (by loading different character-root-fonts), an advantage not found in existing solutions, and a particularly important factor in editing. Our experiments have shown that by adding some more character-roots into the character-root table it is possible to produce almost all of the 48,000 Chinese characters for special users. The size of the object code will be still moderate.

The hardware complexity can be evaluated mainly by following an intuitive approach. A video screen needs, in order to be graphic, a RAM memory bit for every point of the screen. In our case, a resolution of 1024*512 points will suffice; i.e., 64 Kbyte. The remaining part of the hardware is equivalent to that of the corresponding alphanumerical screen. A comparison of this memory size with the 500 Kbyte ROM needed for a medium size character library will show that our method can be much cheaper and less complex than existing ones.

5. Conclusions

Obviously some limitations can be found in our work. For instance, the roots table was built only on the basis of direct experiences acquired in this particular field. There has been little linguistic information from experts of this sector, and the root table is not an authoritative one. However, we do think that this new attempt offers a series of interesting points and may prove to be a further step in the realization of an efficient Chinese Character Information Processing system.

Acknowledgement

We wish to express our most sincere thanks to the Italian National Research Council (CNR) and the Chinese Academy of Science for the support given to this project, and in particular, to Prof. Xue Zhi-Lin and Mr. Li Zong-Jie of the Shanghai Institute of Ceramics, Chinese Academy of Science, who have kindly sent the authors precious information not otherwise available in Italy, and to Dr. S. Trumpy, Director of CNUCE, Institute of CNR, for his constant support. We also wish to thank Mrs. Tao Pei-lin for the suggestions and comments she has given us during the preliminary phase of our work and for the long experimental work she has carried out during the functionality test of our system.

References

[1] The Collection of Coded Chinese Characters for Information Communication;
The 4th Ministry of Machine-Building, China; May 1, 1981.

[2] XINHUA Dictionary;
SHANGWU Publishing House, China; 1981.

[3] Chinese English Dictionary;
SHANGWU Publishing House, China; 1980.

[4] Introduction of Chinese Character Processing;
Technology Reference Room of Shanghai Computer Factory;
Computer Technology n. 4, 1982.

[5] The Processing Abstracts of the First Academic Discussion on Chinese Character Information Processing System;
Chinese Instrument and Apparatus Society; June, 1981.

[6] Lian Jing: The Design and Realization of Chinese Character System Based on Graphic Processing; The Research and Development on Computer, Institute of Computing Technology, Chinese Academy of Science.

[7] Geng Li-da: Function and Conclusion on Chinese Character Processing System Based on PINYIN; Institute of Computing Technology, Chinese Academy of Science.

[8] Shen Jia-lin; Microcomputer System for Chinese Character Information Processing;
Instrument and Control n. 2, 1983.

[9] Standard Telegraph Code; Ministry of Post and Telecommunication, China.

[10] GUANGMING Daily; April 18, 1983.

[11] B.W. Kernighan & D.M. Ritchie: The C Programming Language;
Prentic-Hall, N.J., 1978.

[12] A.V. Aho & J.D. Ullman: Principles of Compiler Design;
Addison-Wesley Publishing Company; 1977.

[13] M.E. Lesk & E. Schmidt: LEX: A Lexical Analyzer Generator;
Murray Hill, N.J.; 1980.

[14] S.C Johnson: YACC: Yet Another Compiler-Compiler;
Murray Hill, N.J.; 1978.

Appendix

The abstract of this paper.

采用字根组合和图象处理方法的
汉字处理系统（摘要）

保罗·基尼　　范存昌

本文研究汉字处理问题．介绍了概况，讨论了现存方法和它们的局限性．提出了采用字根组合和图象处理方法的新的汉字处理方案，並描述了在微处理计算机系统上实现的情况．内存占用量很小，可移植于个人用计算机．输入规则简单，使用者很容易掌握．使用三百多个字根和几条组合规则，系统已能产生八千多个汉字．

Some chinese characters, in the order of XINHUA Dictionary.

阿啊锕腌啊啊啊哎哀锿埃挨唉嗳呆骇捱皑癌毐欸
嗳矮蔼霭艾砹唉爱嗳嫒瑷叆暧馤隘嗌碍厂广安桉氨
鮟鞍庵鹌谙盦按铵俺埯唵揞犴屵按案胺暗黯肮昂盎
凹熬敖嗷嗸廒遨獓熬聱鳌警鏊翱麈拗袄媪岙圠坳抝
奡傲慠鏊奥墺懊澳八扒叭朳巴芭吧岜疤笆粑捌茇拔
胈菝跋魃皱把钯靶坝把爸耙鲅罢鲃霸灞吧罷刮饼白
百佰伯柏捭摆败拜稗竩唪扳攽颁斑瘢般搬癍阪坂
板版钣舨办半伴拌绊柈鞞扮瓣邦帮梆浜绑榜膀蚌棒
傍谤蒡搒磅镑稖包苞胞炮鲍剥煲褒雹薄饱宝保堡
葆褓鸨报刨抱鲍趵豹曓瀑爆陂杯卑庳桮碑背悲北贝
狈钡邶背褙孛悖备惫倍焙蓓碚被鞁琲辈鞴鐾唄臂奔
錛贲栟本苯畚夯奙奔倴笨伻彷崩唪绷甭绷琫泵迸蚌

A piece of news from GUANGMING Daily.

科学工作者经过初步考察研究认为
无锡巨冰可能是陨冰

据新华社无锡四月十七日电 （记者蔡名照） 科学工作者经过初步考察研究认为，六天前在无锡坠落的巨冰，可能是一块从宇宙空间闯入地球的"天外来客"。

本社十二日播发坠冰消息后（见本报十三日四版），立即引起科学工作者的重视。国家气象局研究院、江苏省气象台、紫金山天文台和北京天文台派人赶赴无锡，在无锡市科委、气象站的协助下，进行了现场考察研究。科学工作者认为，它很可能是从宇宙空间飞入地球的陨冰。他们解释说，太阳系中彗星的核心部分就是直径几百米至几千米的冰山，它在运行中与流星相撞，就会有一些碎块脱离原来的运行轨道，这些碎块如果与地球相遇，穿过大气层落到地面就成为陨冰。

科学工作者认为，如果这块巨冰确是陨冰，那将有相当高的科学价值。因为彗星是与地球同时形成的，它的冰体上带有地球形成时的信息，而且彗星冰体上的有机物质与地球上有机物质也有着某种联系，因此，陨冰对研究地球和生命的起源有重要意义。

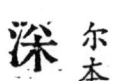

SYSTEMS USED

D. Arnon (p 1), used the Tioga multimedia document system in the Cedar programming environment at Xerox PARC. Figures are integrated into the Tioga document and manipulated as mathematics via CaminoReal or as illustrations via Gargoyle. Paper prepared from Interpress 3.0 masters using a 1200 spi laser platemaker.

P.T. Zellweger (p 19), see D. Arnon.

R. Southall (p 35), formatted with MicroTeX 1.5A1 on an Olivetti M24 personal computer. PostScript output files produced with ArborText's DVILASER/PS program, copy set on a Linotronic machine.

L.D. Wilcox (p 47) see D. Arnon.

J. Behrmann-Poitiers (p 71) produced with Interleaf's Workstation Publishing Software (WPS) Release C on a Sun Workstation, printed on a QMS PS 800 laser printer.

J.-M. de La Beaujardière (p 83), formatted with ViewPoint on a Xerox 6085 workstation. Paper prepared from Interpress 3.0 masters using a 1200 spi laser platemaker.

W. Appelt (p 95), used TeX with Computer Modern Fonts produced with METAFONT, and a QMS Lasergrafix 800 for printing.

R. Furuta (p 109), prepared with LaTeX on a Sun 3/50 under Berkeley Unix, printed on an Apple LaserWriter at 300 dpi.

D.D. Chamberlin (p 121), formatted using Janus (an experimental editor/formatter based on GML, a precursor to SGML). Paper printed on an APA6670, a 240 pel/inch laser printer.

R.A. Morris (p 139), used release 3.0 of Interleaf Technical Publishing

Software, producing PostScript for the Linotronic 300. Spectral figures and character reconstructions produced from Encapsulated PostScript embedded in the document.

W.A. Hegazy (p 157), formatted with TeX, printed on a 300 dpi Canon-based laser printer. Figures prepared using MacDraw and PostScript and printed on an Apple LaserWriter.

H. Trickey (p 171), produced using LaTeX on a Sun. Copy set on an APS-5 phototypesetter (involving conversion of TeX dvi format into troff dvi format).

P.J. Brown (p 183), troff, printed on a Laserwriter attached to a Sun-3 network.

M. Kaplan (p 193), produced with IDE (described in the paper), formatted with troff on a Vax and Imagen.

A.W. Luniewski (p 205), see D.D. Chamberlin.

K. Pier (p 223), see D. Arnon.

R. De Sousa (p 239), LaTeX on a LaserWriter through PostScript.

S. Nath (p 249), used a preliminary batch version of Vidura running on an IBM PC compatible. Printed on a TI Omnilaser 2108 Laser Printer with PostScript Interpreter.

E.H. Dooijes (p 261), used MacWrite on a Macintosh Plus, printed on a LaserWriter Plus. Illustrations (apart from fig. 10) prepared on a penplotter. Paper has been reduced in size.